Totem Poles and Tea

Totem Poles and Tea

Hughina Harold

VICTORIA · VANCOUVER · CALGARY

Heritage House Publishing Ltd.
#108-17665 66A Ave.
Surrey, BC V3S 2A7
www.heritagehouse.ca

Library and Archives Canada Cataloguing in Publication
Harold, Hughina, 1915–2001
     Totem poles and tea/Hughina Harold—2nd ed.

Includes index.

ISBN 13: 978-1-894974-13-4
ISBN 10: 1-894974-13-1

     1. Harold, Hughina, 1915-2001. 2. Teachers—British Columbia—Village Island—Biography. 3. Nurses—British Columbia—Village Island—Biography. 4. Kwakiutl Indians—British Columbia—Village Island—History. 5. Mamalilikulla Indian Day School. 6. Village Island (B.C.)—Biography. I. Title.

FC3845.V54Z49 2006   971.1'103'092   C2005-907554-6

Edited by Karla Decker and Edna Sheedy
Cover and book design by Jacqui Thomas
Front cover: Detail of *Mamalilicoola, B.C. 1928*, woodcut on paper, by Walter Joseph Phillips, Glenbow Collection
Layout by Darlene Nickull
Map by Cecilia Hirzcy Welsford

 The interior of this book was produced on 100% post-consumer recycled paper, processed chlorine free and printed with vegetable-based dyes.

Heritage House acknowledges the financial support for its publishing program from the Government of Canada through the Canada Book Fund (CBF), Canada Council for the Arts and the British Columbia Arts Council.

 Canada Council   Conseil des Arts
for the Arts   du Canada

 BRITISH COLUMBIA
ARTS COUNCIL

Printed in Canada

Dedicated
to my three daughters
Anne, Betty and Kathleen

Thank you to Art Downs for remembering my manuscript and encouraging me to bring it out of its drawer. Thank you to my editor, Edna Sheedy, for taking the time to massage my words and thank you to Rodger Touchie for the many hours spent seeking out and collecting photographs from a bygone era on Village Island.

And to all the First Nations people, the Todds, Muriel Banfield, Kate Mann and, of course, the Guardian Angels—thanks for the memories.

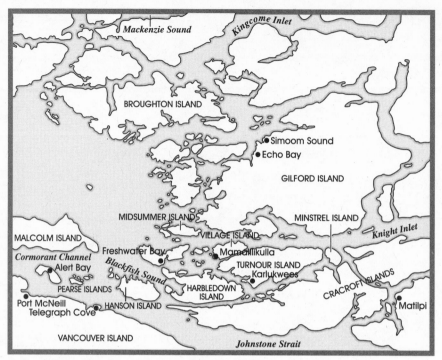

Mackenzie Sound — Kingcome Inlet

BROUGHTON ISLAND

• Simoom Sound
• Echo Bay

GILFORD ISLAND

MIDSUMMER ISLAND

MINSTREL ISLAND

MALCOLM ISLAND

VILLAGE ISLAND

Knight Inlet

Cormorant Channel

Freshwater Bay

• Mamalilikulla

Alert Bay

Blackfish Sound

TURNOUR ISLAND
Karlukwees

CRACROFT ISLANDS

PEARSE ISLANDS

HARBLEDOWN
ISLAND

• Matilpi

Port McNeill
Telegraph Cove

HANSON ISLAND

VANCOUVER ISLAND

Johnstone Strait

Port Hardy
Alert Bay
Port McNeill

Campbell
River

VANCOUVER
ISLAND

Vancouver

Victoria

Getting to Village Island from Alert Bay through the rough, unpredictable waters of Blackfish Sound took about three hours—if all went well.

This 1970 aerial photograph shows the remains of the ancient village of 'Mi'mkwạmlis on Village Island. Current maps usually identify it under the spelling Mamalilaculla.

Contents

Foreword to the Second Edition

Just over seventy years ago, a young woman accepted an appointment as teacher and nurse at Mamalilikulla (now spelled Mamalilaculla) on remote Village Island. Hughina Bowden was only 20 when she left her family home in Victoria to begin an adventure that would expose her to the beauty and danger of coastal British Columbia.

She arrived at Mamalilikulla full of hope and uncertainty about what lay ahead, and her first impressions—of a vast and beautiful but essentially empty wilderness—offered little in the way of reassurance. However, her view of her new home soon changed as she got to know her First Nations neighbours, as well as a nearby farming couple, handloggers and their families, and the friendly crews of itinerant mission boats.

Hughina realized she was part of a story worth telling, so accounts of her experiences travelled home in her weekly letters. Many years later, she came across those old letters, and the memories came flooding back. She was inspired to turn the letters into stories, which were read by Eileen Laurie on her CBC program *Morning Visit* in the 1960s. A nostalgic trip to Alert Bay in 1985 inspired Hughina once more, this time to draft a manuscript that was published by Heritage House in 1996.

Hughina's anecdotes are immediately engaging; her wry observations keep the tone light. Her keen curiosity and vivid storytelling allow us to view an intriguing piece of this province's history. When she stepped off the boat in Alert Bay in 1935, Hughina encountered a civilization that had been impacted by more than 150 years of contact with fur traders, colonialists, missionaries and bureaucrats. She brought with her the views and prejudices typical of the mid-1930s, so it is not surprising that her first impressions were rather dark. But her outlook would change:

> When I first came to Village Island, unprepared and knowing nothing of the Natives and their ways, I had a superior attitude. I thought them dull, unresponsive and unemotional ... it was difficult to get to know or to understand them. But as the months crept by, I learned something of their culture and a few words of their language. I learned to appreciate them as individuals possessing the strengths, dreams and sorrows common to all of us.

Thankfully, Hughina's later review of her original documents did not compromise their integrity: she made no attempt to inject "political correctness" into the manuscript. Although the prejudices of the times are sometimes evident in her opinions, she also demonstrates a remarkable flexibility and open-mindedness.

When she realized, for example, that the curriculum provided by the Department of Indian Affairs was irrelevant to her young pupils, she changed her approach:

> The government curriculum was simply not set up for Native children. When I realized how completely their lives differed from the ones depicted in the readers, I tried to improvise. We would go for walks along the beach when the tide was out, and they would teach me things I didn't know about shells and seaweed. They showed me dulse, which was edible.

Hughina developed strong attachments to her students, and felt deep compassion for her young patients who suffered and sometimes died from the scourge of TB. She also formed a close bond with an elderly woman who could not speak a word of English.

As time went on, Hughina's capacity to understand grew and her attitudes continued to evolve. She experienced moments of revelation when she saw how the proud history and age-old traditions of the Mamalilikulla had been unrecognized and disrespected by the White intruders who descended upon them.

One such moment occurred after she witnessed a clandestine winter potlatch. Potlatches had been outlawed by an amendment to the federal Indian Act in 1884, and in a deeply moving passage, Hughina gave her account of this historic event, then went on to comment on the potlatch system:

> This system worked well for the Kwakiutl, who were among the wealthiest of the Indian nations. They lived in a land of abundance, their living standard one of the highest in the world. Then the White man came, bringing his monetary system—and his diseases; measles, smallpox and tuberculosis killed thousands. The potlatch system broke down. The last great potlatch was held on Village Island in December of 1921, after which 45 people were charged with such offences as dancing, speech making, and gift giving. Twenty of these people were sent to prison ... while their potlatch paraphernalia was pirated away to eastern Canada and the United States. Since that

time, the occasional potlatch, such as the one I had witnessed, was a furtive affair, and but a shadow of its former prominence and glory.

While fine stories emerged from Hughina's experiences teaching and tending the people of Village Island and neighbouring villages, her contacts with the families of handloggers and other coastal inhabitants provided additional great material for glimpses at life on the mid-'30s coast. Most interesting is the insight into the mutual support that existed among these pioneers, who were on their own against the elements. Through her strong friendships with them, Hughina found timely escapes from the rather dour missionary women who were her hosts on Village Island.

Twenty-seven years after Hughina arrived at Village Island, my wife and I began a four-year ministry in the Tsimshian village of Lax Kw'alaams (Port Simpson), 40 kilometres north of Prince Rupert. Hughina's stories brought back many good memories—and some sad ones—of our time there.

The legacy of disrespect and insensitivity on the part of those who came with a superior attitude turned out to be a scourge almost as devastating as the "White man's diseases" that decimated populations and began destroying a sophisticated social order—a destruction that continued with such historic injustices as the potlatch law of 1884.

Today, we are in a new era of relations with the First Peoples of the land now called British Columbia. Fundamental to the success of this new relationship are underlying principles of recognition and respect. The First Nations Summit, the Union of B.C. Indian Chiefs, the federal government and the government of B.C. all recognize the possibilities that will result from new attitudes, mutual partnerships and real trust.

Those of us who have experienced the friendship of First Nations people who have welcomed us into their homes, their ceremonies and their hearts have found acceptance, in spite of our uninformed attitudes—just as Hughina Harold did.

To her relationship with the Mamalilikulla, Hughina brought views that often failed to recognize certain cultural values. But she also brought a keen interest in learning, a commitment to teaching and healing, a respect for the First Peoples and their traditions, and the sense to know when a good story is a good story.

Enjoy these stories—some are sad and lonely, and some hilarious. Others depict circumstances of hair-raising danger.

Through Hughina's eyes, we see a precious time in our history.

—John Cashore, United Church minister and
former B.C. Minister of Aboriginal Affairs

Foreword to the First Edition

"I'm told there is nothing left on Village Island now. No signs of the school, no brown house, no totem poles—just empty spaces filled with weeds and stinging nettles. It seems incredible that for a short time many years ago, this dot on the map was the centre of my universe."

So wrote Hughina Harold.

"In 1985 I returned to northern Vancouver Island. From Port McNeill, a 15-minute government-ferry ride took me and friends to Alert Bay on Cormorant Island. It had been nearly 50 years since I'd laid eyes on this remote town, but a few familiar landmarks remained."

At the end of the shoreline street sat the remains of the regal brick building Hughina once knew as St. Michael's Residential School for Indian children. Layered in peeling white paint, the once-noble structure was a shabby foil for the new Kwakwaka'wakw Nation's U'Mista Cultural Museum that now stood beside it. A museum will preserve some of their heritage, she thought, as her eye was drawn to the crest of the hill beyond which stood the world's tallest totem pole.

"I could also see St. George's Hospital and the totems in the Indian graveyard next to it," she wrote. "That was about as far as Alert Bay extended back then."

Hughina strolled the length of the narrow street, seeking traces of the familiar. "The Indian homes and totems that so influenced my first impressions were gone, replaced by a supermarket, a gift shop and the café where we ate lunch. I did find the house that had once been the home of Murray Todd, the Indian agent who had hired me those many years ago. Farther along I was delighted to see the Anglican Church, a hundred years old now, but looking spruce under fresh yellow paint and white trim."

With her friends, Hughina toured the new museum, occasionally recognizing a name or face on display. Outside again, the majestic totem seemed even taller. She noted sadly that the Thunderbird gateposts, which guarded the entrance to St. Michael's, were faded and rotting. Her visit was near its end when she walked onto the dock and stared across Blackfish Sound and the stormy waters she had crossed so often returning to—or escaping from—Village Island.

Memories of the Todds and the dozen Native children who had been her life seemed to roll out of the mist. She recalled the dramatic waterfront of Alert Bay, and the ghostly settlement of Village Island that had greeted her a half century before. She pictured the two Guardian Angels sipping their tea inside a tilted house against a backdrop of primitive totems.

"The visions I had of a bygone era were fixed and clear," she wrote. "I knew I had witnessed things that should not be forgotten."

Then her mind flashed to *the letters*. In the mid-1930s, while working as a teacher-nurse at the Christian mission on Village Island, Hughina Bowden—or Miss B., as she was generally known—wrote long, detailed letters to her family in Victoria. She explained, "After Mother's death, I found a box full of my letters, carefully preserved. They sat untouched in my cupboard for years. Then one day, during a cleaning attack, I rediscovered the box. I promptly abandoned my chore to read the letters, and relive those memorable days.

"The next day I couldn't wait for my three girls to scurry off to school and my husband to go to his office so I could get on with my *great project*! I was going to once again bring Village Island to life.

"I completed my *great project* in mid-1960. At that time CBC radio broadcast *Morning Visit*, with Eileen Laurie reading human-interest stories. I thought my tales of Village Island might fit the show's format, so I sent Eileen my handwritten effort. To my joy she ran my stories for many weeks as a serial. I acquired a listening audience—and even received fan mail!"

Among *Morning Visit*'s audience was Harry Wolcott, an American anthropologist who had taught on Village Island to collect material for his dissertation. After listening to the CBC, Wolcott contacted Hughina and documented their discussions in *A Kwakiutl Village and School* (New York: Holt, Rinehart and Winston, 1967).

"For a time my literary efforts ended," she tells us. "I knew there was more to say and better ways to say it, but because of great changes in my life, my stories of Village Island sat untouched for 20 years. My 1985 trip to Alert Bay spurred me to action."

Hughina Harold went back to her 50-year-old letters and prior notes to draft this manuscript. She created an honest portrayal of the attitudes of the mid-1930s and the personal concerns and priorities of a 20-year-old woman far removed from the creature comforts of her Victorian home. Surprisingly, due largely to her own humility, her work spent another decade in a drawer, obscured and ignored.

Mrs. Harold passed away in 2001. As she had so clearly recognized in Alert Bay in 1985, she *had* witnessed things that should not be forgotten.

—Rodger D. Touchie

Three Inches East of Alert Bay

*I*T WAS THE SPRING OF 1935 and the Depression was full upon us.

My classmates and I, after three years of training, had just graduated from the Royal Jubilee Hospital in Victoria with our nursing degrees. But what we'd anticipated as a bright future dimmed in the reality of those difficult years. Jobs were scarce and wages low.

But fate consists of odd connections and unexpected opportunities.

Margaret Plunkett, one of my classmates, was lucky enough to become the private duty nurse for Reverend Charles Schofield, the bishop of the Anglican Church. One day he told her about the church's need for a teacher with nurse's training. Such a person, he explained, was required in an up-coast Indian village where there was both a mission and school.

As I had exactly those qualifications, having also graduated from Victoria Normal School, Margaret immediately thought of me. She phoned me one day and gaily announced, "Hughina, I've found a job for you, and it's right up your alley."

"You have?" I asked, pleased at the very idea of working. "What is it?"

"You'll be paid $90 a month," she exclaimed.

Although her answer was evasive, my interest was definitely piqued. In these times private duty work was difficult to get, and general duty paid only $35 a month. She told me what little she knew about the job, then told me the bishop wanted to meet me.

Hughina Bowden trained to be a registered nurse at Victoria's Royal Jubilee Hospital, graduating in 1935.

At this point, despite the alluring salary, I wasn't at all sure the position was for me, but I did consent to hear out Reverend Schofield. He proved to be a delightful—and *persuasive* gentleman. Before leaving his company, I was surprised to hear myself accepting a job at a place called Village Island.

Now committed to going, I thought it a good idea to find out exactly where. No one I knew had ever heard of Village Island, so I resorted to a large map. My eyes scanned from Vancouver until I found Alert Bay, an estimated 200 miles northwest. There it was! I applied my ruler. Three inches from Alert Bay. I measured the island and did more calculations. It was tiny. A mere seven miles long and two miles wide. Village Island suddenly seemed very remote.

For a young stay-at-home who'd grown up in Victoria, it might as well have been another planet. What on earth had I agreed to?

The mission on Village Island was affiliated with the Columbia Coast

Anglican Church bishop Charles Schofield's powers of persuasion led Hughina to accept the job on Village Island. Bishop Schofield had visited Alert Bay in 1925 on the *Columbia* to dedicate the new St. George's Hospital as the ship's base.

Mission, established by Reverend John Antle in 1905 under the wing of the Anglican Church of Canada. Reverend Antle was a seagoing Newfoundlander who wanted to bring medical and spiritual help to the hardy people wresting a living from B.C.'s rugged northern coastline. He amassed a small armada to do just this, and his flagship was the *Columbia*.

Not only did the *Columbia* have a chapel, a hospital room—and doctor— for emergencies, it had a wireless connecting it with Alert Bay. From there, messages could be relayed to St. George's Hospital or other ships in the area. In 1935 communications such as the *Columbia*'s were non-existent for the people working in the remote logging camps or missions dotted along B.C.'s northern shores, so the *Columbia* played an important role in their lives—as it would in mine.

The mission on Village Island was run, I was told, by two dedicated English women, Miss Kathleen O'Brien and Miss Kate Maria Dibben.

Through Miss O'Brien's private funding, a combined church and school had been built, as well as a small preventorium for the care of Indian children suspected of having tuberculosis.

That summer, as Reverend Schofield had indicated, Mr. Murray Todd, the Indian agent for Alert Bay and vicinity, called me to set up an appointment. I was apprehensive, but this pleasant white-haired man proved to be friendly, obliging and more than willing to answer all of my questions. And there were quite a few.

Our mutual employer, he told me, was the Department of Indian Affairs in Ottawa, and my salary was to be $270, paid quarterly. My school and medical supplies had to be requisitioned from Ottawa through him. The Indian people were transient, and the idea that school should open after Labour Day and continue until June didn't impress them. Families returned to Village Island, he said, only when the fish were caught, the clams dug, and the seaweed and berries gathered. Of the dozen school-aged children I would teach, attendance would not warrant opening the school before late October. He would notify me when the time was right.

"And how will I reach Village Island from Alert Bay?" I asked.

"I'll arrange for your transportation," he assured me, smiling. "It's only 15 miles."

Fifteen miles, I thought. That didn't seem like much. Perhaps my trepidation about this position was unwarranted. Surely I'd get to Alert Bay and Vancouver Island now and then.

That summer I attended school to renew my teaching certificate and did shift work at the hospital in the evening. The summer seemed to fly by, and as time passed, I confess the Village Island adventure was losing its appeal. Then, one day, the inevitable letter from Mr. Todd arrived, telling me the people were returning to the island.

It was time to pack up.

Two days later, with mixed feelings, I embarked on a Canadian Pacific Railway boat to Vancouver, where I transferred to a coastal steamer for the overnight trip to Alert Bay.

The following afternoon the boat rounded a point, and I saw Cormorant Island and crescent-shaped Alert Bay for the first time. The town, stretching along the curved shoreline, looked ragged and small. From what I could see, there was only one street in the entire town.

The town was bracketed by two large buildings. Houses and businesses hugged the corridor between these imposing structures, and an assemblage of wharves poked into the sea like a handful of misshapen fingers. But it was the totem poles, tall and ancient, that held my gaze. Tilting at the heavens with uneven grace, the totems defined the Indian section of town. Behind them rose the deep green of uncut timber. I guessed the town was no more than two miles long.

As the ship eased toward the wharf, I picked up my suitcase and prepared to take my first steps down the gangplank—to what, I didn't know.

People stood about the dock and at the open door of a freight shed. Indian children played tag among oil barrels and packing cases. Indian men leaned against those same crates, watching the ship unload. There were many Indian people, and it gave me an odd feeling.

I spotted Mr. Todd immediately. His white hair was in stark contrast to the black hair of the Natives. How reassuring it was to see a familiar face! He grinned broadly as he came to meet me, although I'm sure I looked travel-worn from lack of sleep—and probably scared stiff, too—which I was.

"Welcome to Alert Bay," he said genially. "I hope your trip went well." He picked up my bag. "Now, come and meet Sadie Thompson, my secretary."

I followed as he walked toward a red-haired young woman dressed in a heavy sweater, tweed skirt, and sensible flat-soled shoes. She greeted me warmly.

Mr. Todd shifted the weight of my suitcase. "Let's go along to the house. I'll come back and see to your trunk later."

I nodded, more than happy to let him "see to" whatever he wished.

"You'll be staying with us tonight," he said. "Tomorrow a boat will take you to Village Island."

Obviously my stay in Alert Bay was going to be brief.

After leaving the wharf we walked through the Indian section. As Sadie made small talk in an effort to put me at ease, I tottered clumsily along the uneven road in my best high heels. I became quite envious of those sensible shoes of hers.

But when I wasn't looking for a safe next step, I did look around.

I'd never been anywhere like this and was curious. Small unpainted houses lined both sides of the street close to the rough road. On the beach side, the houses stood on pilings. I imagined them when the tide was high, jutting over the water. Some of the doors were open, showing a stove, kitchen table, and bed in close proximity. I decided a lot of living must be done in one room.

Stout, black-haired women, wearing heavy blankets, sat on door steps, gossiping in their Native tongue. As we walked by, Sadie and Mr. Todd greeted some women by name. They answered the greeting, but I could feel their eyes following me. The same thing happened when Mr. Todd greeted some men lounging outside the general store. When he inquired about their fishing, they answered him, but stared at me.

News travels fast in small places, so I imagine my arrival *was* causing a ripple of interest. And no doubt I looked the oddity, stumbling along in my city shoes that so aptly demonstrated the limited knowledge of Village Island's new teacher.

Totem poles stood here and there between the houses, some leaning awkwardly, others collapsed and rotting among the weeds. If they had ever been bright with colour, it was gone. Now they were weathered to grey.

It took only a few minutes to pass through the Indian village, and I admit I was glad to leave it behind. The stares and silence made me even more nervous than I already was.

A few moments later Mr. Todd said, "Here we are," and turned in at the gate of the most imposing house on the street. Painted a soft cream, the house had a wide veranda, a tidy fenced yard, and faced the sea. Annexed to the house, but with a separate gate and entrance, was the Indian agent's office.

Mrs. Myrtle Todd appeared from the kitchen as we entered. Of medium height, she wore her brown hair scooped back from her face and twisted in a knot at the back of her neck. Unlike her husband, who was smiling and jovial, Mrs. Todd looked to be rather severe and critical. I had the feeling she was appraising me, wondering how long I'd last—not long, from the look she gave me.

She was polite, though, and offered us all a cup of tea; but when that was done, Mr. Todd and Sadie disappeared into his office, and I was left alone with the formidable Mrs. Todd.

Murray Todd, the regional Indian Affairs agent, seen here with workers at the Alert Bay fish cannery, became Hughina's main link with the world beyond Village Island.

Farmland above Alert Bay's St. Michael's Residential School yielded food for its students. The stately edifice stood in stark contrast to the Native village nearby.

She had a point to make and got right to it. "What about your family?" she asked. "Is it a large one?"

"My family? Oh! Yes, it is. I'm the youngest of seven girls, so along with my sisters I have brothers-in-law and nieces and nephews." I wondered where she was leading.

"Then you've never been completely on your own," she stated flatly.

"No, not really." I admitted. "I've always lived at home or close to it. The last three years I've lived in a nurses' residence, but I could always get home on days off for a good meal."

She shook her head dubiously. "I wonder how you'll cope, living on an island with only the missionaries and the Native people for company."

I decided to be honest. "Actually, the more I think about it, the more the idea terrifies me. But if I can get away now and then, I'm sure I'll manage." At least I sounded brave.

"We didn't see much of your predecessor," she said. "She rarely came to the Bay."

"Good heavens, you mean once I'm on Village Island, I won't be able to leave?" I hadn't thought about this possibility.

"It depends on how badly you want to get away. The agency boat goes over now and again to check on things. And the fisheries inspector and the *Columbia* call. And you might be lucky and get to know some of the people living in the area. Other than that"—she paused for a moment—"there's always the Indians' gas boats."

"Tell me about the gas boats." If this was a means of escape, I intended to know about it.

"Most of them are sturdy enough, I guess, but I've seen a quite a few that don't exactly look … reliable."

This comment sent my heart to my boots. I wasn't sure of my own seaworthiness, and now I had to worry about gas boats! My rosy visions of whipping away for jolly weekends were disappearing rapidly. At that moment I was sorely tempted to jump the next ship going south. But I soldiered on, still looking for the golden lining.

"What about the missionaries? What are they like?" I asked.

"Kathleen O'Brien is a dedicated woman, and I admire her for what she's trying to do on the island." She paused again before adding. "I must say she manages well in spite of her handicap."

"No one told me she was handicapped," I exclaimed, afraid to ask exactly what that handicap was. It didn't take long for Mrs. Todd to tell me.

"Oh? Well, she's really quite deaf and uses an ear trumpet."

"My goodness," was all I could say to that. Then I asked, "And Miss Dibben, what about her? What is she like?"

"Ah, Miss Dibben. A woman full of missionary zeal. She's devoted her whole life to the church. However … "

"Yes, go on," I urged.

"She has an affliction too, I'm sorry to say."

"What's wrong with *her*?" I tried not to emphasize the "her," but failed.

"She has limited vision. No sight at all in one eye and only partial sight in the other. Sometimes I'm amazed at the way she manages." With that Mrs. Todd stood and started to clear away the tea cups. Our conversation, it seemed, was over, leaving me with a fresh batch of worries.

The next morning, I awoke to the scream of the seagulls and the unfamiliar putt-putt of gas boats. It took a few moments to figure out where I was. When I did, I sat bolt upright.

This was Village Island day.

Maybe, I thought, if I stay in bed and pull the blankets over my head, I could make it all go away. But I knew it wouldn't, so I climbed out from under the warm covers. The tantalizing aroma of brewing coffee wafted up the stairs, so I dressed and followed its trail to the kitchen. Breakfast was on the table, and as I took my place, Mr. Todd spoke.

Secured in front of St. George's Hospital in Alert Bay, the flagship *Columbia* was the Columbia Coast Mission's link with the winter villages of the nomadic Kwakwaka'wakw families and the remote logging camps.

"I've arranged for your transportation to Village Island. Mr. Cameron, our fisheries inspector, is going that way today. He'll be leaving around noon."

"Thank you. That's very kind of him," I answered feebly. If either of the Todds detected my lack of enthusiasm, they didn't show it.

I offered to help Mrs. Todd with the dishes and we chatted amiably for the rest of the morning. I found her to be a frank, forthright woman who found no middle course. She either liked you or didn't. It was as simple as that. I sensed she liked me and the thought pleased me. It was as though I'd passed a test of some kind.

When it came time for me to go, she said briskly, "Now remember, we'll always be glad to have you stay with us if you can get away from the island now and then."

I nodded rather glumly.

She smiled. "Now, cheer up, Hughina. I'm sure you'll make the best of it."

I'm glad someone was sure, because at the moment I certainly wasn't.

Mr. Todd carried my suitcase to the fisheries wharf to where a boat called the *Black Raven* was tied. There on its afterdeck sat my trunk.

And so my adventure began.

The *Raven's* Journey

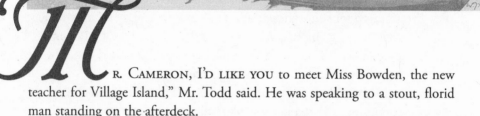

"MR. CAMERON, I'D LIKE YOU to meet Miss Bowden, the new teacher for Village Island," Mr. Todd said. He was speaking to a stout, florid man standing on the afterdeck.

"Welcome aboard, lass," came the man's reply in gruff, Scottish tones.

Smiling nervously, I climbed aboard the *Black Raven*, which was not black at all. Being a government boat in the service of the British Columbia department of fisheries, it was painted a serviceable grey. Mr. Cameron disappeared into the wheelhouse and signalled the engineer. In minutes we were underway. As we reversed away from the wharf, Mr. Todd raised his hat in salute, and reluctantly I waved goodbye. A moment later he was gone.

I was on my own.

"Ye'd better come inside, lass. It's a mite chilly out here today," Mr. Cameron called from the wheelhouse.

I joined him, and through the windows, I watched Alert Bay recede into the distance as the *Black Raven* moved out into the inlet. Soon all I could make out was the hospital and the totems in the old Indian graveyard.

Then it was behind us, and we were making our way over choppy water, skirting small rocky islands, while the sturdy chugging of the engine held us on course. I soon lost all sense of direction and could only trust Mr. Cameron knew where he was going. As far as the eye could see, there was nothing but grey rocks, overcast skies, churning sea and green trees.

"Doesn't anyone live out here?" I asked, straining my eyes to find some sign of life, a house, a narrow pier, a boat. There was nothing.

"Aye," Mr. Cameron replied. "A lot of people live hereabouts."

"Where?" Strain though I might, I could see nothing and no one, not even a puff from a campfire.

"Oh, they're here, tucked away in a bay or a sheltered cove. It's a big country, lass."

I thought back on my long journey from Vancouver.

"It sure is," I mumbled, still scanning the horizon. There seemed to be endless miles of water and hundreds of islands. I was grateful when Mr. Cameron identified some of the larger ones for me.

"That's Malcolm Island," he said, pointing left. "It was settled by Finnish people years ago. Sointula is its largest settlement. I'm told the name means "harmony." The first people to arrive there planned a utopia of some kind, intended to keep their own customs and language. It worked for a while, until they ran into money trouble. After that a lot of them left. The ones who stayed are good fishermen. Sointula is a nice town." He squinted, then pointed to the right. "Look. Over there. That's Pearse Island, and Hanson Island lays over yonder."

As the *Black Raven* nosed through the channels formed by the islands, he continued to tell me what he knew of this sea-swept country. Until, suddenly, the islands were behind us and we were in open water aboil with angry whitecapped waves.

"Where are we now? Isn't it terribly rough?" To me the answer to the last question was obvious, but in my apprehension I asked it anyway.

Mr. Cameron smiled by way of comfort as the boat smacked each wave in turn. "We're in Blackfish Sound," he said. "And it isn't at all bad today. There's times you can barely make it across, and it's not wise to try in a small craft when the sweep of wind and tide comes south from Johnstone Strait. When *that* funnels through here, it can be a dangerous stretch of water."

I didn't even want to think about it.

"I'm glad that's behind us," I said ardently when we were safely across the sound and in the lee of the islands once more.

"If you're going to be in this country long, you'll have to get used to a bit of rough weather, lass. Worse than today by far."

I was pondering my ability to "get used to it" when he announced, "I guess we'll say hello to the folks at Freshwater Bay." With that, he gave a mighty blast on the boat's whistle.

In the distance, Freshwater Bay seemed to consist of a dock, a couple of sheds and a house. Smoke came from the chimney and someone waved from the doorway.

This sign of life provided only minor comfort. To my eyes the land still appeared vast, empty and lonely. Its primitive, unspoiled beauty was awe-inspiring, but also cold and uninviting. I felt small and very much alone.

Nearly two hours later, Mr. Cameron said, "We'll soon be there now."

I quickly peered through the wheelhouse windows, but all I could see were more tree-covered islands, one looking much the same as the other. A few minutes later, he signalled for half speed and we rounded a point, the *Black Raven* cautiously making her way between great, jagged rocks.

Village Island came into view.

Then I saw it—the home of the Mamalilikulla.

The tiny Indian village was tucked into the coastline, dwarfed by the land that contained it. Weather-beaten houses made a haphazard row above the beach, each one facing the sea. The few that had once been painted had long since shed their colour in favour of a dull grey. Shacks stood dejectedly atop pilings on the beach, while to the left, on a knoll, was a building that, unlike the rest, faced the village. It had a newness about it, and over the entrance, it had a belfry topped by a wooden cross. I assumed it was the school. To the right, at the far end of the row of houses, I could see a large square building with a log frame. Beside it was a tall totem. Other totems stood along the path and between the houses.

One house stood apart from the rest—a small, brown house floating on the water. It was just below the building with the belfry.

The whole place was deathly still, a stillness punctuated only by the odd wisp of smoke pluming from one of the tin chimneys. The backdrop for this drab cluster of houses and totems was the forest, its trees—thick, dark and impenetrable—reaching for the very sky.

I would be living in one of these houses, I thought dejectedly. I was afraid to ask which one it would be. None looked inviting. My heart sank.

I did not want to live in this awful old place.

If Mr. Cameron sensed my despair, he said nothing, and the *Black Raven* relentlessly plied her way through the rocky channel to my new home.

The Brown House

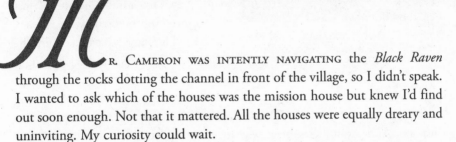

*M*R. CAMERON WAS INTENTLY NAVIGATING the *Black Raven* through the rocks dotting the channel in front of the village, so I didn't speak. I wanted to ask which of the houses was the mission house but knew I'd find out soon enough. Not that it mattered. All the houses were equally dreary and uninviting. My curiosity could wait.

We skirted the full length of the village and nosed toward the float in front of the floating brown house. The water lapped around the front edge of the raft on which the building sat. The back of the raft reclined on the pebbled beach. As the boat was being made fast to the float, two middle-aged women emerged from the house.

"Good afternoon, Mr. Cameron," said the smaller of the two.

"Miss O'Brien." He nodded, then turned to the other woman. "And how are you, Miss Dibben?" Without waiting for a reply, he gestured toward me and went on. "This is Miss Hughina Bowden, your new teacher, and she's to help with the nursing, too. Or so I've been told."

Miss O'Brien spoke first. She was prim and polite. "I'm glad you've had a safe journey. Now, do come in and have a cup of tea."

I smiled through my anxiety and followed. The women led the way from the float onto a plank walk, then onto the raft that both supported and formed the veranda of the brown house. Mr. Cameron and I followed them through the kitchen to the sitting room.

Kathleen O'Brien, right, sporting her ever-present hair ribbon, poses with her visiting niece from England and Miss Kate Dibben on the village path, as a cool breeze makes its presence felt.

Miss O'Brien instructed us to sit down, then turned to Mr. Cameron. "What's the latest news from Alert Bay?" she asked.

"Yes, do tell," put in Miss Dibben. "And have you heard when the *Columbia* is due?"

While Mr. Cameron proceeded to bring them up to date on the latest from Alert Bay and beyond, I had time to study the women I would be living with in the months to come.

Miss O'Brien was short, on the dumpy side, but her quiet voice was laced with a pleasant English accent. Her hair was dark, liberally sprinkled with grey, and around her head, just above her eyebrows, she wore a black ribbon. Her hair was tucked in the ribbon at the sides and back, giving it a puffy, bouffant style.

Her attire was plain, consisting of a shapeless sweater over a loose-fitting blouse, a baggy skirt, and sturdy brogues. And around her neck was an ear trumpet resembling a miniature banjo, its flat, open cup attached to a tubular handle with an earpiece at its tip. As I was looking at it, she put it to her ear, and Mr. Cameron leaned forward and bellowed into it loud enough to make her jump.

I stared. I had never seen such an oddity in my life. When I could drag my eyes from the ear trumpet, I studied her face. A good face, I decided. And gentle, with a decided twinkle in her warm brown eyes.

Miss Dibben was of a more robust build, with mounds of white hair piled high above a pale face. Her eyes, which had probably once been blue, looked colourless and strained behind thick-lensed glasses. She too was simply clad, in a navy-blue dress topped by a sweater. I didn't see a twinkle in Miss Dibben's eyes; instead I could almost feel the missionary zeal.

Two very different women, I decided.

My eyes skipped furtively around the room while the ladies busied themselves with Mr. Cameron's news and preparing tea.

A wide window overlooked the channel in front of the house, giving a picturesque view of water and islands. There was a piano near the kitchen door

In 1926 Kathleen O'Brien used her own resources to establish a floating home at Village Island and dedicate her life to missionary work, nursing and educating the Mamalilikulla children.

and, at the opposite end of the room, a potbellied stove sat snugly between two wicker armchairs. A drop-leaf table, host to a coal-oil lamp, stood under the window. Other lamps perched on wall brackets in strategic places around the room. The varnished floor was covered with braided rugs. Pictures, many with religious themes, hung in an uneven arrangement on beaverboard walls. Neat piles of magazines were stacked in a corner near the window. I spotted *Punch*, *Sketch*, and *The Daily Mirror*. As well, there was a bookcase holding prayer and hymn books. The room had a prim, old-maidish look—which wasn't surprising, considering its occupants—but it was also comfortably lived-in and not unfriendly.

"And now it's time for tea," Miss O'Brien said, passing the cups and pound cake.

After we'd been served, she turned to me. "We're glad to have you with us, Miss Bowden, and we do hope you'll be happy here. We're so gratified to have a qualified nurse as well as a teacher. Sometimes we run into medical problems that do worry us."

I nodded politely and sipped my tea. "How many children will be starting school?" I asked tentatively.

"Not many," Miss Dibben replied. "The Indian people haven't yet settled in for the winter. Of course, there are the children in the *Hyuya-Tsi*, but we tutor them separately."

Many days during her first months, Hughina would walk along the shoreline and look back at the village or stare down the channel to Alert Bay with yearning eye, wondering what she had taken on.

"What's the *Hyuya-Tsi*?" I'd never heard such a word before.

"It's our tuberculosis preventorium. We gave it an Indian name meaning place of rest. We have three girls at present." She sighed sadly. "TB is such a scourge among the Indian people."

Both ladies then inquired politely about Victoria and my training school, probing into my ability as a teacher. I answered as best I could, all the while hoping my inexperience didn't show too much.

Finally, Mr. Cameron got to his feet. "I must be off," he said, then turned toward me. "Goodbye, lass. Sometime when I'm coming this way, I'll call and take you to Alert Bay."

I said my goodbye, all the while wondering if he would remember his promise. I hoped he would. I'd been here less than an hour and I was already looking forward to leaving.

I watched the *Black Raven* creep out of the channel, and as she chugged into deep water, my mood turned dismal. I had one thought.

There goes my last link with civilization.

Marooned!

S O, HERE I WAS STRANDED on a remote island—all because a small band of Kwakwaka'wakw families chose to winter here, and my government was intent on educating them. My sole companions were two middle-aged spinsters of whom I was in awe.

Miss O'Brien distracted me from my gloomy thoughts, her voice full of cheer. "Now, I'm sure you want to get settled, so I'll show you to your room."

We didn't have to go far. I followed her through one of the three doors in the sitting room to my bedroom.

"I hope you'll find everything you need," she said, quickly scanning the tiny room. "I'll leave you now to unpack." She closed the door then, leaving me in my cell.

I couldn't think of a better word for it. But luckily, in this case, there were means of escape. The room, no more than eight feet long and six feet wide, boasted three doors and two windows. I checked the doors. One led to the bedroom next to mine, which was also entered from the sitting room; one was the door I'd just come through. The third door opened outside—to nowhere. Well below its sill were the logs of the raft on which the house rested. Strong cables attached to the cribbing of logs were set into the bank. These, I guessed, were all that kept us from floating out to sea.

Through one window I could see the path along the beach and the houses of the village above and to the right of it. The other window was beside my door to nowhere, and through it I could see the hillside and a new-looking building. The preventorium, I assumed. Beside it was a tiny house with a peaked roof.

My bed was a narrow cot with a lumpy mattress, but the sheets were spotless. A two-drawer washstand held a basin, a jug and the usual accessory for where there was no indoor plumbing. A corner of the room was curtained off to form a closet of sorts. The only other piece of furniture in the room was a straight-backed chair. My trunk sat under the window with the view, leaving just enough room for the bedside rug.

Recessed into the wall above the bed were shelves holding small volumes of Shakespeare, Tennyson, Longfellow and the Brownings. The room, with its sloping ceiling, looked as if it had been added as an afterthought. But despite the room's size and Spartan furnishings, I was grateful for the view and the privacy. I set about unpacking my trunk.

I unpacked slowly, daydreaming of my home in Victoria, only vaguely aware of the sound of the sea lapping beneath the house. As the hour passed, the sound gradually diminished, but as my hands were busy and my mind a couple of hundred miles away, I paid no attention.

A soft tap on the door brought me back to reality with a start. Miss O'Brien called through the closed door, "Would you please come for supper now?"

"I'll be right there, Miss O'Brien." As I left my bedroom and stepped into the sitting room, I had the oddest sensation. Was it possible that, since my arrival, I'd developed a short right leg? I realized everything in the room, including me, was slanted toward the sea. Was it me? Or some kind of optical illusion? I was almost afraid to ask, in case my added weight had affected the balance of the house in some way.

"Miss O'Brien," I said timidly.

There was no answer.

I realized then she hadn't heard me, so I spoke louder. "Miss O'Brien, is there something wrong with the house? It seems to be on a slant."

"Oh," she said, smiling. "Yes, of course you *would* notice it. The tide is out, you see."

I didn't see at all. "The tide is out?"

"Yes, dear. When the tide is out, the house rests on the beach," she explained reasonably, and with that comment went into the kitchen.

I went to the window, and sure enough, the sea was a good 30 feet from the house, and the floating dock was resting at an awkward angle on the rocky shore. This was certainly nothing like my perfectly stable home in Victoria.

Miss O'Brien came back into the sitting room and continued. "You see, the house rises and falls with the tide." To hear her, you would think it was the most natural thing in the world.

At low tide the little brown house was left high and dry, allowing winter winds to assault the floorboards. The school/church sits in the background.

My reaction to this latest bit of news about my new home was mixed. Having always lived on a firm foundation, the thought of a floating house made me uneasy. But it was a relief to know both my legs were still the same length and my vision intact. I followed Miss O'Brien into the kitchen, still atilt and trying to digest this new oddity.

The round kitchen table was set for dinner. It stood under a window, affording a view of the *Hyuya-Tsi* across the path on the hillside.

I took the seat assigned to me and looked around. On the opposite side of the kitchen, in an alcove overlooking the channel, was a range and a sink with a tap. The tap surprised me. I'd assumed we'd pack water from the village pump, so this discovery was a happy one. The stove had a large reservoir for heating water, confirming the tap provided only cold. Nevertheless, it gave a welcome flavour of civilization.

The meal was good, but the ladies were stiff and formal. As we ate I wondered if they were as much in awe of me as I was of them. What conversation there was centred on the village.

They told me about people with names such as Beans, Mountain, Salmon and Sewid. I heard about the girls in the *Hyuya-Tsi* and the women's hopes for arresting at least some of the incidents of TB.

After supper Miss O'Brien asked if I'd like to check the dispensary.

"Oh, yes!" I said with enthusiasm—and relief. This was familiar ground and I was intensely curious. "Where is it?" I asked, expecting to see something shining with glass and white enamel, with neatly labelled bottles in straight, tidy rows.

"Over in the corner," Miss Dibben said, gesturing with her head. "As you know, all the medical supplies are provided by the federal government."

The corner indicated by Miss Dibben was in the shadow outside the circle of light cast by the coal-oil lamp, and I could see nothing either white or shining in the gloom. On investigation, I found open shelves with curtains instead of doors. Behind the curtains were demijohns of cod-liver oil, mineral oil, cough syrup, Aspirin and soda mints. A further search revealed bottles of iodine and Mercurochrome, bandages, adhesive tape and absorbent cotton. The topper was a medical-style black bag, which would be the badge of office of Miss Bowden, village nurse. Now, this was exciting!

The next day I tried to behave like a teacher. Through the window I viewed the school with alarm. As it would be my domain in the months to come, I decided I should accustom myself to it. So, at breakfast, I asked Miss O'Brien for the key.

I walked up the hill to the schoolhouse door, unlocked it, then stepped into a small vestibule. A sturdy rope dangled in one corner. It was connected to the bell that would call the children to school. On one side of the entrance there was a low shelf holding galvanized buckets, above which were rows of hooks, each holding a mug and toothbrush. Split wood and a box of kindling sat against the wall on the other side.

When Hughina arrived, the school was a decade old. This 1926 photo shows Reverend Comely of Alert Bay, a former bricklayer, starting to build the chimney. The teachers await completion.

Hughina's photo shows her school, which had high, narrow windows facing away from the sea. The tall trees nearby cast a sombre gloom on the place.

I opened the inner door, which led into the main room. Daylight filtered in through high, narrow windows on one side only, the side away from the sea view. Whoever designed the school had no eye for beauty. Tall trees grew close by, shutting out the sunlight and casting a sombre gloom. The walls were unpainted and had darkened to a nondescript brown, and the floor, composed of rough planks treated with oil, was almost black. The desks, sitting in straight rows, were old and scratched from long use—not new when they arrived here, I guessed.

A plain teacher's desk sat at the front of the room, and an old organ stood off in the corner. Sundry coal-oil lamps rested on wall brackets around the room, the largest one sitting atop the organ. A blackboard covered the wall behind the teacher's desk and a wood-burning stove stood midway along the left-hand wall. In cupboards I found scribblers, pencils, readers and arithmetic books. No frills, but all the basic necessities. There was only one thing missing—the pupils.

I was about to light the fire and prepare for my first day of teaching when Miss O'Brien arrived.

"I've just checked through the village," she said. "And the families with children seem to have gone again. Sometimes it's hard to pin them down at this time of year, but I'm sure they'll be back in a day or so."

It seemed I'd been granted a reprieve. I wondered where the families had gone. Fishing, perhaps.

"If I'm not teaching," I said, "I might as well do some exploring."

"Do, by all means. I know Miss Dibben will be happy to show you the *Hyuya-Tsi.*"

I walked down the path from the school and up the uneven steps to the door of the preventorium. Miss Dibben greeted me and invited me to meet the patients.

She ushered me into a bright, airy room—not at all like the school—with the sun shining through windows on three of the four walls. With its southern exposure, and facing the sea, the solarium caught light from sunrise to sunset.

The room held four beds, but only three were occupied. Miss Dibben stood by one of them.

"This is Eliza," she said, then indicated the other girls in the room. "And this is Christine and Kathleen."

I smiled and said, "Hello."

"Hello," they chorused, then ducked under white bedspreads, giggling as young girls do.

"We hope we're making progress," Miss Dibben said quietly. "This project is just underway, you know. The doctor is hopeful Christine and Kathleen's illness has been caught in time, but there is cause for concern regarding Eliza. But we are doing our best with rest, fresh air and proper diet." When the girls surfaced from under the covers, she changed the subject. "Now, come and see the Gables."

"What are the Gables?"

"It's the house next door, where I sleep so as to be near the children. I also prepare their meals there."

It turned out the Gables was the tiny house I'd spotted from my bedroom window. Under its peaked roof there was only one room, furnished with a bed, a chair, a cookstove and cupboards for food storage. The Gables was more cell-like than my room. I couldn't help but feel Miss Dibben, given her age and affliction, should have things easier. I guess I was the soft one, for she seemed quite content with her life of hard work and austere living.

My tour of the Gables didn't take long, and after thanking Miss Dibben for showing me her special place, I decided on a walk through the village.

Earlier I had stood on the steps of the school and looked along the hillside path leading to the village. Now I walked along it, the Gables and the *Hyuya-Tsi* above, and the brown house below. The path was wide enough to walk two or three abreast, and the surface was hard-packed from years of wandering feet. Tall dry grass, thistles and stinging nettles grew where no houses stood. If there was a plan for the village, it wasn't obvious, except to ensure every house faced the sea. It seemed each builder had chosen a site on whim. A few had

Kate Dibben, shown here surrounded by children from the local day school, taught in Alert Bay before her move to Village Island.

been built with care and an eye to design, while others were jerry-built shacks, old and weathered to a soft grey. Few had seen a coat of paint, and the ones that had were dulled by time and salt spray. The shacks on the beach were the worst of all, looking as if they would collapse at any moment. Rickety steps led from the top of the bank to the doorways, and moss encrusted the curling shake shingles on their roofs.

Totem poles, ancient and lonely, told their timeless stories, but no one was there to listen. They kept their silent vigil, and their reason for being seemed long forgotten. They appeared forlorn, standing here and there along the path, almost like intruders. But the true intruders were the houses, elbowing these monuments of the old culture aside to make room for the new.

The stories were told in the carved designs, by the figures set one on top of the other—the Bear, the Salmon, the Raven, the Orca and the mightiest of them all—the Thunderbird. The carving on some was still distinct and fine, the adze marks plainly visible, while on others the elements had bleached them smooth and silvery, turning them hoary with age.

In an open space between two houses, the grass grew tall. Wood, neatly stacked, stood ready for the cold winter nights. A kitchen range, rusting in the wind and rain, stood abandoned beside the woodpile. There was something else.

Thrown in an untidy heap near the old stove and the fresh-cut wood were several carved images. About five or six feet in length, they depicted dwarfish men with round moon faces. These effigies must have been held in high regard at one time but now, their significance diminished, they'd been tossed aside. I studied three phases of history in this grass-grown corner—the ancient images, the middle-aged stove and the neat woodpile, a necessity of the present.

I walked on, passing a few empty, though obviously lived-in, houses. Then I came upon an open field where, at the edge of the path, an archway, guarded by a totem, stood stark and bare. The arch was at least 10 feet tall and constructed of peeled logs 4 feet in diameter. The ends of the lintel lay in grooves chiselled into the tops of the vertical columns. Time had lent a soft patina to this portal of the past. In the field beyond, traces of an ancient building's footprint were barely discernible. Grass now reigned where once stood a mighty house.

Next I walked toward the great square house which I'd first glimpsed through the glass of the *Black Raven*'s wheelhouse. I recalled how, from the sea, it had dwarfed the dwellings nearby. Now I stood just outside it, peering through the arched doorway into its shadowy past.

The skeleton of this great house was a grid of enormous logs and a triumph of primitive engineering. It easily measured 50 feet from the entrance to the rear wall, and each roof support was a single straight-grained log with a circumference greater than the span of a man's arms. The corner posts were embedded firmly in the ground, and the beams, which formed the rectangular shape of the house, rested easily in grooves chiselled into the tops of the corner posts. At the rear, the ends rested on the heads of two mighty Thunderbird totems. With their all-seeing eyes, enormous beaks and widespread wings, they stood tall and silent. Because they were protected from the wind and weather, their colours glowed bright and clear. These were indeed two treasures of the Mamalilikulla culture. I stood, utterly still, and admired the magnificent structure.

Hughina would walk this path many times as she set out from the little brown house to respond to the latest village emergency. It was a far cry from wandering down Government Street in Victoria.

These discarded effigies must have held some significance for the Mamalilikulla at one time.

No nails were in evidence in the construction framework, and I knew the great timbers had been raised above the ground only by equal amounts of will and manpower. The length of each beam and corner post and the straightness of their grain suggested these beams had been selected with meticulous care.

In the centre of the room were ashes and half-burned logs, remnants of what had been a roaring fire. Directly above, light filtered through the opening in the shake roof, cut there to allow the smoke from the fire to escape. Raised platforms defined the inside perimeter, and a dais sat at the feet of the great Thunderbirds. The floor was hard-packed earth. Standing in the doorway to this old house, I could only wonder what stories of ancient cultures it could tell. But the guardian Thunderbirds would keep the secrets of this special place, as would the dense forest at its back and the sea on its doorstep. I turned to go.

I faced that sea then and felt the harsh wind chill my face and whip at my hair. I listened to the sigh of evergreens and the slap of waves on the rocky shore. As far as the eye could see there was only water, islands and more water. Not a living soul was in my sight. There was beauty in abundance, but at that moment—to me, at least—there seemed to be nothing else.

The G.A.s

URING THE NEXT FEW DAYS, I had an opportunity to become better acquainted with the G.A.s. (It was later in my stay that this private nickname popped into my head. They always seemed to hover about, concerned about my every move, so the name Guardian Angels just came naturally; the abbreviation to G.A.s came next. But *never, never* did I address them as anything other than Miss O'Brien and Miss Dibben.)

I became known as Miss B.

The G.A.s were content with their chosen life, and Village Island, manless and circumscribed, was their world. They accepted without complaint what to me was sheer and deadly isolation. To them, dedicated as they were to doing good works, the hardships and inconveniences were but a small price to pay for greater accomplishment. What I saw as difficult or burdensome was to them simply everyday life. Living without modern conveniences didn't trouble them in the least. I was the maladjusted outsider.

Of the two, I found Miss O'Brien, despite her poor hearing and the astounding ear trumpet, the easier to talk to. She had flashes of humour and usually a merry attitude. Kathleen O'Brien had first come to Village Island as a nurse in 1920 and had lived here ever since. Her life was one of true dedication. If she had a foible, it was "pros and cons." Nothing was ever decided without debating her pros and cons. At meals when we were all together, she had a great time jumping from one to the other and leading us into the discussion. She was a kind and trusting person who saw the best in everyone. A few unscrupulous souls often played on her sympathy and giving nature, well aware she could never say no to anyone with a mournful expression and an outstretched hand.

Hughina found Kathleen O'Brien to be a kind and trusting person who saw the best in everyone.

Miss Dibben was pious and proper. She abided by the law of the church and the law of the land—to the letter. I never found her as approachable as Miss O'Brien, although no one could fault her for her good intentions and hard work.

Their tasks were divided. Miss O'Brien was the housekeeper and financial manager, while Miss Dibben took care of the children afflicted with tuberculosis. Miss Dibben also organized and led church services in the school on Sundays, and prayer meetings, which were held each weekday evening in the sitting room. She played both the piano and the wheezy old organ, and always led the singing in a lusty voice.

There were two other inhabitants on Village Island besides the G.A.s, the Natives and myself. A couple of days after my arrival, Miss O'Brien called excitedly from the kitchen alcove, "Here comes Mr. Oiens." As I'd never met our neighbours, some of her excitement transferred to me.

I watched through the window as a clumsy-looking gas boat was being skilfully guided through the rocky channel. A big man in a windbreaker and gumboots jumped onto the float and made the boat fast. He unloaded a heavy milk can and a full gunny sack, then carried them to our door.

Miss O'Brien greeted him and introduced me, rather proudly I thought, as their new teacher.

Immediately my hand was lost in an enormous paw, and my ears were treated to a strong Norwegian accent. "How do, Miss? Mrs. Oiens, she'll be glad to meet you, too. Yah!" he said, shaking my hand.

To me, he looked like a Viking of old. In his youth, I'm sure he had been a handsome man. He was tall, with a muscular build, and the strong aquiline features of his face were topped by a thatch of iron-grey hair.

After greeting me, he turned back to Miss O'Brien. "Here's the milk, yah? I go get the eggs and butter. And some mail I have for you." Then he returned to his boat for the rest of the supplies.

The Oiens had a farm on the island, about a mile from the village. It was the G.A.'s source of eggs, milk and fresh vegetables when they were in season. Today, he was also the mailman, it seemed.

Mail was something I had yet to learn about.

When he returned to the house with the mail, he told us his wife had asked us to come for tea. I was pleased when Miss O'Brien accepted. It gave me a pleasant glow to hear there were other friendly people in the vicinity. Despite Mr. Cameron's assurances that there were lots of people "in these parts," I had yet to meet anyone other than the G.A.s. Mrs. Oiens's invitation was a welcome chance to alter that.

We boarded the boat, and after rounding a point and entering a bay, we tied up to the Oiens' jetty. Their unpainted farmhouse sat in a field about 50 feet from the shoreline of the protected cove.

A tall, raw-boned, white-haired woman waited at the door. She looked harried and work-worn, but so rich was her accent, you'd have thought she had arrived from her native Scotland only yesterday.

"Glad to see you, lass," she said, pumping my hand. "It's fine to see a nice young face again. We get a bit tired of the auld ones." She chuckled.

"Now, do come and have some tea and scones," she said, herding us inside. She served us the most delicious scones this side of heaven—warm, golden and dripping with butter and strawberry jam.

Mrs. Oiens talked non-stop, as someone does who lacks companionship, and I immediately felt I was a kindred spirit. I was sure she experienced the loneliness that plagued me.

While we had our tea, our hostess told us the story of the Oiens on the British Columbia coast. She had come from Scotland years before to cook in logging camps and, in one of them, had met her husband. For years they lived in remote places such as this one. Their last place of residence, before settling on Village Island, had been on Smith Inlet, farther north on the coast. There, they had lost all their equipment and possessions in a forest fire, forcing them to move and start over again. Mrs. Oiens asked about Victoria and Vancouver as though they were foreign countries. It had been years since she'd been anywhere near either of B.C.'s major centres.

"Ye'll come and see me often, won't ye, lass?" she asked as we were leaving. There was no mistaking the pleading note in her voice.

I assured her I would, while dreading the thought I might become as bushed as she was. From what I'd seen of Village Island and the emptiness of the waters around it, it looked decidedly possible.

I soon discovered that the only contact with the outside world was by written word, carried to and fro by whoever passed our way. This casual dependence came to light in my early days on the island and did nothing to endear it to me.

It wasn't until the middle of October that enough families with children returned to warrant opening the school. The thought of teaching filled me with alarm, and the gay adventurous spirit which I'd been brimful of during the summer was slowly but surely evaporating. However, the inevitable day arrived, so I rose from my cot, shivered across the cold floor of the sitting room to the kitchen for my jug of hot water, and returned to my room to perform my chilly ablutions.

After breakfast I walked up the hill to the frigid school. As I was also the janitor, it was up to me to light the fire and draw a bucket of drinking water from the well. These tasks marked the beginning of my workday.

While I was setting out scribblers, pencils and readers, there was a tap on the door and Miss O'Brien poked her head in.

"I wanted to remind you to raise the flag. I noticed you hadn't done so," she informed me politely.

"Yes, Miss O'Brien," I said. "I'll do it right away."

As the Union Jack sailed to the top of the pole and began flapping in the wind, I told myself to remember to lower it at sunset. Obviously, *the flag* was critical to the smooth running of the mission.

When the flag was properly dealt with, I dashed back into the school, poked the sluggish fire and took a final look at my lesson plans. At precisely five minutes to nine, I gave the bell rope a hefty tug; its clanging filled the still, frosty air. Then I waited for my first day as teacher of the Mamalilikulla Indian Day School to begin.

A few minutes went by before I heard the knob of the outside door turning, followed by a rustle and a whisper in the vestibule. The door opened and three children sidled in. For a moment I studied their unique faces, round with slightly slanted eyes over flat-bridged noses. Straight ebony hair. I waited for more children to follow them, but no one else appeared.

"Good morning, children," I said in my best teacher's voice. "Where are all the others?"

"Dunno," said the one boy.

"Went to Turnour Island last night," chirped a bright-eyed, light-skinned girl.

"I see. And when will they be back?" I asked, wondering if this so-called school was ever going to get underway.

"Dunno," the children chorused, shrugging.

"Well, in that case we'll carry on," I said. "Tell me your names, please."

The boy spoke first. "Wilfred," he said, then gestured toward the bright-eyed girl. "And that's my sister Stella."

"And what is your name?" I asked the other girl.

"Emily," she whispered shyly.

Another question yielded surnames, and I filled in the register with the names of Stella and Wilfred Hanuse, and Emily Beans, marking three Xs on the large sheet, which somehow looked very empty.

We followed this with the Lord's Prayer, then headed outside for toothbrush drill. Each child had his own mug and toothbrush on a hook in the vestibule. The children brushed vigorously, and it soon became a game to see who could spit the farthest. The first teacher on Village Island had instituted this daily routine, and I saw no reason to abandon it, as it was the only time many of the children brushed their teeth.

Later on I decided on another aid to sanitation and to the peace of the classroom. Nose-blowing time. There is nothing worse than a roomful of sniffling children afflicted with constantly running noses. As none of them ever had handkerchiefs, old sheets torn into squares served the purpose and were readily disposed of.

I wasn't too sure of myself in the classroom, but as the days progressed, I found the children had forgotten almost everything they'd been taught the year

Below and next page: Hughina's students pose outside the schoolhouse, on a rare day of full attendance.

before. This gave me more confidence because I felt we were, more or less, starting on an equal basis. The exceptions were Wilfred and Stella, who were the bright sparks of the group, and who had no trouble remembering their lessons.

By the end of October, enrolment had increased to 10. Families that had left in spring for the fishing season gradually returned to their winter island. I was yet to learn that days off to go clam digging, family outings to Alert Bay, long visits to neighbouring villages and just plain not coming to school in the morning made the children's school year short indeed.

My first impression was that the children were dull and unresponsive, and nothing in my year at Victoria Normal School had prepared me for this. Then I realized the government curriculum made no special provision for Indian children. In their homes they spoke mainly Kwak'wala, their Native tongue, and any extra-curricular reading was limited to funny books.

Much of the children's poor reaction to my curriculum stemmed from its irrelevance to their environment and Native culture. The parents were fond of their children, but verbalizing didn't seem an important means of communication. There were no crayons, cutouts or children's books in their homes, nor, as far as I could see, were they taught nursery rhymes or songs. Their education was geared to life on the island. They were perfectly familiar with gas boats and fishing boats, and while learning to be wary of the sea's dangers, they enjoyed all its freedoms. This was a far different school than the alien one they were thrust into on weekday mornings, where they were told to sit still—and where they were disciplined by a strange White person.

The standard readers of the day were written for the middle-class White child and geared to that child's environment and experiences, none of which bore the faintest resemblance to life in an Indian village in the year 1935.

Many of the children I taught had never been farther from the island than Alert Bay. To them "car" was just a word with no meaning, and the pictures in the readers of Mummy in her sparkling kitchen, wearing a frilly apron, with two little White children and their sweet puppy and kitten had no relevance at all. Certainly, the idea of Daddy going off to his office in the car was no simile for what their own fathers did. Still, the days took on a routine of sorts, and I hoped the children were learning something that would be of use to them.

There were days when I had my doubts.

The one thing that didn't become routine was the flag. For some reason I could never fathom, I would invariably forget about it, and either the children or Miss O'Brien would have to remind me. I didn't mind the children jogging my memory, for then I could ask one of the older boys to deal with it for me. But Miss O'Brien always looked so hurt whenever she had to mention my omission. The flag, and whether it was up or down, was important to her. Had she stormed a little, perhaps I'd have felt less guilty, but she never did. It was always, "Miss B., *do* try to remember the flag tomorrow," or "Miss B., it's sunset and the flag is *still* flying." Then I would tear outside to pull the bally thing down!

However, on this tiny island, lost in the vast maze of the B.C. coast, the Union Jack could usually be seen fluttering from the top of the flagpole—its red, white and blue glory visible to any passing boat.

Whether it impressed the Natives or not, I never knew, but it certainly warmed the cockles of the G.A.'s stout British hearts.

Y SPIRITS WERE AT A low ebb. I was lonesome, homesick, maladjusted and disenchanted, and after only a few weeks—bushed. Civilization seemed a distant memory. I kept thinking, shades of Mrs. Oiens!

Then on a Saturday morning in mid-November, I heard the chug of a boat's engine. As the island wasn't exactly a busy port, the sound of sturdy engines breaking the silence was notable, something new and different to the ear. Who could it be?

My hopes soared when the *Black Raven* turned into the rocky channel and headed toward our float. Then salvation appeared in the rotund form of Mr. Cameron, who had brought me to this lost and lonely place. He had said he would call by some weekend when he was going to Alert Bay, but I'd dared not hope he'd remember his promise.

When the *Black Raven* was fast to the float, he called to me, "I'm on my way to the Bay, lass. Would ye care to come along?"

"Would I!" I yelled back, already mentally packed. "I'll be with you in a minute."

I filled my suitcase at the speed of light, and in minutes had my coat on and was aboard the boat. I believe Mr. Cameron was quite nonplussed at my alacrity— and I know the G.A.s were. I'm certain they'd never seen me move so quickly.

My next worry, as we headed to Alert Bay, was whether the Todds would remember their invitation that I stay with them if and when I got back to

Alert Bay. But at this point I'd have gladly slept on their doormat. I'd make out somehow. For now I would simply enjoy the ride.

Alert Bay looked like a mighty metropolis after my cloistered weeks on Village Island. With quaking heart I made my way to the Todds' house and knocked on the door. Mrs. Todd opened it.

"You made it back then. Good," she said, then herded me inside. "You're just in time for lunch."

And I was. Mr. Todd and Sadie were already at the table, and in no time a place was laid for me. Visitors appearing from nowhere seemed not to faze Mrs. Todd at all, so from then on, I felt I'd be welcome anytime I could devise a way of getting off the island—which was fast becoming an obsession.

Lunch with the Todds had none of the formality the G.A.s insisted on; instead it was warm, relaxed and peppered with easy conversation.

"How are things going on Village Island?" Mr. Todd asked.

I gave him a rundown on the village and the school—not that there was much to report—then I requested a few more supplies. I thought I might as well make use of my time here and do some good for the village.

Mrs. Todd interjected, "What about you? How are you making out?"

"If it's a change I wanted when I took this job, I'm getting it," I replied. "I certainly hadn't imagined living in a house that rises and falls with the tide. And when the tide is out, and there's a gale blowing, you wouldn't believe

This photo, taken by Indian agent William Halliday, Murray Todd's predecessor, shows Alert Bay from the Todds' front yard.

how cold it is. My feet haven't been warm since I left Victoria." With that I snuggled closer to the warm kitchen range and wiggled my toes, the heat and company making me contentedly giddy. I went on.

"There's one thing I'll never get used to, and that's not having a bathtub."

"How do you manage?" inquired Mrs. Todd, looking at me quizzically.

"Water comes by the jugful from the kitchen, so the best I can do is sponge bath in my—" I shuddered for effect "—heatless room.

"There's a cold-water tap in the kitchen, and a reservoir attached to the cookstove. That heats the water, and we dip into it for dishes and to fill jugs to take warm water to our rooms."

"Quite different from what you were used to at home, I expect," Mrs. Todd said. I wasn't sure, but I think she was testing me.

I smiled. "There's more. Something that gives the place quite the air of modern living."

"Oh, and what's that?"

"Well, next to the outhouse, there's a—" I stopped, not quite sure what to call the thing. "An arrangement of sorts. Miss O'Brien showed it to me. She's quite proud of it. It's kind of a shower, rather ingenious actually."

"'Kind of a shower?'" she repeated, looking puzzled.

"It's a galvanized bucket suspended by a rope from the ceiling. The bottom of the bucket is perforated. The idea is to fill it with hot water—cold if you're hardy enough—then get under it as the water trickles through the openings. There's no drainage problem, of course. The water simply runs through the cracks and knotholes in the floor to the beach below." I remembered Miss O'Brien showing me the enclosure, telling me with a flourish to have a shower whenever I wished to.

"Have you tried it?"

"No! The thought of taking a shower in that flimsy enclosure, with the wind whipping through all the apertures, gives me chills! I stick with the jug in my room. That way, at least I only have to expose one portion of my anatomy at a time to the cold drafts. I've never seen anyone actually using that shower," I said. "And I know *I* never will."

I guessed she was finding it difficult not to smile at the firm tone in my voice. "Then by all means, help yourself to the bathtub," she said. "You'll find towels in the cupboard in the hall."

These were words I longed to hear.

In minutes I was wallowing in steaming water up to my chin. Never had a bath felt so divine. I'm sure the Todds thought I was going to spend the rest of the weekend in their bathroom. But I emerged at last, and although

I was rather weak in the knees from being submerged so long in hot water, I'm sure I was considerably lighter and a few shades whiter than when I arrived.

I floated downstairs, clean and pure as new snow, and Sadie immediately invited me to her place to meet someone named Muriel Banfield.

As it turned out, Muriel was the field nurse for the Indian population of Alert Bay, and to our delight we found we had mutual acquaintances in Victoria. It was like meeting a long-lost friend.

As it was Saturday afternoon, everyone was out on the town's one and only street. There were no cars so everyone walked. As a result, it was practically impossible *not* to meet a good portion of the town's population. During the course of the afternoon, I discovered there were a lot of young people in this area, and although we were separated by only 15 miles, which in Victoria

Public-health field nurse Muriel Banfield poses with 104-year-old Charlie James in Alert Bay.

would have been nothing, I now knew out here those miles covered a stretch of tricky, unpredictable ocean.

As well as Muriel, I met Percy Wickett, who taught at the Alert Bay Indian Day School, and a woman named Kay Weymouth, also a teacher at the school. I also met the resident doctor, some of the nurses and a few teachers from the residential school. In the short space of an afternoon, I felt I had friends, and after my lonely time at Village Island, the feeling was a welcome one.

That night I slept cozy and warm—and level—in the Todds' comfortable home. In the morning I had another bath. I had the suspicion it might be weeks before I had the luxury again. All too soon, the *Black Raven* blew its horn. It was time to go. But this time I boarded with a lighter heart, knowing now I wasn't entirely alone in an alien world.

Monday morning, after my short taste of fun and freedom, it was back to business: lighting the fire, raising the flag, brushing teeth, blowing noses and trying to teach a few reluctant children. After school, with the black bag

Percy Wickett's Alert Bay Day Indian School classroom had 31 students in 1935.

tucked under my arm, I switched roles and became village doctor. It had been Miss O'Brien's habit to make rounds once a day, so I carried on with this routine.

Because I had my RN, it was assumed I knew the answers to *all* medical problems. The G.A.s had coped quite well before my arrival with the aid of government supplies, Doctor Somebody-or-other's encyclopedia on the ailments of the human race and a St. John's Ambulance *First Aid to the Injured*, but once I made my appearance, nothing was done without consulting me. This was complimentary but worrisome, as I wasn't at all sure my abilities deserved this much confidence.

The bright spot in this part of my job, and the most helpful, was the arrival of the mission ship, *Columbia*, which normally called every couple of weeks, except during winter, when the weather proved too hazardous.

The member of the crew I was happiest to meet was the doctor, David Ryall, a young man who had only recently finished his internship. This was his first job, and he was as new to the Indians and their ways as I was. Together we would make the rounds of the village, checking on anyone needing attention. I found it a great relief to discuss my problems with him and get some assurance that the treatments I'd prescribed were not going to prove fatal. I'm relieved to say I had no horrible disasters.

After Dr. Ryall and I were through in the village, we would board the *Columbia*'s kicker, the motor launch used to bring visitors ashore, and follow the rocky shoreline to call on Mrs. Oiens. She had high blood pressure, and I often thought she was glad of it, for the attentions of the "nice young doctor" appeared to be a highlight in her otherwise drab life. After he'd

The 106-ton hospital ship *Columbia* was launched in 1910 and plied the coast until 1957.

After the first hospital was destroyed by fire, the new St. George's was opened May 13, 1925, and dedicated by Chief Whonnock of Fort Rupert as "the house of salvation and the house of hope." Inset: In the mid-1930s Dr. David Ryall (left) stands next to his wife, whom Hughina knew as Frances Salmon. Dr. Ryall's hospital staff of five served the entire coast.

checked her heart and blood pressure, on would go the kettle and out would come the homemade scones or bread and jam and fresh butter. All the while her Scottish tongue never ceased its chatter. It was a pleasant hour and a reminder the world went beyond Blackfish Sound.

While the doctor and I were busy with things medical, the G.A.s bustled about with the *Columbia*'s parson in tow, organizing a church service. Because there were no communications to the island, visits such as these came out of the blue. There was no time for advance preparations. But when the *Columbia* blew its whistle, the village people knew within the next hour there would be a service.

The school served as the church, and hasty preparations were made by simply placing a hymn and prayer book on each desk, lighting the lamp on the organ and covering my desk with a cloth. That accomplished, Miss O'Brien would ring the bell to signal all was ready.

Most of the older people attended, as well as a few of the younger ones. Miss Dibben played the organ and stoutly led the singing, and the parson would read lessons and give a short sermon.

The parson was a joy to the G.A.'s hearts. Reverend Henry Dance was a bachelor, perhaps 40 years old, tall and angular, with a touch of grey in his hair. My early impression was that he was pious, humourless and somewhat

Reverend Henry Dance served aboard the *Columbia* in 1936, but felt the mission sacrificed its religious mandate to provide medical and social work. The next year he took up shore duty with the diocese in Alert Bay.

condescending toward the Native people. But he was actually quite shy. Particularly of maiden ladies, I think. And here on Village Island, the poor man was surrounded by them. In what seemed a bored manner, he would carry out his ecclesiastical duties, but when he strode resolutely up the hill in his black cassock and white surplice, he looked impressive indeed.

Regardless of the parson's attitude, during his time there, the shabby little school was transformed into a place of worship, and the G.A.s, bless their good hearts, would afterward carry on their work with renewed zeal and vigour.

The Golden Smile

*I*F I THOUGHT I'D BEEN cold in November, by the time December came I looked back on it as being semi-tropical. Now the winds blew in from the sea, harsh and icy, and the ground was bound by frost. When the tide was high and the house afloat, its floors were warm enough, but at low tide, with no water beneath for insulation, every nook and cranny in the house oozed cold, biting air. Even the schoolhouse, on dry land with an enclosed foundation, was uncomfortably cold despite its wood-burning stove.

I felt as if I were walking, not on two feet, but on two blocks of ice. I'd clump along the village path, most of the time feeling nothing below my knees, and at every opportunity I'd prop my feet on the sitting-room heater or a hot water bottle. I should have known better, because this habit led to a severe case of chilblains twice as painful as icy feet. When the soreness became unbearable, I'd soak my poor appendages in a bucket of hot salt water, all the while feeling immensely sorry for myself.

I never went to bed without a hot water bottle, bedsocks and a sweater worn over my flannel pyjamas. The G.A.s, when they realized my discomfort, supplied me with a noisome coal-oil heater. Although it emitted a dreadful smell, without it I think I'd have frozen solid.

It was impossible to heat the floating house adequately, as due to its peculiar motion, none of the windows or doors fit properly. The only sources of heat were the kitchen range and the potbellied stove, which would only be

The little brown floathome, purchased by Kathleen O'Brien and Eleanor Nixon independently of the Columbia Coast Mission, was towed to the Village Island beach by the *Columbia* in 1926. A year later the two women were officially recognized by the mission.

lit for the usual four o'clock tea.

At night the house was a symphony of sound. The cold and frost caused the dwelling to crack and bang like so many exploding firecrackers. Stormy nights were worse, for then the wind was a banshee wail that could keep the dead from sleep. When the tide was high, the house rocked with the waves, while the anchoring cables creaked and groaned continuously. I'd shiver in my cot, listening to the storm rage outside the thin walls and watching the curtains billow—even though the windows were tightly shut. And when the waves lashed over the logs of the raft and crashed up the bank outside my door to nowhere, I'd cross my fingers and hope that, in the morning, I wouldn't wake to find us all floating out to sea.

During a spell of this bitter weather, I took my first trip on an Indian gas boat.

It was Friday noon. I'd just dismissed the children and started toward the house, anticipating a hot drink and warm food. I noticed a dilapidated gas boat tied to the float, and on entering the kitchen, I found Miss O'Brien vainly attempting to communicate with a young Indian couple in their mid-to-late teens. Miss O'Brien didn't seem to be making any headway. The pair just sat quietly, making no response to her gentle voice, which was all but drowned out by the screams of an infant the girl held on her lap. The child was no more than eight months old.

"Oh, Miss B.," Miss O'Brien said, the relief in her voice evident. "I believe we have a little problem here." She gestured toward the young couple.

"What seems to be the trouble?" I asked.

"These young people are worried about the baby," she replied.

I glanced at the young parents where they sat, still as stone.

"They're from Gilford Island," she went on. "At least I think so. They don't speak much English. Hardly any as a matter of fact, so I'm not sure exactly what's wrong."

"Let's have a look," I said.

The child, a boy, was wrapped in filthy rags that smelled to the heavens, and when I removed them, I discovered a half-starved little body. He screamed louder when I touched his back, and on turning him over, I discovered an ugly bruise. One side of his face was swollen from an abscessed ear encrusted with discharge. I gave the parents a disapproving look, but they registered no emotion. I turned my attention back to the little boy.

This was a real emergency. I knew treatment was beyond my resources, and it would be hopeless to send these young people home with instructions. How could I make them understand when they spoke virtually no English? We couldn't keep the baby at the mission house because we had no facilities for such things. There was only one option.

"This child needs to be seen by the doctor," I said to Miss O'Brien, raising my voice to be heard over the crying infant. "And as soon as possible."

She nodded. "That was my thought, too." She glanced at the silent parents. "Can we make them understand, do you think?"

"We'll have to at least try."

We then told the parents the baby should go to the hospital in Alert Bay. They nodded, but I felt uneasy and not at all sure they understood the seriousness of the situation.

"Miss O'Brien," I said. "I think it's best I go along and make sure the doctor sees this child."

"By all means, Miss B., I feel this is enough of an emergency to warrant closing the school for the rest of the day. I'll see to it immediately." And out she went.

I turned to the mother. "When did you last feed the baby?" I asked.

She shrugged. I couldn't tell if she didn't care or she simply hadn't understood me. But from the looks of the baby, it was obvious he hadn't been fed too regularly, so I made up a formula of milk, water and corn syrup. He gulped it hungrily and almost immediately went to sleep. The silence was heavenly!

I cleaned up his ear and refilled the bottle, then I ate a hasty lunch and set about preparing for the trip. The day was cold and blustery, so I piled on some extra clothes, then wrapped the baby snugly and carried him to the boat with the parents following behind.

Up close, the boat was even worse than I'd first thought, and for a moment, I considered a hasty retreat. But duty called, so I stepped aboard the dirtiest, smelliest boat it was possible to imagine. No more than 15 feet in length, it hadn't seen a paintbrush—let along a scrub brush—since its original primer. There was a cabin of sorts that housed the engine and provided a place to sit out of the wind. When I poked my head in, I was instantly overwhelmed by the odour of stale fish and gas fumes. I immediately decided I'd rather freeze outside than be asphyxiated inside. I looked around for a place to sit, but there was nowhere except the narrow ledge of the well deck, and I could hardly stand erect holding a sick infant for 15 miserable miles. I went back to the house, where Miss O'Brien scouted out a wooden apple box. It would have to do.

When I stepped back aboard, I found more than half the well deck occupied by another passenger. I assumed she'd shown up while I was getting my apple box. Certainly she hadn't been in the cabin or I'd have noticed.

She was a large woman and almost enveloped in a thick, green blanket. If she was a relative of the young couple, no one chose to enlighten me, and the woman, although she stared constantly in my direction, didn't utter a word. But when I'd glance her way, she would grin broadly, almost blinding me with a fantastic display of gold teeth.

My previous trips over this stretch of water had been on the *Black Raven*, a substantial boat of respectable size with a roomy wheelhouse as protection against the weather. I felt secure on her, knowing there was something solid between me and the deep waters below. Not so on this flimsy contraption! I was sure if I put my foot down too heavily it would go right through the bottom of the boat. The water, dark and cold, was as close as if we were in a rowboat. Much too close. For a moment panic closed my throat. But when I thought about the number of miles between Village Island and Alert Bay, I decided I couldn't hold my breath that long; I'd have to make the best of it. I settled myself on the apple box, held the baby close and tried to relax.

The young father was working with the reluctant engine. It would start, then stall, then start again with a blurp, while clouds of blue smoke and sickening gas fumes polluted the air. At last it started, and we began weaving our way between the rocks of the narrow channel toward the more open water of Village Pass.

The pass usually had some protection from the islands on either side, but on this day, a biting wind blew out of Knight Inlet. I was grateful for the warmth of the hot water bottle I held to the still-sleeping baby's ear.

We passed Freshwater Bay, so I knew we'd soon be in Blackfish Sound, an open stretch of water, which, from what I could see, was a boiling mass of whitecaps. When the first waves struck her, the frail gas boat shuddered from bow to stern. The wind came at us from all directions, lifting spray, then blowing it hard over the gunwales. The dark sky, filled with scudding clouds, seemed only inches above our heads.

The boat struggled on, and we reached the point of no return in the middle of an angry sea. The battle between the shaky craft and the powerful wind and water seemed hopelessly unequal. While I worried which would be the victor, I held the baby close to warm him and find my own reassurance from the contact.

At that moment the engine sputtered—and died.

I looked quickly at my blanketed companion, but she sat impassively. If she was fearful, it didn't show. The young mother stayed in the shelter of the cabin as her husband went unhurriedly to the engine, even as the wind tossed the boat about as if it were cork.

I was in a panic. I knew we were being blown off course. I had no idea what might happen, but I was thinking the worst. Time seemed like eternity. Then as suddenly as it stopped, the temperamental engine started, and the young man pointed us again in the direction of Alert Bay.

I relaxed my grip on the infant, only to tighten it again, and yet again, as the engine repeated its stop-and-go performance twice more before we made the final run of Blackfish Sound.

The tip of Cormorant Island loomed ahead, and I sighed with relief when I saw the totems in the Indian graveyard, for next to it was our destination—the hospital. For the first time since entering Blackfish Sound two hours before, I started to relax. I was so stiff with tension, I wondered if I'd be able to walk.

My travelling companion flashed me her golden smile, no doubt greatly amused by this nervous newcomer, for she had sat serenely through the whole rugged trip, looking perfectly at ease.

The man made the boat fast to the hospital dock, and I struggled to my feet, barely able to hang on to the baby, who, miraculously, had slept through the entire ordeal. My feet were numb. I could hear but not *feel* them as I clumped over the wooden planks that made up the pier. As I staggered along the pier, I was followed by the mother and father and the woman with the golden teeth.

At the hospital I gratefully handed the baby to one of the nurses.

What happened to the baby and his parents?

I could never be sure.

I never saw or heard from them again.

Just A-Wearyin' for You

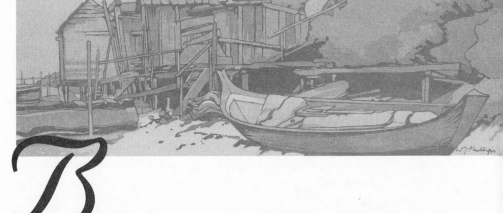

B Y DECEMBER, SCHOOL WAS IN full swing with a fairly consistent attendance of 12—unless someone slept in or a family decided to go visiting. With Christmas approaching, I was mulling over an idea, had been for a few weeks. I broached it one night at the supper table, figuring it was time to test the waters.

"I've been thinking of having the children put on a Christmas concert," I announced.

The G.A.s met my idea with some surprise and for a long moment were silent. Miss O'Brien spoke first.

"Now that's an interesting idea," she said, obviously impressed with my diligence and concern for the children. "No other teacher has had a concert. A party, yes, but never a concert." She turned to Miss Dibben then. "What do you think, Dib? Shall we discuss the pros and cons?"

Miss Dibben nodded, and the discussion began.

The pros won, and the concert fuelled conversation morning, noon and night for the next week. We thrashed out a program—and I do mean *thrashed*! Before we were through, I felt it had been beaten to a pulp. But the G.A.s had never been less formal or more animated, so I thought it was worth it.

"It would be nice to have a real party, wouldn't it, Dib?" enthused Miss O'Brien one day. "We could ask everyone to stay on for tea and cakes."

The prospect seemed to please Miss Dibben. "I think we should, O'Brien," she said. "Most everyone is back in the village now, and we haven't had a social get-together for a very long time."

My idea now loomed large, destined to create a bang-up evening. I hadn't expected such an enthusiastic reaction.

"Now, Miss B.," instructed Miss Dibben, "you work out a practice schedule for the singing, and I'll do my best to be available to play the organ."

When I told the children about my plan for a concert, I had to explain at some length exactly what "concert" meant. Most of them had never heard of one, but once they understood, they happily entered into the spirit of things.

We worked out a simple program. The children would sing "Away in a Manger" and "O Little Town of Bethlehem," then they would recite "The Night Before Christmas." As for me, I planned to bone up on my rusty repertoire and sing a song and recite a short poem. The audience would join in the singing, and the high point of the evening, before we brought on the tea and cakes, would be the Nativity scene, with Miss Dibben at the organ playing "Silent Night." All in all, we were certain it would be a spiritually uplifting as well as fun-filled evening. The village was rife with anticipation. But before all these events could take place in an orderly way, there was a lot of practising to do.

The exciting part of the extravaganza was the Nativity scene. All the children were in the cast. Stella Hanuse was the obvious choice for Mary, and her brother Wilfred, being the tallest boy, was picked as Joseph. Wee, black-eyed Margaret Rose was chosen to play the infant Jesus, and all the rest were to be wise men and shepherds. This was the costumed part of the entertainment, and the children were looking forward to it.

From her hoard of odds and ends, Miss O'Brien unearthed old curtains, a bedspread, and bits and pieces of material. Stella made a beguiling Mary draped in a sheet with a cheesecloth headdress, while Wilfred looked handsome in his bedspread robe. The others were fitted out in appropriate costumes, and a manger was devised from a wooden box.

We scouted the woods for a Christmas tree and found a well-shaped pine, which the bigger boys had a fine time chopping down. The children, taking turns with the carrying, carted it back to school, where we decorated it with paper ornaments, another project from the handiwork period.

Meanwhile, the G.A.s were busy organizing the after-concert feast, gaily baking slab cakes and mounds of cookies. The concert was going to be the most exciting event of the winter, and whenever I made rounds in the village, the people would nod and smile.

"Pretty soon concert, eh?" they would say. "Ike. Ike. Good. Good. We come!"

The concert was set for the evening before school closed for the Christmas holidays, so the day before that we had a final practice, put the finishing touches on the tree and tidied the classroom. We were ready. Through hours of practice the children had mastered the verses and carols. I was delighted by their enthusiasm and excitement.

I went to bed that night confident my first term as teacher had gone well, and I was, I hoped, about to end it in a blaze of glory.

The truth was I was feeling quite smug.

The next morning I was up as usual, raising the flag and lighting the fire. The school smelled of fresh-cut evergreens and looked cheerful and Christmasy. I rang the bell and waited for the familiar scrape of boots in the vestibule.

The minutes ticked by but all was silent.

I looked at my watch. Nine o'clock. Then five after. And still no chattering voices or scuffing boots. Puzzled, I went outside and looked the length of the village. Other than the occasional plume of smoke in the frosty morning air, there was no sign of life.

I decided to seek out Miss O'Brien.

I entered the kitchen to find her doing the breakfast dishes. "Miss B.?" she said, obviously surprised to see me home at this odd hour. "What's the matter?"

"I'm not really sure," I said. "But not one child has come to school. The village seems to be completely deserted."

"Oh, my! This needs to be investigated." She wiped her hands with a towel, donned her coat, and together we walked along the village path. We knocked on each door in turn, but no one answered until we came to Mrs. Joseph's.

"Where are the people and children?" I asked.

"Clam digging," she replied.

"Why are they clam digging now?" I exclaimed.

"Clam buyers come last night. Everybody gone to dig clams," she said flatly, as if it were the most logical thing in the world. Which to her, no doubt, it was.

I had my answer. Every able-bodied man, woman and child, which included the whole school, had harkened to the call of the clam buyers and the jingle of silver.

"When will they be back?" I asked.

"Dunno. Maybe tomorrow. Maybe next week."

Miss O'Brien and I looked at each other, stunned to silence. There was nothing to do but thank Mrs. Joseph and head home.

"Who will eat all the cakes?" Miss O'Brien murmured, shaking her head. Then, with remorse, added, "Poor Miss B., you've worked *so* hard."

I *was* feeling a bit sorry for myself—not that it did any good. "Well, if there are no children, there'll certainly be no concert. Surely you'll find someone to eat the cakes."

What I almost said was maybe we could feed them to the clams!

I wondered about the clam buyers who manned the boats at this festive time of year, plying the coastal waters, gathering clams for the gourmet appetites of city folk. Surely some of them were family men with children performing in Christmas concerts. I wondered if they knew of the disappointment their untimely arrival had wrought, and if so, if they would have a twinge of conscience.

There were a few old people left behind, so we invited them to come to the school that evening. On the insistence of the G.A.s, I recited my poem and sang my song, which, if I remember correctly, was "Just A-Wearyin' for You." Appropriate for the occasion, I thought. After my performance we attempted to rally a chorus to sing Christmas carols, but as the old people didn't know either the words or tunes, and Miss O'Brien couldn't sing a note, it ended up a duet—Miss Dibben and me.

After this half-hearted effort at a bang-up evening, we started on a long line of cakes and cookies.

Thus, with a resounding thud, ended my first term as teacher of the Mamalilikulla Indian Day School, Village Island, B.C.

Do Re Mi

*T*HE THOUGHT OF SPENDING CHRISTMAS on the island was more than I could bear, so I announced my intention to go home for the holidays. This caused no end of a stir and a great many sessions of pros and cons. But finally it was settled.

I needed transportation desperately and, for once, luck was with me. The Oiens had visitors with a good, sturdy boat who were on their way to Alert Bay. After a brief visit with the Todds, I caught the first coastal steamer going south. Soon I was in the bosom of my family, regaling them with tales of my life in the wilderness. It was time well spent. The laughter and love bolstered my flagging resolve.

I returned to Village Island determined to make the best of my lot.

There was little activity in the village during the winter, and the people were content to stay home around warm fires. I suspected this suited them well. Not so the G.A.s; missionary work was their calling, and they laboured ceaselessly in their chosen field.

Each evening after supper, we knelt in prayer for half an hour in the sitting room. Often it was just the three of us, but it gladdened the G.A.s' hearts when some of the village people came. Miss Dibben was then spurred to even greater piety and I often wondered, as I eased the pressure on each knee in turn, if the session would ever end.

A prayer meeting was held in the school on Friday nights. This was the high point of the week for the G.A.s. I did my part by giving the schoolroom an extra spit and polish on Friday afternoon. The fire in the heater was kept burning and the lamp wicks trimmed. I avoided the actual meeting, after attending once and once only. I very alertly offered my services as official sitter for the TB patients. Miss Dibben accepted graciously, as this meant she was free for the whole evening.

These Friday-night sessions were long and noisy, sometimes lasting three hours. They took on the aspect of evangelistic revival meetings, rather than time spent in quiet meditation. There was hand clapping, foot stomping and lots of loud "Amens" and "Hallelujahs"—all of which I heard plainly, even in the Gables. There were testimonials, confessions of sin and sincere promises of future reform. Voices became louder, higher-pitched and more excited as the evening wore on. The Indian people left exhausted, while Miss Dibben glowed with happiness and elation.

On Sunday morning Miss O'Brien would ring the bell, and the families would stroll along the path to the school-cum-church. No one ever hurried. Time meant nothing in the off-season, when there was no fishing, and to the old people it was of no consequence all year long.

They would come slowly into the classroom and find places to sit. The stouter ladies had trouble squeezing into the children's small desks, while the men sat with feet jutting into the aisles. Many of the faces were wrinkled and wise with age, some were expressionless, others jolly and chuckly—like old Auntie. And except for one small boy who had blond curls, their eyes and hair were black and their skin swarthy.

To my eye, Gertrude Hanuse was the beauty of the village. She spoke both English and Kwak'wala fluently and, when the need arose, acted as my interpreter. This happened often, as many of the older generation spoke no English. She was also the mother of Stella and Wilfred, the bright lights of the classroom.

I was told then that womanly beauty in the eye of the Indian male was typified by a round face, flat-bridged nose, almond-shaped eyes and straight black hair. But how any male, Indian or otherwise, could fail to appreciate Gertrude's beauty, I couldn't imagine. Her skin was a clear olive, and her features bordered on the classical. She had flashing black eyes and shiny hair she wore in a long braid down her back. She was tall and carried herself like a duchess.

The women loved bright, splashy prints, coloured beads and jangling bracelets of Indian design made of gold or silver. Most of the women had generous proportions, and their dresses were cut with blousy tops and full skirts. The older women wore shawls that served as a head covering, and their

In 1926 Donald New, a forest service engineer, photographed this group when two Alert Bay teachers visited Village Island. Alex and Dan Hanuse stand left of Eleanor Nixon, soon to be the local teacher. Flora (Hanuse) Dawson and Dora (Speck) Alfred surround Kate Dibben, who was still years away from moving to Village Island. Fred Hanuse stands next to his mother, Gertrude, and baby sister, Stella. A decade later Stella was Hughina Bowden's shining star.

hair hung in long, thick braids. Most of the younger girls followed the trend of the times and had short hair, often with frizzy permanents.

The men, for the most part, were dark-complexioned and stocky, except for Harry Mountain. Tall and handsome, he was every inch the chief, or *Gikumi*.

Miss Dibben conducted the Church of England Sunday service in both languages from hymn and prayer books that had been compiled by a missionary who came to Fort Rupert in 1877. He had devised a phonetic written form of Kwak'wala, which must have been a considerable undertaking. But as few of the old people could read, they still followed the service by rote. However, many of the younger ones could read some of both languages.

As for me, I attended church on Sunday and prayers in the sitting room during the week—which I couldn't very well avoid. I felt I was doing my part.

Miss O'Brien had other ideas.

"Miss B.," she said one evening at the supper table, "I was thinking it would be very nice if you held a music class for the young people."

I almost dropped my fork. "But I don't know how to teach music," I protested. "I barely know the scales. And any singing I do is all by ear."

"I'm sure you'll do beautifully, dear," she insisted calmly. Apparently there were to be no pros and cons. The issue was settled.

My heart wasn't in it, nor were the hearts of my reluctant pupils, consisting of teenagers out of school and some young married couples. Miss O'Brien decided they needed cultural diversion, and they were going to get it. But what good "Do Re Mi" was to them, I failed to see.

About 10 students came the first night, mostly out of curiosity, I think—and on the insistence of Miss O'Brien. They sat slumped in the too-small desks, ankles crossed in the aisles. They watched and listened stoically, their expressions deadpan, while the light from the coal lamps cast weird flickering shadows on the walls and ceiling. No doubt they were wondering what on earth they were doing here. As was I.

I made these ghastly sessions stretch to about three-quarters of an hour. By this time my students were yawning and shuffling their feet, and I was almost to the point of handing out squares of old sheets for "nose-blowing time."

"That will be all for tonight," I'd say. Their change of expression was immediate. Faces wreathed in smiles, they'd jump to their feet and stampede for the door as if a gun had gone off.

They were faithful for a few nights, but soon their numbers dwindled. If *anything* more interesting came up, such as a clam-digging tide or a boat ride on a calm night, they were off—for a less *cultural* but more exciting evening.

The young people liked cowboy music. They listened to records on the few windup gramophones in the village and could imitate the nasal twang of the singers almost perfectly. This was much more fun than singing scales in a gloomy nighttime schoolhouse.

And, as I was to learn, they had music of their own, its roots deep in their tribal past.

One clear evening, I was standing at my window admiring a ribbon of moonlight on the smooth sea when I heard singing. Into the moon's path came the silhouette of a canoe, gently paddled by four young men. They were singing in their Native tongue. The song had a primitive rhythm, a throbbing cadence, unique and unfamiliar. I could only wonder at its meaning. Was it a folk story of some kind? A tale of a great chief perhaps? Or an epic telling of a young brave's courage? Or was it a song of love?

The silhouette faded. The sight and sound lingered.

Northern Exposure

ACH DAY AFTER TEACHING SCHOOL, I'd have a cup of tea with the G.A.s, then switch roles to become the village nurse. With the black bag tucked under my arm, I'd trudge along the path, calling at every house to pass the time of day and inquire after the health of the family. Usually everyone was fine, but when medical attention was necessary, I did what I could. In this way I got to know the villagers and gained their confidence. Because of this, my nursing duties increased, not only in the village, but in the surrounding area.

Often my tea with the G.A.s was delayed when I'd come home to find some of the people waiting for me at the house. Then the kitchen became a dispensary and nurse's office. The complaint might be a scratch, a headache or a splinter—and there was always someone with a cold. Cough mixture was in great demand, for they loved its sweet taste, and the bright red of Mercurochrome cured any number of things. This, along with an imposing bandage, sent many patients home happy.

On occasion I was called to a neighbouring village. When I'd arrive home and see a gas boat tied to the float, it usually meant my services were required. So I'd don my coat, grab the black bag and board whatever uncertain mode of transportation happened to be waiting. Our destination might be the village of New Vancouver, a few miles away on Harbledown Island. Or possibly Turnour Island or Midsummer Island. Perhaps the more distant Gilford Island. At first I had no clear idea of where I was going. I just hoped for the best and went.

When I think of winter on Village Island, the word grey comes to mind. Cloud and heavy mist cast a sombre gloom over land and sea for days at a time, often hanging so low the peaks of the mainland mountains were completely obscured. At times like these, the villages, with their rows of houses facing the sea like idle, old men hoary with age, were doubly dreary. Yet, wind and salt spray had lent to the planks, log walls and curling shake shingles of their exteriors a soft rain-soaked grey, and when approached from the sea, they were unique in their picturesque solitude.

Many of the emergencies were not emergent at all, as with a little effort on the ailing person's part, they could have come to me. For reasons of their own, they chose not to, so I obliged by hopping into the waiting gas boat and going to them. I worried about leaving pills or rubs, for I was never sure they took them as instructed. I counted the pills carefully and never left enough to do any harm, even if taken all at once. Mostly, they were Aspirin or a mild laxative, and soda mints cured many an excruciating pain.

On my first visit to New Vancouver, I met Cheeky Joe. He had grizzled grey hair and a wide, broken-toothed grin that cheerfully displayed discoloured teeth. He talked a steady stream of *very* bad English. I decided his name suited him perfectly.

"You doctor?" he asked.

"No," I replied. "I'm a nurse."

"Almost all same doctor. Here. You fix," he said, extending his arm.

"Fix what?" Nothing was visible to the naked eye.

"Here," he said, pointing with a grubby finger to his wrist. "Sore long time—two years, mebbe."

I felt his wrist and moved his hand in all directions. The movements were free, and he didn't wince with pain.

"I'll fix," I said.

From the black bag I took scissors and adhesive tape which I cut into strips. With these I strapped his wrist. He gave it an experimental twist and then broke into a snaggle-toothed grin.

"Yeah, yeah. You fix. Feel good. All better now!" He went off, happily displaying this instant cure to his friends and relations. I was an immediate success in the village of New Vancouver.

There was one weather-beaten shack on Village Island that I never failed to visit. Moss grew in the chinks between the logs and encrusted the roof. Two broken steps led to the sagging door and a small window let in the light. The one room held a stove, a couple of iron beds, two chairs, a table and a couple of chests. This was the home of Auntie and her brother Sam.

I never knew Auntie by any other name. She spoke very little English and understood less, and I knew no Kwak'wala—but we got along beautifully.

When I'd tap on the door and walk in, she would beam me a toothless smile and immediately start talking in Kwak'wala, all the while gaily chuckling at her own humour. If it was a nice day, I'd sit in the sun on her steps while she entertained me with a stream of happy chatter.

One such day she patted me on the shoulder and said, "You my *kwunuk*."

From her tone, I understood she'd said something especially nice, but I had no idea what. "Kwunuk?" I repeated. "What do you mean, Auntie?"

"You kwunuk!" She chuckled again, pointing at me with a grubby finger. Just then Gertrude strolled into view so I called her over.

"Auntie keeps calling me a kwunuk, Gertrude. What is she saying?"

"'Kwunuk' means daughter," said Gertrude, smiling broadly. "She's calling you her daughter."

"Dot her. Dot her," Auntie repeated, nodding gleefully.

"Imagine that," I said, proud and pleased. "What's the word for mother, Gertrude?"

"*Ubumpus*," she told me.

"Hello, Ubumpus," I said to Auntie.

"Yeah. Kwunuk. Ubumpus." Auntie laughed, rocking to and fro in delight.

From then on, Auntie and I were mother and daughter. My new parent was short, dumpy and never too clean. Her face was framed by long, grey braids, and she wrapped her head in a kerchief tied in a style all her own. Usually, she wore a baggy dress and one of Sam's raggedy sweaters, but she always had a twinkle in her eye and a wonderful sense of humour.

I found her irresistible.

Auntie, Hughina's self-appointed mother, stands beside the tallest totem in the village, near the remains of a community house.

As Auntie was my self-appointed mother, I guess that made Sam my uncle. No one knew how old Sam was, or Auntie either, for that matter, but Sam looked *very* old. His frame was spare and bent, and he shuffled along with the aid of a stick. He had long ago lost most of his teeth, his face was sunken and wrinkled, and what hair he had was wispy white. His eyes were rheumy and red-rimmed. He never said much, apart from a few guttural phrases, and rarely left the little shack or ventured far from his own doorstep.

So it was surprising to come home one day to find Sam in the kitchen, sitting on a chair, clutching his stick as if to keep from falling off.

The G.A.s were there, too.

Glancing up from her pastry-making, Miss O'Brien said, "Sam is waiting to see you, Miss B."

"What's the matter, Sam?" I asked.

"Sore leg. Me got sore leg," he answered. This was the longest speech I'd heard him utter.

"Where exactly is it sore?"

Without a word he got to his feet and laid his stick on the chair. He fumbled with a piece of string tied around his waist, undid the knot, and calmly dropped his pants to the floor, and there he stood—in front of the horrified eyes of the missionaries—without a stitch of underwear.

Miss Dibben, for all her dim eyesight, seemed fully aware of Sam's naked state. With a shriek, she flew out the door, slamming it behind her.

Miss O'Brien proved equally agile. One stricken look, and in a flash she was through the door into the sitting room, hands still covered with pastry and leaving a trail of flour behind her. I heard the key being turned in the lock.

Sam stood, pants puddled at his feet, and watched this speedy exodus with a puzzled expression.

"What-za matter dem?" he muttered with a jerk of his head.

I didn't bother to explain these were maiden ladies of virtue. In the first place he wouldn't understand, and in the second, I was so helpless with laughter I couldn't utter a word. Poor old Sam. He'd probably never caused such a sensation before.

At last I got down to the business of finding out about Sam's complaint. As it turned out, he really did have to remove his trousers, for he had a running sore in his groin—although this didn't entirely justify the lack of underwear.

After I'd applied a dressing to the affected area, he hauled up his rumpled trousers, tied the string securely and shuffled off home, still obviously mystified at the commotion he had caused.

The poor G.A.s were badly shaken by this episode. After Sam was safely out of sight, O'Brien came sheepishly into the kitchen to finish her pies. We didn't see Dib again until she was called for supper. Neither lady said a word.

In fact, Sam's visit was *never* mentioned; it was as though it hadn't happened.

To spare them further embarrassment, I changed his dressing at home, where he made a satisfactory recovery,

And, as Auntie said, "Him a little bit good."

Lonely Beach

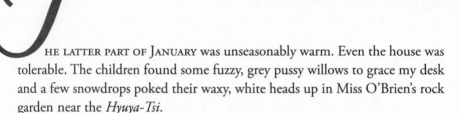

*T*HE LATTER PART OF JANUARY was unseasonably warm. Even the house was tolerable. The children found some fuzzy, grey pussy willows to grace my desk and a few snowdrops poked their waxy, white heads up in Miss O'Brien's rock garden near the *Hyuya-Tsi*.

After school I often walked through the woods to visit Mrs. Oiens. Along the path, midst the scent of moss and rain-damp earth, I would stop and listen. The sounds were the songs of the wild—the winds sighing in the tall trees, the rustle of an unseen woodland animal, a scolding squirrel skittering up a tree trunk. Through the forest came the sounds of the seashore and the everlasting screeching of the seagulls. Enclosed by the dense woods, I sometimes felt as if I were the only human in the world.

Other days, when the teaching day was done and the sick attended to, I'd leave the confines of the house and go exploring.

On one such day I found the mouth of a tiny stream and followed its meandering path into the woods. It rippled clear over a bed of smooth stones as it made its determined way to the sea. Its gentle banks were moulded, green with moss. Everything was in perfect miniature. Did fairies waltz along its banks when the moon was full? I wondered. Deep in the woods the stream disappeared under an outcropping of grey-green boulders, its source secret and mysterious.

My favourite walk was out onto the rickety old Indian wharf, whose bleached skeleton clung to the rocky shore. When the tide was low, I would scramble off the end of the wharf, over the rocks and around the point. On that pebbly beach, my solitude was complete. No sign of the village was visible, nor could I hear a sound other than the sea and the gulls.

Looking to the right, I could see Knight Inlet, and straight ahead, off the inlet's far shore, the green mound of Gilford Island. To the left was the beginning of Village Pass, which led to Alert Bay and its enticing hint of civilization. As far as the eye could see, there was neither sign nor sound of human habitation.

As I walked the beach, I'd often disturb the gulls at a seaside dinner. This initiated a raucous chorus of complaint as they rose to the sky. Gleaming white, they'd wheel overhead in ever-widening circles, then land with graceful precision to strut and scold, farther along the beach. Cormorants lazily rode a floating log, sitting perfectly still, like black-robed monks in quiet meditation. Sometimes a pair of eagles would glide silently overhead, looking for unsuspecting prey, or a school of porpoises would appear out of Knight Inlet, playing tag like happy children, rolling and diving, wet skins gleaming and flashing in the sunlight. When a boat would appear on the horizon, I would speculate as to its destination and who might be aboard.

One day, as I sat quietly on a log, my mind miles away, I was brought back to reality by a sound coming from Knight Inlet. I watched and waited, slightly alarmed, for it was a sound I'd never heard before. Finally, into my line of vision, came an enormous whale. He would dive, then surface; blow a huge spout and dive again, his immense black bulk cleaving the water, leaving waves and whirlpools in his wake. I fixed my eyes ahead of him, trying to guess where he'd surface again, mesmerized by the animal's rhythm and grace. He kept a straight course through the water, heading only he knew where. And then he was gone, the sound of his great spouts floating back on the clear, still air.

I would return from these solitary walks to the realities of the shabby little village: tummy aches, pregnancies, cuts and bruises—the depressing scourge of

Hughina's favourite getaway spot looked out on Knight Inlet, the lush coast of Gilford Island and the distant mountains.

"This was Main Street," says Hughina. "We headed straight down the channel to go to the Bay. It faces almost due west." This 1936 photo was taken from the end of the wharf.

TB. Then it was back to a classroom of not-too-eager children. I felt as though I were two people, one the proper nurse-teacher, the other the daydreamer sitting on a log on a lonely beach.

Potlatch

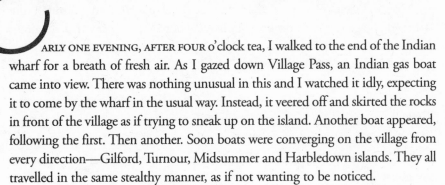

ARLY ONE EVENING, AFTER FOUR o'clock tea, I walked to the end of the Indian wharf for a breath of fresh air. As I gazed down Village Pass, an Indian gas boat came into view. There was nothing unusual in this and I watched it idly, expecting it to come by the wharf in the usual way. Instead, it veered off and skirted the rocks in front of the village as if trying to sneak up on the island. Another boat appeared, following the first. Then another. Soon boats were converging on the village from every direction—Gilford, Turnour, Midsummer and Harbledown islands. They all travelled in the same stealthy manner, as if not wanting to be noticed.

Later that night, at supper, I said, "There seem to be a lot of visitors in the village tonight. I wonder what's up."

Miss O'Brien was curious too, and after the meal was cleared away, she went to call on the chief, Harry Mountain. In a few minutes she was back, obviously excited.

"The people are having a potlatch," she said. "And it's well underway."

My excitement matched hers. "I'd love to see it. Do you suppose they'd mind?"

"I'm sure Harry Mountain will agree," she said. "And I think you should see it. I'll go along with you."

I didn't waste a minute. "I'll get my coat," I said, and turned quickly toward my room. Before I'd reached the door, Miss Dibben rose in mighty indignation.

"Miss O'Brien!" she said in a voice so loud poor O'Brien could hear it without her ear trumpet. "You are well aware the potlatch has been outlawed. It is a *heathen* ceremony. If you attend, it will appear you are condoning such conduct. What kind of an example is that to set for the Indians?" She was in high dudgeon.

"Now, Dib, this is more like a party," said Miss O'Brien gently. "It would be a shame if Miss B. missed seeing the dancing. This might be her only opportunity."

"It is against the law," Miss Dibben reminded us sternly. "And I will have nothing to do with such goings-on and you should not either." With that she stomped off to the Gables.

Miss Dibben was right, of course. The potlatch, part ritual and part celebration, and at one time integral to traditional Native society, had been outlawed by the government since 1884. Because of this, part of an ancient culture had been lost, and what might have been passed from generation to generation had been forgotten. Potlatches now were rare—and clandestine.

I was thrilled at the opportunity to witness one.

Miss O'Brien, old sport that she was, walked with me through the darkened village to the community house. A couple of men stood at the door. One of them was Simon Beans.

"Evenin', Miz O'Brien. Evenin', Miz B." he said.

"Good evening, Simon," answered Miss O'Brien. "Do you mind if we watch for a while? Miss B. would like to see the dancing."

"Sure. Okay. Go in," he said hospitably.

"No, thank you, Simon. We'll watch from here."

"It's warm in there. Cold out here," Simon said. A practical observation, I thought.

"No," Miss O'Brien said firmly. "Out here will be fine."

Evidently she condoned the potlatch only so far, but as I wasn't in a position to argue, I held my tongue, happy to participate in any way I could.

Through the knotholes and cracks in the walls, and a half-open door, I witnessed a fantastic scene. It was as though I'd walked back through the pages of a history book, to the time before the White man came; a time when these people were free to celebrate their culture and live as they chose.

The community house, ordinarily full of echoes and a ghostlike emptiness, now glowed with vibrant life and colour. A huge pile of logs blazed and crackled in the centre of the earthen floor, the flames leaping high, while the smoke curled upward to escape through the hole in the roof. The roaring fire was the only illumination, and it cast distorted, dancing shadows on the old plank walls.

My eyes were drawn to the far end of the long room where the Thunderbirds stood. The colours—yellow, red, green and white bordered in black—that formed the unique design of their feathers and eyes glowed in the orange light of the fire. In daylight, they were beautiful specimens of Native art, but now they were animate! Was it my imagination, I wondered, or were their eyes watchful, their wings curled to guard against evil from without?

People sat in the gloom on the platform around the edge of the earthen floor. Each was wrapped in a blanket of red or green, while children, laughing and happy, played in the glow of the fire. Two tall figures in ceremonial robes stood on the dais at the feet of the Thunderbirds. The taller of the two was covered from shoulder to ankle by a splendid green robe, heavy with buttons of mother-of-pearl that outlined the intricate appliquéd design. He wore a crown of ermine tails and animal claws, and in his hand he held a beautifully carved speaker's staff, or talking stick.

It took me a few minutes to realize the picturesque figure was Harry Mountain, chief of the Mamalilikulla tribe. What a different Harry to the work-a-day fisherman I had come to know. He was the *Gikumi* now, these were his people, and time had reverted to past glories.

The other man was also arrayed in the raiment of chief. He wore a long blanket fringed with ermine tails and adorned with pearl buttons. His headdress was designed from abalone shells and eagle feathers, and he, too, held a talking stick, the emblem of a chief.

Harry was speaking to the people, his voice resounding through the great house. He spoke dramatically and emphasized each phrase with sweeping gestures. As he spoke, the children continued to play in the firelight, and the people laughed and chattered in the shadows around the walls. The fact no one listened didn't seem to bother him. His speech went on and on. It was obvious he was saying complimentary things about the man at his side. I wondered why.

"What's going on?" I finally asked Miss O'Brien.

She turned to Simon, who was still standing near the door.

"Why is the potlatch being given, Simon?"

"Fort Ruper' chief die. His son is now chief."

"Ah, then this is a celebration," said Miss O'Brien, who knew something of Indian customs. She turned to me. "The guest of honour is the new chief of the Fort Rupert people. Watch. Harry will probably do something to show him great honour."

Just then Harry picked up what looked like a shield about four feet high and a foot or so wide that had been resting at the feet of the Thunderbirds. He presented it to his guest with a dramatic speech. The Fort Rupert chief accepted it. Then, with a few modest words, he gave it back to Harry. This was repeated several times.

"What are they doing now?" I asked. This was getting more confusing by the minute—and intriguing.

"Harry's given him a copper. To be presented with a copper is a great compliment to the new chief. But tradition requires he, in all humility, must refuse it at first. In the end he'll accept it. It's all part of the ceremony."

"What's a 'copper'?"

"They're sheets of copper that have been beaten into the shape of a shield. The shield is then embossed and incised with a design depicting family crests which, in most cases, is an honoured animal from their Native lore.

"Traditionally the copper was considered a standard of social prestige and could be inherited by the descendants of the owner. It was also a unit of monetary value, the value depending on its potlatch history. It has no real value in itself, but I'm told it could possibly double in price each time it's sold or given away. Each copper is given a name and its history is always known."

"It must be very valuable then?"

"Indeed." She nodded before going on. "Before the White man came and introduced money as we know it, the blanket was the standard of monetary value among the Natives. Back then they were made of cedar bark or animal skins. Later, they used the Hudson's Bay blanket. Theoretically, a copper could be worth any number of blankets, which might be owed by one man to another. On occasion a copper was destroyed or tossed into the sea. When this was done, all debt was cleared and the slate wiped clean. Its display at a potlatch was always a dramatic event." She turned her attention back to the ongoing ceremony.

The *Gi-Gikumi*, or chiefs, had at last finished their orations when the guest accepted the copper.

Then the music began. But such strange music! The musicians were seated below the dais near the feet of the Thunderbirds. About 10 men sat either side of a long board and with sticks, beat out a pulsating rhythm. They accompanied the rhythmic beat with droning, guttural singing. They sang in chorus, keeping perfect time to their own accompaniment. I found my cold feet tapping to the captivating ONE, two, three, four ONE, two, three, four beat.

Out of the shadows, from around the walls, the women slowly rose and came into the circle of light cast by the fire. They took up the rhythm of the music with dancing feet. Round and round the fire they whirled, turning, weaving and swaying in the time-honoured way of their ancestors.

Every dancer wore a button blanket of red or green or blue. Each blanket was ornamented with a family crest—a whale, a bear, a salmon or a seal—that had been cut from flannel or cotton and appliquéd on the blanket so the design lay on the back of the wearer. The crests were outlined with mother-of-pearl buttons and bordered with more buttons in geometric designs.

As the dancers twirled and swayed around the fire, the glow picked up the rainbow colours of the pearl buttons, causing them to sparkle and flash in the light. It made a brilliant picture; the blazing fire, the stout, blanket-draped women, surprisingly light and graceful on their feet, dancing to the throb of the music. And there, in the background—the chiefs in all their magnificence, standing between the Thunderbirds with the copper gleaming at their side.

The music faded, the women returned to the shadows, and for a few minutes there was silence. Then, from outside the walls of the community house, came the sound of a weird and haunting whistle. Immediately, the musicians took up a frantic drumming, and from behind the Thunderbirds, into the circle of light, leapt the hamatsa. A startling sight!

His face was painted and he was scantily clad in a brief shirt and trunks. His ankles and wrists were ringed with bracelets of shredded cedar bark and animal claws, while on his head he wore a circle of coloured feathers and abalone shells. He was the cannibal, awesome and savage.

He leapt and crouched, weaving with fantastic energy around the fire—all the while emitting blood-curdling howls. While he danced with abandon, four stalwart youths circled the room, staying between the people and the hamatsa.

"What are the boys doing?" I asked Miss O'Brien.

"Legend has it the people must be protected from this unearthly being, lest he attack or capture a victim to drag away to his lair in the forest. The young men are intended to be those protectors."

The hamatsa cannibal dance stemmed from the initiation of a novice into a secret society. The novice was kept secluded in the forest and spent many days fasting. He was taught the rules, dances, songs and rituals, and when his training period was complete, a special feast was arranged. The people would gather in the great house, around the fire, and await his arrival. The signal was given by the eerie whistle, and in those early days, he would leap into their midst through the hole in the roof. He would dance and mime uncontrollable hunger, uttering cries of "Eat! Eat!" Sometimes he would actually bite a person who had been singled out for this dubious honour. Through the dance he would tell how he was possessed of evil spirits. Gradually his mentors would show him how to control them, and he, interpreting through the dance, would reveal he was ready to return to human society. [Editor's note: It is the common belief among contemporary scholars that the hamatsa was present only at the Winter Ceremony, an event distinctly separate from the potlatch. Given the time of year and various factors that had influenced village life by

Villager Jimmy Sewid identified this as a photo taken in 1912 at Harry Mountain's house, where 16-foot poles show the mythical cannibal birds (which Hughina took to be Thunderbirds) and grizzly bears. Based on revelations in his later autobiography, it was most likely Jimmy Sewid who was behind the hamatsa mask on the night of Hughina's one and only potlatch.

the 1930s, it is possible that Hughina Bowden witnessed a rare consolidation of two First Nations celebrations on this occasion.]

As I watched the hamatsa dance around the blazing fire in time to the wild music, I was lost in times past. Then—abruptly—the music stopped, and he was gone as quickly as he had appeared. Again there was silence.

The drumming started again but with a slower beat, and another figure appeared from the shadows and began to dance around the fire. He was dressed in long fringes of shredded cedar bark, one from armpit to waist, the other from waist to knee. His anklet and bracelets were of animal claws. He was less wild than the hamatsa and his dance was slower. What tale was he telling? I wondered.

Just then Miss O'Brien tugged at my sleeve, and I realized she must be as cold as I was. Still, I was reluctant to leave.

She tugged again.

We left the people to their dancing and gift giving, and I never found out what story the dancer was telling.

Miss O'Brien and I made our way through the night using a flashlight to pick out the path, while I continued to feel the presence of wood spirits and wild men.

Later in my stay on Village Island, Harry Mountain showed me a collection of old photographs of a potlatch that had taken place in Alert Bay years before. Both sides of the narrow street were piled high with blankets, sacks of flour and sugar, and stacks of dishes. Thousands of dollars' worth of merchandise stood in the street. He told me how the givers of the potlatches would try to outdo each other in gift giving. This increased their standing in the community, while they fully expected their bounty to be returned a hundredfold.

This system worked well for the Kwakiutl, who were among the wealthiest of the Indian nations. They lived in a

The decline of village life by 1939 is evident in the state of the community house. For many years, the house poles rested outside the home of Henry Bell.

land of abundance, their living standard one of the highest in the world.

Then the White man came, bringing his monetary system—and his diseases; measles, smallpox and tuberculosis killed thousands. The potlatch system broke down. The last great potlatch was held on Village Island in December of 1921, after which 45 people were charged with such offences as dancing, speech making and gift giving. Twenty of these people were sent to prison and served short sentences, while their potlatch paraphernalia was pirated away to eastern Canada and the United States. Since that time, the occasional potlatch, such as the one I had witnessed, was a furtive affair and but a shadow of its former prominence and glory. But I would not soon forget it.

The sitting room looked drab after the excitement of the community house, and Miss Dibben was still huffy with Miss O'Brien for going, and taking me. But I didn't care. I sat with my cold feet on the heater, sipping hot cocoa, still under the spell of the wildly beating drums.

Two Small Ripples

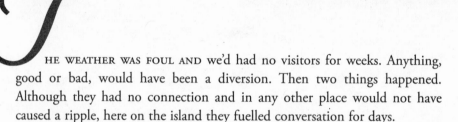

*T*HE WEATHER WAS FOUL AND we'd had no visitors for weeks. Anything, good or bad, would have been a diversion. Then two things happened. Although they had no connection and in any other place would not have caused a ripple, here on the island they fuelled conversation for days.

The first momentous occurrence was a social evening. This was Miss O'Brien's brainchild, for she also felt our lives needed livening up. The pros and cons were discussed with every meal, including afternoon tea. While listening to the plans being laid, I couldn't help but think a potlatch would be much more fun. I suspect the village people thought so too.

"I think Thursday would be the best evening," Miss O'Brien said. "Maybe you would render a song and recitation, Miss B. There were so few to hear you at Christmas; it would be nice for you to have a larger audience. I've passed the word through the village, and I'm sure most everyone will come. I've also mapped out a program of games. After that, I thought we'd have tea and cakes."

On the appointed day, I kept the school fire burning and arranged the desks in a friendly circle. People started arriving about 7:30, and everyone who could walk was there.

The older women chattered and giggled, but the men, as is common with men the world over on such occasions, looked somewhat sullen, as if they'd been dragged away from their hearth-sides much against their will. The young people sidled in, looking bashful and unsure of themselves.

Miss O'Brien got the party underway with a couple of mixers, a game known as "Jacob and Rachel" and the good old standby "Pin the Tail on the Donkey." The people played these games with childish glee, and there was much chuckling and laughter when the tail landed on a spot far removed from the target. This went on until everyone had a turn.

When things quieted down, I sang my song and recited my poem, neither of which evoked much enthusiasm from my captive audience. They were much more eager when Tom Mountain was led to the platform.

Tom was Chief Harry Mountain's nephew. Blind from birth, he had to be accompanied everywhere. Tom had an ear for music, and he'd taught himself to strum guitar and sing by listening to records. He had, without a doubt, learned the worst selection of cowboy songs I'd ever heard. However, he was the only one in the village who played a musical instrument, other than Miss Dibben, and she would play nothing but hymns. Because of his talent, he was always the centre of the young people. This was a blessing for him, but his music was very hard on my sensitive ears.

Tom twanged his *gee-tar* while doing a perfect imitation of the nasal drawl of the pseudo-cowboys. The verses went on and on, and still the audience pleaded for more. Tom was the hit of the evening.

The grand finale, prior to the tea and cakes, was dancing—the French minuet.

Although Miss Dibben didn't approve of dancing as such, the minuet passed muster, as in her eyes, it was more of a folk dance. Miss O'Brien, who had danced in her youth, saw no harm in this sort of gaiety. Miss Dibben couldn't play the appropriate music on the wheezy old organ, so someone brought a windup gramophone and a stack of records—all of them cowboy tunes, except for the "Isle of Capri."

"The last item on the program will be the French minuet," announced Miss O'Brien. "Will you please choose your partners. Miss B. and I will lead off to demonstrate the steps. It's very simple. I'm sure you'll be able to follow." With this she stepped confidently to the dance floor with me in tow.

"Miss O'Brien," I said. "We've no music."

"Pardon, Miss B.?"

I spoke louder this time. "We've no music," I repeated.

"Oh, my, but surely there's a suitable record."

"No," I told her. "There's nothing but cowboy tunes, except for one, and it's not the right rhythm."

"No matter," she replied airily. "I'm sure it will do nicely. Now, let us begin."

Someone cranked the gramophone and "The Isle of Capri" blared tinnily forth.

She and I joined hands, and she counted aloud, "One, two, three, point. One, two, three, point. One, point. Two, point. Turn and bow."

Miss O'Brien tripped along, blithely unaware of the deafening beat in the background. The village people fumbled through the steps of the stately dance as best they could. The stout women, who had danced so lightly and gracefully at the potlatch, now clumped heavily, causing the very floor to tremble—all the while shaking with laughter. The men and the young people were a lost cause, for they couldn't seem to keep from introducing some of the fancy footwork of the Indian dances, which didn't mix at all with the French minuet.

Never before, I'm sure, has the elegant minuet been danced to such inappropriate music by such an odd assortment of people in such an unusual setting.

Miss O'Brien glowed with pleasure while she served the tea and cakes.

The other noteworthy event was the annual visit of the school inspector. Rumour had it he was in the vicinity, but with no direct communication to anywhere, I had no idea when he might pounce on me. His name was Mr. Barry, and he was the inspector for all Indian day schools on Vancouver Island and the central B.C. coast.

The older children knew him, of course, as he came every year, but he was an unknown quantity to me. This would be my first experience at being assessed as a teacher, and I quaked at the thought. I figured preparedness was my best defence, so I worked with renewed energy. We went over the number work and practised reading, spelling and writing. We picked out the best art work and displayed it nicely around the walls. We took special pains to keep the room tidy and made sure the mugs and toothbrushes were hung in neat rows in the vestibule.

Each morning, as the flag flew to the top of the pole (and this was one time when I never forgot), I would wonder if this would be the day he'd arrive. I was becoming a nervous wreck.

As time went by with no sign of him, I reached a point where, for long periods of the day, I forgot all about him. It was during one of these periods that he knocked at the school door and walked in, taking me completely by surprise.

He was of medium height with a heavy build and a round, florid face. I studied him. He didn't *look* as if he were going to eat me alive.

As he walked briskly up the aisle, the children stood and chorused, "Good morning, Mr. Barry"—just as we'd practised.

"Good morning, class. Good morning, Miss Bowden."

The class resumed their seats, sitting as still as mice for a change. Even the sniffling subsided for the time being. He perused the attendance sheet and then said, "Now, we'll hear some reading and see how these young ones are progressing."

As the class was grades one to four, more or less, the standard was set by the reader, which was the only way they could be graded, due to irregular attendance and the short school year. But this was arbitrary at best. One boy of 12, although still coping with the grade two reader, excelled in his Native art.

The government curriculum was simply not set up for Native children. When I realized how completely their lives differed from the ones depicted in the readers, I tried to improvise. We would go for walks along the beach when the tide was out, and they would teach me things I didn't know about shells and seaweed. They showed me dulse, which was edible. Sometimes we'd ramble in the woods gathering fungi from old stumps. On the smooth upper surface of the fungi, they would draw and colour figures from their own experience. They could draw whales, Thunderbirds, fishboats and fish in detail, as well as community houses complete with totems and house posts.

They loved to sing and the song they liked best was "Frère Jacques." It amused me to teach these Indian children a French folk song, but try as I might "vous" always came out "boo." In school, and up and down the village path, they would chant:

> Frera Jacka, Frera Jacka,
> Domay Boo, Domay Boo,
> Somay la Matina,
> Somay la Matina,
> **BING BANG BONG!**

For the purpose of Mr. Barry and his inspection, I carried on with reading, writing and arithmetic in each grade. Little Stella didn't let me down. She read nicely in a clear voice, knew her tables and wrote plainly, shining like the star that was her name.

Hughina and two of her students peer tentatively at a beached mud shark.

Reverend John Antle, founder of the Columbia Coast Mission, and his successor, Alan Greene, often took photos to supplement the message in *The Log*. This photo of Miss O'Brien, Hughina's star pupil, Stella Hanuse, and a friendly pup likely had that purpose.

Mr. Barry sat quietly at my desk while I plodded through the long, *long* morning. When noontime came—at last—he and I went down the hill to the brown house for lunch. He chatted amiably, and I found he was human and not a monster after all.

He knew I was a registered nurse, so all through lunch, instead of discussing teaching and school problems, he talked about his heart condition, providing a blow-by-blow description of every symptom. He cheerfully informed me he should never walk uphill, as, in all likelihood, he'd drop dead at any moment. Looking at his heavy-chested build and florid complexion, this didn't surprise me. I can't say this grim prospect made me feel better about his visit.

He didn't stay for the whole afternoon. Instead he dismissed the class early. Much to my relief, and the joy of the children, the dreaded inspection was over.

I was curious as to what kind of report Mr. Barry would give Mr. Todd. I was doubtful of my teaching ability, yet he had neither criticized nor praised. I was completely in the dark as to his opinion. It was sometime later that Mr. Todd told me I had passed inspection, and that Mr. Barry had found Stella to be one of the brightest pupils in any of the outlying schools. I often wondered what had impressed him more, my teaching ability or my sympathetic understanding of all his cardiac ailments.

We've Caught Up with the Indians

*T*HE DEEP-THROATED WHISTLE OF THE *Columbia* echoed through the frosty air, and soon the putt-putt of its kicker could be heard, heading for the village. Joy reigned supreme!

The *Columbia*'s visit meant news, fresh faces and someone different to talk with.

It meant the G.A.s had the parson for a service in the school and an hour's chat beside the living-room heater while they had a cup of tea. It meant I had the doctor to tell me of civilization beyond the shores of Village Island. Added to this, I had a couple of cases causing me concern, one of them a pregnant woman with a hernia.

I took him to see her first.

"Go to Alert Bay in a couple of weeks," Dr. Ryall told Mrs. Dick Charlie. "You'd better have *this* baby in the hospital."

"Hokay, Doc," she nodded. "Dick'll take me to 'Lert Bay."

"I don't think you need to worry," he said to me when the visit was over. "She's had babies before, without trouble, but she should be in the hospital for this one. Besides, she has a while to go yet."

I sighed in relief at his reassuring words.

The doctor and I then climbed into the kicker for the short journey to visit Mrs. Oiens. We skirted the shore of Village Island on one side, while on the other lay the small islands that formed the channel. Most of them were nothing more than jagged rocks, while a few were larger and topped with evergreens.

A couple of these tiny islands were Indian cemeteries with burial houses built high in the branches of the trees. They were very old, but the colours of the family crests, which had been painted on the walls, were still faintly visible. This style of burial was common practice before the White man came. The remains of the departed one, along with their earthly treasures, were laid away in these little houses. By choosing these islands with their sheer rock faces rising out of the sea, they were safe from marauding animals. The Native people were superstitious about such places, for they believed the graves to be haunted by the spirits of their ancestors. Consequently, the houses were never molested.

Mrs. Oiens was delighted to see the doctor, and although I visited her often by way of the woodland trail, she greeted me as if I'd been away for a year.

After our tea, we made our way back to the village to where Reverend Dance waited on the float. The *Columbia* was ready to leave. Too soon. But the break from routine had been welcome. And now we had a whole new batch of pros and cons to be discussed.

Early the following morning, I was awakened from a sound sleep by Miss O'Brien, knocking on my bedroom door in a state of agitation. "Miss B., Miss B.," she called.

I sat up groggily. "Yes? What is it?"

"Miss B., Mrs. Frank Joseph had her baby last night."

This brought me out of my stupor and onto the cold floor in a hurry. I hadn't known Mrs. Joseph was pregnant, let alone full term—and as far as I knew, she was *long* past child-bearing age.

I opened the door to find Miss O'Brien in a great flutter.

"Are you sure it was Mrs. Joseph?" I said loudly.

"Oh, dear, did I say Mrs. Joseph? I meant to say Mrs. Dick Charlie."

"Good heavens, she isn't due yet and she's supposed to go to hospital. I wonder what it's done to her hernia." One day after the *Columbia*—and the doctor—leave, I was thinking. What bad luck, for me and Mrs. Dick Charlie.

I threw on my clothes, grabbed the black bag and raced along the village path in the cold morning air. I arrived at the Charlie residence out of breath, knocked on the door and went in.

The Charlies' main room, as was common, was kitchen-bedroom-sitting room combined, with a lean-to on the back for overflow beds. Mrs. Charlie was in bed in the main room, looking serene, while her newborn baby slept peacefully in a wooden cradle beside the kitchen range.

I asked the obvious question. "How are you feeling, Mrs. Charlie?"

"Ike. Ike. Good, good," she said cheerfully.

"Who helped with the baby?"

"Old Sarah. She come in the night."

Old Sarah was a crone-like creature who lived in a shack behind the community house. I'd been told she was a midwife.

I checked Mrs. Charlie's abdomen, particularly the area of the hernia, but it didn't look any worse. The infant was a good colour and everything seemed normal. As there was nothing further to do, I went back to the house for breakfast, then to school.

Mid-morning, there was a knock on the door and Miss O'Brien walked in. She wasted no time.

"Miss B., come quickly. The baby is hemorrhaging."

I left off being teacher and became nurse with a flick of the little black bag and for the second time that morning, ran through the village to the Charlie residence.

Mrs. Charlie was still in bed, but this time the room was filled with village women. They were murmuring and chattering in great concern.

I went to the infant's cradle and pulled back the covers. His abdomen was soaked with blood.

"Yaksum. Not good," said the women, shaking their heads.

I removed the blood-soaked band swaddling the baby's abdomen, then bathed the area to discover the cord was oozing slowly and obviously had been for some time. It was a small matter to retie the cord, and the bleeding stopped immediately.

The Indians had their own way of tying the cord, leaving it about twice as long as we consider necessary. Then a long string is tied to the cord's tip with the ends fastened behind the baby's neck.

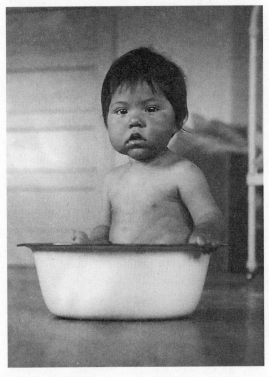

Hughina's young patient shown here may have been one of the last children born on Village Island.

Once the bleeding stopped and the baby was tucked in again, I turned to leave. But the women wouldn't let me go. They surrounded me, faces wreathed in smiles. They shook my hand, patted my back and stroked my arm. Never before had I seen them so demonstrative. It was much later before I was able to leave the house.

That afternoon I checked on mother and child and all seemed well. The following afternoon I visited to find Mrs. Charlie was up and had been all day. She'd done her washing and her usual household chores and was now preparing the evening meal of dried fish and eulachon grease.

"Why aren't you in bed? You shouldn't be up yet," I scolded. "My goodness, the baby was born only yesterday."

"No bed. All fine now," she said, grinning broadly.

I was really alarmed at this turn of events. My training had taught me maternity patients should remain in bed for at least a week to 10 days after confinement. Now the pendulum has swung the other way and new mothers are encouraged to get up almost immediately.

So it seems we have caught up with the Indians!

Ada

O

N VILLAGE ISLAND THE GRIM battle with tuberculosis never stopped.

The G.A.s worked constantly toward their goal of stamping out the disease in the village, and Miss Dibben, despite her failing sight, did a valiant job of caring for the patients in the *Hyuya-Tsi*. Of the three girls in the preventorium, Eliza was the worst. But there was one other case of TB in the village, a young girl, who was by far the most gravely ill.

She was 17 and her name was Ada Wallace.

When I first came to Village Island, unprepared and knowing nothing of the Natives and their ways, I had a superior attitude. I thought them dull, unresponsive and unemotional. Except for Auntie, who didn't let a language barrier interfere with communication, it was difficult to get to know or understand them. But as the months crept by, I learned something of their culture and a few words of their language. I learned to appreciate them as individuals possessing the strengths, dreams and sorrows common to all of us.

Ada and her mother knew all about sorrow.

Ada, the only child of her widowed mother, was seriously ill when I came to the island. There was no hope for her recovery, so it was Mrs. Wallace's wish she remain at home. Ada's bed was by the window, enabling her to see the people as they strolled along the village path and to watch the activities of the gas boats. Everyone either waved or stopped at the doorstep to talk awhile. As neither Ada nor her mother could read, and Ada was too sick to do handiwork, no doubt this friendly village gossip helped to pass the time.

I met Ada soon after I came to the village. A quiet girl with limpid brown eyes and soft black hair, she had the typical high colouring of the TB casualty. Her young body was frail, already wasted by this dreadful disease.

Mrs. Wallace was a big, handsome woman with an intelligent face. She was always silent, and I was never sure what she was thinking during my visits to Ada—although I was sure she understood more English than she could speak. She was a very caring mother, and once the importance of cleanliness regarding Ada and herself had been explained, she was careful to keep their dishes separate and faithfully burned the sputum containers.

There was little to do for Ada except to keep her comfortable, so each day I would rub her back and fluff her pillows. On Saturdays, when I had more time, I would give her a sponge bath and change her sheets. Then I would fuss with her hair and tell her how pretty she was. She would smile quietly, obviously enjoying this extra attention, although I was never sure how much she understood. She was shy at first, but after a while I knew she looked forward to my visits, for her eyes would light up when I came in the door.

Mrs. Wallace, on the other hand, would sit stonily by the kitchen range, giving me only a curt nod of recognition. Never once did she smile or respond to my greeting, and I was always uncomfortable in her company.

Then, one day as I was leaving, she picked up a bulky roll from the floor and shoved it at me. "Here. You take," she said.

I took what she offered, so surprised by her words that all I could do was stare at the bundle in my hands.

"You look," she commanded.

I unrolled the bundle to find a lovely hand-hooked rug. For a moment I was speechless.

At last I stammered, "Thank you, Mrs. Wallace. It's beautiful."

My gratitude evoked no response, so I fumbled for more adequate words. "Ike. Ike. Good, good." I said.

Only then did her expression soften, and a fleeting smile crossed her handsome face. I looked at Ada, propped up on her clean pillows, and she smiled and nodded. Then Mrs. Wallace turned away and took up her place beside the kitchen range. This ended the conversation, so I thanked her again and left. This time, however, I left with a glow of pleasure.

There was a chest beside Ada's bed. Made of clear yellow cedar, its lid was expertly carved, and it had brightly painted totems at each corner. It was fine Native art and I often admired it. One day Ada indicated I open it. When I lifted the lid, I found it filled with new clothes, as well as new sheets and blankets.

I exclaimed over the soft blankets and crisp sheets, as well as sweaters, slips, underwear, stockings and dresses. There was two of everything—a complete wardrobe in duplicate. Ada smiled happily when I told her how lovely everything was. But while I admired the finery, I kept wondering why it was there. I left the Wallace house still curious about the chest.

When I met Gertrude on the village path, we chatted for a moment, then I asked, "Gertrude, can you tell me something? Why does Ada have a chest beside her bed filled with new clothes?"

"Those are for when she dies," Gertrude said matter-of-factly.

"Does she know what they're for?"

"Sure, she does."

"Doesn't it bother her?"

"Oh, no. Ada wouldn't like it if she didn't have any new clothes for when she dies," answered Gertrude, surprised at my ignorance.

"But why two of everything?"

"Because," she explained patiently, "they have to last a long time. You see, she has to take plenty with her. Some for when she dies and some for later."

It seemed having sufficient clothing for the hereafter, tucked away in a cedar chest, was common practice. From then on every time I went to see Ada, I would eye the chest, knowing the time was not far off when, sadly, she'd be wearing this new finery.

She rallied again, however, and for a time was able to dress and get out of bed for part of each day. I suppose the temptation was too great, for soon I noticed she was wearing some of the new clothes. Maybe it was a last, faint hope they wouldn't be used for their original purpose. Whatever the reason, I was glad she'd had a little while to enjoy her new things, because she was soon confined to bed again, this time never to leave it.

Early one morning, just before Easter, I was called to the Wallace house. Ada was in a deep coma, her life flickering to its untimely end. There was nothing to be done but wait, and I was filled with sadness for this girl who'd never had a chance to really live. I stayed with Ada until she died, then turned to leave. The village women had gathered in the room, and as it was customary for the relatives to prepare the body for burial, I didn't want to intrude.

As I moved toward the door, I heard Mrs. Wallace speaking quietly to Gertrude. Then Gertrude turned to me and said, "Miss B."

"Yes, Gertrude, what is it?"

"Mrs. Wallace wants you to fix Ada. Will you do it?"

This request took me completely by surprise. "Yes, of course," I said. "If that's what she'd like."

I looked toward Mrs. Wallace. She still had the stolid expression, but I could see the quiver of her lips as she nodded her head. I was deeply touched to be asked to give Ada this final attention. Mrs. Wallace, in a special way, was bestowing an honour on me.

The small room was hot and crowded with women who sat on the few chairs or squatted on the floor. Each sat with her shawl-covered head bowed in grief. As I started the task of preparing Ada for burial, they broke into high-pitched wails, rocking back and forth in unison. I was listening to sounds of mourning that stretched back to antiquity. The air vibrated with it.

"Ah eeh! Ah eeh! Ah eeh!" they cried in concert.

I bathed Ada, then the cedar chest was opened. With Gertrude's help, I dressed her in the new underwear, slips, stockings, dresses and sweaters. I noticed the few things she'd worn had been replaced with new ones. When she was dressed, we wrapped her in the white sheets and soft blankets.

The keening of the women grew louder and louder, ceasing suddenly when we finished our task. The room went strangely quiet.

The men waited outside with a casket in which Ada was placed. The casket was then carried in a slow procession along the village path to the school. The women took up the keening again as we plodded through the village, then stopped as we entered the school.

When paying their respects to the dead, the Natives clung to their ancient customs—customs the missionaries viewed as heathen. Yet, on the surface, they accepted the rites of the White man. They dutifully listened to Miss

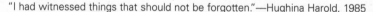

"I had witnessed things that should not be forgotten."—Hughina Harold, 1985

Dibben read the prayers for the burial of the dead from the *Book of Common Prayer*. How much did they understand? I wondered. And did it matter? Perhaps their vision of the hereafter was not so far removed from our own, and who's to say one way is better than the other. We were gathered to honour Ada. For now she was our bond.

When the memorial service ended, the casket was carried to a waiting gas boat for its final journey to Alert Bay.

I stood at the end of the old Indian wharf and watched the boat disappear down Village Pass.

I would miss Ada.

She had become part of the pattern of my life on Village Island, and her life was too soon at an end. Her quiet acceptance of the inevitable gave solemn and sobering thought.

Blackfish Sound

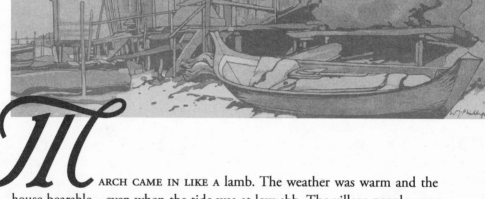

ARCH CAME IN LIKE A lamb. The weather was warm and the house bearable—even when the tide was at low ebb. The village people were getting the wanderlust, and from day to day, I never knew how many children would come to school. One day it might be 12, the next, 3 or 4. Even the G.A.s were restless, and I had developed a major case of spring fever. However, our desires were poles apart. They eagerly awaited a weekend visit from the parson, while I was champing to get off the island.

The *Columbia* hadn't called for some time, and there was no definite word of when she'd appear. Nevertheless, the pros and cons went with every meal, and the G.A.s laid plans for Reverend Dance that would leave the poor man limp as a wet rag before the prospective weekend was over. The days crept by with neither word nor sign of the *Columbia*.

Saturday arrived and, as usual, I did my washing. This was done on the back porch, a portion of the raft behind the kitchen. There was a hand-cranked washing machine with a wringer and galvanized tubs for rinsing. Lines were strung under the lean-to roof. I'd finally mastered the scrubbing board, so the amount of skin I removed from my knuckles was now barely noticeable. Nor did my arms ache as much when pumping the clunking old washing machine, and I no longer got my feet soaked when dumping the wash water over the edge of the raft to the beach below.

In the afternoon, I walked through the woods to the Oiens'. Mr. Oiens had been to Minstrel Island for mail, and I happily read my batch of letters. About four o'clock, after we'd had our tea, I started back through the woodland trail, enjoying the late-afternoon sun filtering through the trees. I came to a rise in the path, and just as I started up, who should pop over the top but the parson. He gave me a terrible start, for, in all my walks through the woods, I'd never before met another human being. He muttered something about "a lovely day" and strode on, never slackening his pace.

When I arrived at the brown house, the G.A.s were busy. Miss O'Brien was moving out of her room to make way for the parson, while Miss Dibben sent messages through the village telling the people to listen for the bell calling them to evening prayers. The parson was on the spot with every escape route cut off, so the G.A.s

Reverend Dance and Hughina's G.A.s pose during one of his infrequent visits to Village Island.

planned to make the most of it. By the time Sunday night arrived, he looked worn out.

He occupied Miss O'Brien's room next to mine, muttering and snoring, while the bedsprings complained at his unaccustomed weight and length. The good man would probably have been mortified had he realized how clearly I could hear through the paper-thin walls.

On Monday morning the school was again a school, for which the parson was deeply grateful, I'm sure. The *Columbia* wasn't due to return until Tuesday morning, so he spent an aimless day with nothing to do and nowhere to go. When the whistle sounded Tuesday morning, he was waiting on the dock, suitcase in hand, long before the kicker was anywhere in sight, looking happier than he had all weekend.

With the parson's visit over, the G.A.s settled back into their groove and happily carried on their chosen work, while I was becoming more and more like a caged beast. I hadn't been away from the village since my return after the New Year, except to visit Mrs. Oiens or make a few calls to care for someone on a neighbouring island. All my happy plans for gay weekends in Alert Bay, which looked so easy on a map in Victoria, had been to no avail. Regardless of my New Year's resolution to make the best of my lot, I was stale and unsettled.

The week after the parson's visit, I heard Simon Beans was going to Alert Bay the following Saturday. Simon and his wife Emma were a nice young couple with two well-behaved children, Emily and Henry, in school. Emma made excellent bread and often sent us a pan of hot buns for supper. Simon owned the *Helen B*, a 15-foot gas boat in much better repair than many of the village boats. So, with the weather settled and the sea calm, I decided to join Simon for the trip to Alert Bay.

Early Saturday morning I walked through the village to the jetty where the *Helen B* was tied and climbed aboard. There were other passengers. Three of them were husky young men from the village and last, but far from least, there was Fat Maudie. She was a relative of Simon's and came by her name honestly, for she must have tipped the scales at 250 pounds. She sat in the well deck on an apple box, shrouded in an enormous blanket and, like a sphinx, neither moved a muscle nor uttered a word.

Determined to enjoy this day, I made myself as comfortable as possible, sitting on the hard edge of the well deck. It was a glorious morning with a sun already warm and a sea like glass. Every rock and island had its perfect reflection. The silence was broken only by the sound of the gas boat's engine. I sat back and relaxed in the mellow spring sunshine, happy in the fact I was off the island and on a journey.

We made a steady course through the island waterways and arrived in Alert Bay in something over two hours. A perfect crossing. As I stepped out of the boat, I smiled benignly at Simon and the boys and even at Fat Maudie, who had sat like a statue the entire trip.

"We leave at four o'clock," Simon said as I headed down the dock.

"I'll be here," I answered with a wave. Even the thought of returning so soon didn't dampen my enthusiasm.

Alert Bay looked magnificent after my cloistered months on Village Island, and I made straight for the Todds', praying someone would be home.

They were, and Mrs. Todd seemed genuinely pleased to see me.

So I spent a few happy hours talking and hearing about something other than school, sick people and the narrow round of village gossip that went with every meal on the island. Later, I visited

Two of Simon and Emma Beans' children stand beside their grandfather's house post.

Muriel Banfield (back row, left) and Murray Todd's secretary, Sadie Thompson (back row, right), started a young mothers' club in Alert Bay in 1935. Muriel left the area at the same time as Hughina and donated many of her old photos to the provincial museum in 1973.

Sadie and Muriel and listened with envy while they told me of the social whirl they'd been in all winter.

All too fast the hours flew. Sadie and Muriel walked with me to the wharf where the *Helen B* was tied and, with great reluctance, I climbed aboard.

Fat Maudie had already settled herself into immobility, and the boys were lounging on top of the cabin roof. I waved goodbye as Simon pulled away from the wharf and watched the bay until I could no longer see the tall totem poles.

About then I realized we were heading into a stiff breeze. The sea had lost its mirror-like appearance of the morning and was whipped into choppy, whitecapped waves. However, the engine was chugging along competently, so I gave the weather no thought. Cormorant Island now lay behind us. Soon Hansen Island loomed into view and beyond it Blackfish Sound. I could see whitecaps ahead, and though they looked menacing from this distance, I consoled myself with the thought the Natives were wise to the ways of the weather and knew these waters from time immemorial. And I felt safe with Simon and his *Helen B.*

But when we came out of the lee of the islands into the sound, the wind and waves hit with fury. In moments, we were surrounded by threatening, roiling water—but nothing, I was sure, Simon couldn't handle. Surely he'd seen much worse. As no one spoke to me, all I could do was work to quiet my mounting fear.

The boat plowed on, straining and plunging over each wave. The farther we went into open water, the angrier the seas became. A liquid, sluicing sound filled my ears while I watched great, undulating waves bear down on the small boat. Each was topped by whitewater, curling like witches' talons, ready to claw us under.

The *Helen B* climbed her full length up the side of the next wave to teeter precariously on its crest, then plunged into the trough, only to meet the oncoming surge and climb, teeter and plunge again. The small craft, with Simon straining at the wheel, stubbornly fought the fury of the sea, but I was beginning to wonder if it might be a losing battle.

With every sickening descent into the troughs between the great rollers, we would be surrounded by cold, green water. The sky seemed to vanish from sight. Then I saw, as from a lookout on a mountaintop, one roller mightier than all the rest, rushing toward us. I watched, horrified, the steady, relentless progress of this wall of water. The *Helen B* plunged to meet it, and as we climbed its side and reached its peak, spume splashed into the well deck, soaking my feet but far worse, spraying the labouring engine with salt water. There was a feeble sputter and then a dreadful silence. Only the roar of the sea remained. The boat, with its terrified passengers, was at its mercy.

Simon flew to the engine, leaving the steering wheel free, all the while shouting in Kwak'wala to make his voice heard above the roar of the water. One of the boys leapt from the cabin roof, where all three had been lying on their stomachs, clinging to the sides, and grabbed the wheel. Simon was still shouting commands as the other two boys scrambled off the roof, disappeared into the cabin, and appeared again, each with a paddle in his hand. Then, kneeling one on each side of the prow of the *Helen B,* they paddled furiously to prevent the boat from turning into the trough of the waves. If this happened, she would either be swamped or turn turtle.

While Simon worked desperately to dry and start the engine, the three boys kept us on a straight course. Hours seemed to go by as we rode the cresting waves, then the engine gave a few wheezy coughs and started. Relief was written on all faces, even the immobile Fat Maudie's, but it was short-lived. The engine sputtered and stopped again. As we rose to the crest of each wave, I saw ahead to Freshwater Bay, which meant shelter and safety. Then we would descend into the trough, and it would vanish.

Fat Maudie, who had been sitting all the while in complete silence, now seemed to come to life. She began keening, rocking back and forth on her apple box.

"Ah eeh, ah eeh!" she wailed, almost drowning out the roar of the sea.

I had last heard this mournful, high-pitched cry when Ada died, and to hear it now, when I was sure we were doomed to a watery grave, sent chills down my spine.

"Ah eeh! Ah eeh!" she cried, her eerie lament mingling with the wind.

The engine sputtered and coughed, inching us nearer to Freshwater Bay before stalling once more. And as the boys paddled with furious rhythm, Fat Maudie wailed on. I hung on, silent and numb.

Suddenly, the engine took with more determination, then with a desperate effort, as if being kept going on the willpower of those aboard, it made the final run out of the clutches of Blackfish Sound. Now past Freshwater Bay and into sheltered water, everyone sagged with relief. Fat Maudie stopped wailing and actually smiled. The boys climbed back to the roof of the cabin and lay panting from the strain of the last hour. I released my grip on the edge of the well deck, my fingers so stiff I could barely flex them.

The boat chugged along sluggishly through the sheltered water between the islands. There was a little chop, but after what we'd been through, it felt as if we were riding on velvet. Our progress was slow, but a least the engine was going.

Then, as if to say "Oh, the heck with it," it stopped completely. But this time there was no panic. Except for going nowhere, we were in no danger.

"Rough trip, eh, Miss B.?" said Simon as he began working on the engine again.

"Goodness, yes, Simon. Thank heaven, it's over. Have you ever seen it worse than that?"

"Pretty bad today, for sure. Blackfish Sound can be bad place sometimes."

The boys were talking in Kwak'wala and laughing uproariously, for now it was something of a joke. But not Fat Maudie. She had again lapsed into total silence.

It had grown dark and very cold; I envied Maudie her voluminous blanket. Simon now worked on the engine by the light of a lantern. I watched with half interest, for I'd become so cold I was paralyzed and my wet feet were numb. All I wanted to do was get home to Village Island.

Exactly what happened next or how, I had no clear idea. All I heard was a yell from Simon as the silence was rent by an explosion and the dusk was filled with blue flames. Simon leapt to his feet, shouted some order in Kwak'wala, and from somewhere one of the boys threw him a wet sack. He beat at the flames and as quickly as they'd come, they were gone. Again, all was in darkness.

I wondered if this nightmare trip would ever end, and if so, how? At the rate we were going—no rate at all!—we could float idly the rest of the night, unless someone happened by. At this time of night, that was a very remote possibility.

Simon and the boys had a long conversation, none of which I understood, while I sat shivering and miserable, wondering what to expect next. At this point I thought nothing would surprise me. But I was wrong.

One of the boys picked up a paddle and crawled to the prow of the *Helen B* where he knelt and began paddling as if the boat were a dugout canoe. The other two brought a blanket from the cabin and, after jumping to its roof, stretched the blanket between them, where it billowed in the light wind, thus forming a makeshift sail. The wind was behind us and we were running with the tide, so the boat picked up a little speed. Our progress was slow, but at least we were moving—and in the right direction.

By now it was completely dark. The moonless sky was laced with a myriad of stars, and the islands we passed so slowly were jagged, black silhouettes. Sparkling phosphorescence made a glowing tail to each paddle stroke, so the boat seemed surrounded by a million flashing diamonds.

We travelled at this snail's pace for over an hour while Simon worked on the engine by lantern light. We were getting close to the village and had only to pass a few more islands before turning into the channel. Then, suddenly, the silence shattered as the engine gave a couple of experimental coughs, then started with determination. What a wonderful sound! The boys took down the blanket sail and stopped paddling. In no time we could see the lights of the village. They never looked brighter or more welcoming. We'd be home in minutes.

Or so I thought.

The *Helen B* turned into the narrow, rock-filled channel with the tide on the rise, but not yet fully in. And while Simon had felt his way through this channel a hundred times, this time he lodged the boat on a rock directly in front of the brown house. And there we sat, cold and hungry, a stone's throw from warmth, hot food and dry feet. The boys pushed and pried with paddles to no avail. There was nothing to do but wait until the tide rose high enough to float us off—an interminable half-hour.

By the time Simon secured the *Helen B* to the dock, I'd been on the briny for five hours, most of the time in a state of panic.

When I staggered into the kitchen, I could hardly believe I was there. I collapsed into the chair beside the heater and related my tale to the hovering G.A.s as they plied me with hot drinks and warm food.

At that moment, they truly looked like Guardian Angels.

Simoom

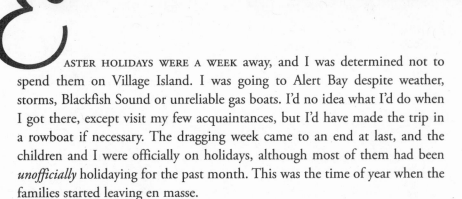

ΕASTER HOLIDAYS WERE A WEEK away, and I was determined not to spend them on Village Island. I was going to Alert Bay despite weather, storms, Blackfish Sound or unreliable gas boats. I'd no idea what I'd do when I got there, except visit my few acquaintances, but I'd have made the trip in a rowboat if necessary. The dragging week came to an end at last, and the children and I were officially on holidays, although most of them had been *unofficially* holidaying for the past month. This was the time of year when the families started leaving en masse.

On Monday I found a boat going to Alert Bay and hopped aboard. I was jittery approaching Blackfish Sound, but this day it was on its best behaviour. It was impossible to believe that, just over a week ago, it had almost been my nemesis.

At Alert Bay, I scrambled off the gas boat and, clutching my suitcase, started along the road toward the Todds' house.

"Hi, there." I heard a voice call from behind me. I turned to see Dr. Ryall from the *Columbia* hurrying toward me.

"I saw the *Columbia* at the hospital dock," I said. "I was wondering if I'd see any of you."

"On holidays?" he asked.

"Yes. I don't know what I'm going to do with them, but here I am."

"How'd you like a trip on the *Columbia*?"

"I'd love it." I was thrilled at this unexpected invitation.

"We're leaving this afternoon for Wakeman Sound and Kingcome Inlet. The parson's at Kingcome now, so you can have his cabin. We'll be gone a couple of days."

"I'd love to go," I said, "but I'll have to check with Mrs. Todd first. She invited me to stay with them when I was here last."

"See what you can do. We'll be leaving about two o'clock. Try to come, you'll meet some nice people, and I think you'll have a bit of fun." He smiled.

Fun! About now I'd do anything to have some of that. Perhaps the doctor had been to Village Island often enough to realize there wasn't much levity in my life. It was pretty dull most of the time for a young girl with my gregarious nature.

We said our goodbyes and I raced to the Todds' house.

"I've been invited to go on a trip on the *Columbia*," I excitedly told Mrs. Todd as she ushered me toward the kitchen.

"Well, for goodness' sake, go," she said. "It'll make a nice change for you."

Bless the woman. I didn't even have to unpack.

At two o'clock, I was at the hospital dock ready to board.

I walked up the gangplank and onto the solid deck of the 100-foot-long *Columbia*. After travelling this very morning on a boat resembling an orange crate, and after my near-tragic journey of the previous week, it was reassuring to be on a substantial craft like this one.

"Stow your bag, then come and join me," called Captain Ed Godfrey through the wheelhouse window.

By the time I climbed the companionway into the wheelhouse, we were backing away from the dock.

"We'll make Simoon Sound tonight," he said, genially.

"That's an interesting name. Where's Simoon?"

"About 35 miles north of here," he answered, pointing it out on one of his marine charts. "On the maps it's spelled 'Simoom,' but everyone around here mispronounces it."

"I think 'Simoon' is prettier. Romantic somehow."

"And a lot easier to say." He laughed, then turned his attention to the route. "Fine people live around there. Just about the best. You'll meet some of them tonight or tomorrow."

With the speed at which the *Columbia* travelled, it was no time before we entered Blackfish Sound; it didn't look nearly so fearsome from the *Columbia*'s wheelhouse as it had from a 15-foot gas boat.

Captain Godfrey skilfully guided the ship through the narrow channels formed by the multitude of islands. Most of them appeared uninhabited, but there were some surprises. Often we'd round a point to see an A-frame and a belch of smoke from a donkey engine. There would be a floathouse, a bare patch on the hillside, and a boom of logs in the water.

At one of these lonely places, he said, "Let's say hello to Ben Jones and the missus." Then he'd sounded a friendly blast on the ship's whistle.

Someone waved from the doorway of the house and we'd wave back. Probably Mrs. Jones would go to bed that night happy in the thought she and Ben were not the last man and woman on earth.

We passed Native villages. One a mere cluster of empty shacks gazing toward the sea, another more lively, with a gas boat tied to a wharf, and a curl of smoke coming from a beach fire. We carried on, and again I was struck by the vast emptiness of this land. In this labyrinth of islands and waterways, where the rugged, towering Coast Range plunged its roots into the sea, I was but a speck of admiring humanity.

About six o'clock we arrived at our destination in Simoom Sound. As the Captain eased the *Columbia* to the wharf, I had my first look at one of the floating communities on the B.C. coast. A number of substantial buildings were constructed on great rafts, all lashed together and secured to the rocky shoreline.

The *Columbia* was a lifeline to the outside world and the defined legacy of John Antle, the mission founder. Inset: Captain Ed Godfrey.

A girl about my age, dressed in slacks and a sweater, stood on the float watching our arrival. She was smiling, and the minute our feet touched ground—or what passed for it—she greeted us cheerily. Her name was Irene Dunseith.

She gave me a big grin, perhaps pleased to see someone so close in age to herself. "Come on in for coffee and meet the rest of the family. We go through the store to get there," she said. On the way she filled me in on the family business.

John Dunseith, Irene's father, had established his store and post office at Simoom Sound many years before. The store was the focal point for the scattered community and stocked many items never seen in city stores, but necessary to meet the special needs of the local residents.

This was also a port of call for the Union steamships serving the smaller communities of the B.C. coast. The post office was a hive of activity on boat day, she told me, as most of the local shopping was done by catalogue and mail order. On that day people came from miles around to collect parcels and mail, and the floats were jammed with boats.

Irene led the way through the store and into the house adjoining it. We entered a big, comfortable kitchen, and I immediately noticed electric lights and a sink—with two taps. Hot water? Here? I stared. Yes, that was definitely a hot-water tank connected to the kitchen stove. Was it possible the Dunseiths also had a bathtub? After living all winter with coal-oil lamps and cold water, to find electric light and hot water in such an out-of-the-way place was a stunning surprise. What luxury!

"Where do you get your power and water?" I couldn't help but ask.

"We're piped to a stream up the shore a piece, and we have our own generator for the lights," Irene told me. "A lot of people have them. What do you have on Village Island?"

"Nothing as civilized as this, I can tell you."

I met Irene's mother and younger sister, Joyce. Mrs. Dunseith was a soft-spoken, white-haired lady, and Joyce was as friendly as her sister. I liked them both immediately. The company of young people after being cloistered for so long with the G.A.s was a special treat.

"I think I'll turn in for an hour," announced Captain Godfrey after we'd had our coffee, "but you're all invited aboard later for some of Doc's pancakes."

"They are?" the doctor asked, then smiled. "Okay, but bring your own soda bicarb!"

I was still in my bunk, or I should say, the parson's bunk, when I was awakened early the next morning by the throb of the engine. I scrambled out of bed, dressed quickly and dashed out on deck to find Simoom Post Office receding around a rocky point. My new-found friends were probably still fast asleep. I took a few breaths of the dewy, fresh air and realized I was starving. So when the aroma of frying bacon and brewing coffee wafted through the open galley door, I followed it.

"Sleep well?" Dr. Ryall asked. He was relaxing with a cup of coffee.

"Yes, thank you. Very well. And it's a *beautiful* morning. Where are we going today?" I poured myself some coffee and joined him at the table.

"We're stopping at Manns' camp farther up the Sound—just to say hello. From there we'll go to Wakeman Sound. After that we'll go up Kingcome Inlet and pick up the parson. He's staying with the Hallidays."

"What's at Manns' camp?" I asked.

"It's an independent logging operation run by Harry Mann and his two stepsons," he said, taking a drink of his steaming coffee. "Kate and Harry have three younger children, too, a girl and two boys. But what makes their place unique is that it has a schoolhouse on floats. As far as I know, it's the only floating school in B.C."

This I had to see.

A short time later the *Columbia* turned into a cove, and I could see buildings floating serenely on their large rafts at the foot of the rocky shoreline. On one side of the main house was a long, narrow bunkhouse and on the other, a substantial schoolhouse, which the doctor pointed out to me. It looked like any other one-roomed school—except for its watery foundation. As well, there was a woodshed and a workshop. The buildings were anchored together in an uneven row.

However, I paid little attention to the buildings, for something much more unusual, and far more beautiful, caught my attention. I could scarcely believe it. Surely the impossible had been created here, for around this floating camp was a glory of a garden. The perfume of its spring flowers wafted on the sea air, heady and unexpected. As the boat drew nearer, I could see this was not a garden in the ordinary sense; it was a labour of love. And a riot of colour.

There were blue, white and pink hyacinths in hanging baskets around the veranda roof. Yellow daffodils and white jonquils bloomed in planters along the edge of the float, and red and yellow tulips grew in hot-water tanks that had been split in two and placed under the windows. There were window boxes filled with grape hyacinths and yellow primulas, trellises for climbing vines and fat flowerpots waiting for geraniums.

The *June M*, seen positioning a boom, was the Mann family's workhorse and link with civilization.

Every teaspoon of earth must have been transported, then the entire garden carefully tended and nurtured, to produce this blazing array.

When the *Columbia* was tied alongside the float, I stepped off, still gaping, and almost bumped into the woman who came out of the house. She was of small, neat build with dark hair and friendly brown eyes. Her smile was a wide one. The doctor introduced us. Her name was Kate Mann.

"What an amazing garden," I said. "It smells just like home and it's so … unexpected."

"I don't know what I'd do without my garden. It's a wonderful diversion." Kate said, laughing softly before changing the subject. "You're at Village Island, aren't you?"

"Yes. How did you know?"

"You'd be surprised how news travels in this country. How is Mrs. Oiens? We were neighbours at Smith Inlet. My husband and I have known the Oiens for a long time."

"I see her often," I told her. "I feel sorry for her at times. She rarely leaves the island, and she's always so glad of company. I'd go crazy if I had to live that way all the time. In fact, I almost do."

"Well, then it's nice you're having a change. Seeing some of the country during your holiday. Come in now and meet Ruth. She's my niece and she's visiting from Vancouver."

We went into the kitchen, where a pretty, dark-haired girl was pouring cups of coffee. Her name was Ruth Mason.

The captain and the doctor joined us, and while we drank our coffee, Kate caught up on the news. I was only half-listening to the conversation, for again

I was eyeing a sink with two taps instead of one and a hot-water tank piped to the kitchen range. Then I saw it, behind a door that was slightly ajar—a bathtub. I stared at this symbol of cleanliness with longing.

I not only wanted, I *needed* a long, hot soak. My last encounter with a bathtub had been at home, during the Christmas holidays, and now it was Easter. Inwardly, I sighed. I couldn't very well ask to take a bath when all I'd been invited for was a cup of coffee.

As I pondered my dilemma, I heard Captain Godfrey say, "How about Ruth coming with us?"

"May I, Aunt Kate? I'd love to go!" The girl pleaded.

"Of course you can," Kate said. "Run and pack your bag."

An hour later we again boarded the *Columbia.*

Our course lay north through Sutlej Channel, and late morning found us changing course to a northeasterly direction as the *Columbia* nosed into the mouth of Kingcome Inlet.

The long inlets of the B.C. coast snaked between towering mountains, rising from sea to sky like stepping stones for the gods. Snow glistened in their higher reaches, melting now to form waterfalls. Cascades like lacy bridal veils poured over cliff faces, white and filmy against the grey-green backdrop.

It was peaceful lazing on the deck below the wheelhouse, and Ruth and I delighted in both the scenery and the mellow spring warmth.

Kingcome Inlet is about 22 miles long and meets Wakeman Sound about midpoint. We reached the entrance to Wakeman about noon.

"See there," the captain said, poking his head out of the wheelhouse window above our heads. He was pointing to a mountainside where a gigantic triangular patch of snow still lingered.

"That's Wakeman slide," he told us. "A few years ago most of the mountaintop fell into the sea. A handlogging outfit is buried under there somewhere. No one was home at the time, thank God, so no lives were lost."

Hundreds of tons of shale lay in mounds at the foot of the wounded mountain, shelving steeply into the sea. The slide had savaged it, ripping away all life and vegetation. Snow covered its scar like an enormous bandage.

Somewhere in the fastness of a bay or snug cove lived the family the doctor was going to visit. I wondered what sort of people they were, and why they'd chosen this life of isolation in preference to community living? We found their logging operation tucked into a bay at the foot of a mountain. The doctor went ashore in the kicker to make his call while the *Columbia* lay at anchor in the quiet water.

When Dr. Ryall returned, the captain weighed anchor, and we retraced our course to the mouth of Wakeman Sound on our way back to Kingcome Inlet.

"Where to now?" I asked the doctor, who had joined us on the deck.

"First up Kingcome River to the Indian village, then on the way back, we'll pick the parson up at the Hallidays'."

The Kingcome River empties into the uppermost regions of the inlet, and as we drew nearer the river's mouth, we heard, before we saw, thousands of seagulls. They looked like a great, wind-whipped cloud, and their cries were almost deafening.

"Look!" Ruth exclaimed. "They're diving for fish."

"This must be the start of the eulachon run," Dr. Ryall said, sounding awed. "I've never seen anything like it."

The eulachon, or candlefish, a traditional staple in the diet of the Indian people, were swimming by the thousands from the river's mouth, turning the sea into a mass of bubbling silver. The gulls would dive straight to the water's surface, pluck a fish, then soar into the air with the wiggling creature flashing in the sun, squirming in a hopeless bid for freedom. The air was electric with this struggle for survival.

From the outboard, the scene was even more spectacular. The surface of the water, just inches below us, was a churning mass of silver fish. Ignoring us completely, the screeching gulls circled the boat, intent upon their prey, while the fish swam blindly and instinctively toward the sea.

Dr. Ryall guided the boat to the river mouth, and as we headed upstream the cries of the gulls grew fainter, leaving us to river music and the solid chug of the outboard.

The river meandered through the delta, then passed great evergreens, growing straight and tall on its banks. The trees eventually gave way to open fields and acres of cleared farmland. The doctor told us how the Landsdownes and the Hallidays had settled in the Kingcome Valley years before, carving productive farms from the rugged virgin country.

The Hallidays had settled in the valley in the spring of 1895. Ernest Halliday first explored the area alone in 1893, travelling by canoe and sail from Comox on Vancouver Island, a distance of over a hundred miles.

The original Landsdowne was a young Englishman from Bristol who came to Kingcome around 1897. At that time the Indian people, resentful of the White settlers, were far from friendly and as the Hallidays and the Landsdownes cleared and cultivated the land, there was more than one skirmish.

Soon we passed the farmhouses, one on each side of the river and set back from its banks, and reached the Indian village, the largest I'd yet seen. It had the same leaning totems characteristic of the old villages, but here the houses along the bank were built on stilts as a safety measure in time of flood. Ruth and I explored the village from end to end, finally scrambling down the river's bank to see it in its entirety. It was in a secure pocket, flanked on either side by snow-capped mountains.

The medical, religious and educational needs of the village people were looked after by two missionaries, who lived in the village. After Dr. Ryall had finished his rounds, they gave us tea, inquiring politely after the G.A.s and the people of Mamalilikulla. Then we boarded the outboard for the return trip downriver, a much faster one, as the river was swift from melting snow.

The Landsdowne farmhouse soon came into view, and the doctor turned the boat toward their riverside dock. We walked along the path to the house, but before we could knock, the door opened. "Hello, Doctor. We saw you going by earlier, so we've been expecting you," Mrs. Landsdowne said.

"Come in. Come in. It's always nice to have company." She smiled at us, then bustled us into the airy farm kitchen. "The men are finishing the chores, but they'll be in soon. Have you had supper?"

When we told her we hadn't, she said, "We'll fix that in a jiffy."

In no time we were sitting with the family around the kitchen table, facing a feast of fried potatoes, homemade bread, pickles, cold roast beef, preserved fruit and lots of steaming coffee. We were starving from our day in the great outdoors and ate ravenously.

"Are you planning to return to the *Columbia* tonight, Doctor?" asked Mrs. Landsdowne, after we had finished and were replete.

"Yes," he said. "I'm going to call at the Hallidays for the parson, then carry on to the *Columbia*."

She frowned slightly. "You know, by the time you do that, it will be dark. Why not let the girls stay here for the night? You can stay with the Hallidays, then come back and pick up them up in the morning."

"That's a good idea—if you don't mind," he said.

"But Ruth and I didn't bring our overnight bags," I said. "They're still on the *Columbia*."

"Don't let that worry you, dear," Mrs. Landsdowne said genially. "We're always ready for visitors. I'll give you something to sleep in."

So, at nine o'clock, we followed her into the guest room. She placed the coal-oil lamp on the dresser, then opened a drawer from which she lifted two neatly folded garments and laid them on the bed.

"There you are. Now sleep well, and I'll wake you in the morning." So saying, our charming hostess left the room.

We picked up the garments and shook them out to find we were each holding a nightgown the size of a pup tent! Obviously Mrs. Lansdowne was prepared for visitors of any size. The nightgowns were finely sewn and trimmed with delicate embroidery. Their puffed sleeves ended in frilly cuffs, and yards of skirt fell from daintily tucked yokes. More frills edged their high, demure necklines.

We donned these quaint, old-fashioned night garments, giggling hilariously at the sight of each other, and climbed between the chilly sheets.

About seven the next morning, Mrs. Landsdowne called, "Breakfast in 15 minutes."

We scrambled out of bed, washed in the icy water from the jug on the washstand and went into the kitchen for an enormous breakfast.

The doctor had told us to be ready by eight o'clock, so after thanking Mrs. Landsdowne for her hospitality, we hurried to the dock. We saw the kicker cutting across the river current, with the doctor at the tiller and the parson standing in the prow like a figurehead. He held the boat to the dock just long enough for us to jump aboard.

As we rushed toward the sea and the waiting *Columbia*, my ears filled with the bubbling song of the river, while the scent of mossy earth and the tang of evergreens stung my nostrils. The day was mirror clear. I breathed deep and all remnants of sleep vanished.

Soon we heard the raucous cries of the seagulls, still busily devouring the little silver eulachon. Almost there.

We came from the river's mouth to find the *Columbia* at anchor in water so calm the image of each rock and tree along the shoreline was impressed in flawless detail on its surface. I watched the perfect reflections waver and distort as the *Columbia* moved out to sea, taking us to our next destination.

Horse Pants and Rattlesnake Boots

E ARRIVED BACK AT MANNS' camp in the early afternoon. During our absence a massive log boom had been secured in front of the camp. The captain tied the boat to it, which meant we had to walk the boom to reach the house. The logs were big and rolled gently, so if one stepped quickly from log to log, there was no danger.

Kate greeted us as we jumped onto the float.

"Did you have a good time?" she asked.

"Wonderful," I enthused. "I feel as though I've been away from Village Island for centuries."

"When do you have to be back?"

"The weekend. Sunday at the latest."

"Why don't you stay on with us, then?" she asked.

"Why not?" urged Ruth. "You'd be here for the party Saturday night."

A party! There was a word that captured my full attention. I had only one worry, which I quickly put into words. "But how will I get back to Village Island?"

"Don't worry," Kate assured me. "There'll be a boat going your way, I'm sure. If not, we'll take you back on the *June M.*"

That was all I needed to hear, and I quickly accepted their invitation to stay.

Now accustomed to life on a floathouse, I still found the Manns' home different. It was level, not at all like the brown house on Village Island, which rose and fell with the tide. The house sat on a substantial raft, fully afloat, so that no winds whistled beneath. But what made it a palace in my eyes was the indoor plumbing. The bathtub fascinated me beyond reason.

I liked Kate Mann. She was a warm and friendly person, and although I'd known her only a matter of hours, I felt I could ask her the all-important question.

"Would it be possible for me to have a bath?" I ventured timidly.

"Why, of course. Help yourself."

"Thank you so much. This is going to be simply wonderful!" I exclaimed with such enthusiasm both Kate and Ruth looked a bit startled.

"I haven't actually had a bath since Christmas," I said, in an attempt to explain.

This seemed to startle them further, so rather than have them question my hygiene, I explained the "plumbing" at the mission house. After that I had full access to Kate's glorious tub. I soaked and soaked, then asked for cleanser to remove the considerable ring around the bathtub. I staggered out of the bathroom, slightly weak from shedding an accumulation of three months' epidermis.

Ruth was waiting for me.

"Come on, I'll show you the rest of the camp," she said. And so I had my first conducted tour of a floating logging camp.

The flowers were blooming in their various baskets, tubs and hot-water tanks, filling the air with their heady scent. I couldn't get enough of it. Then I stopped in mid-sniff and listened, thinking I must be dreaming.

"Do I hear a rooster crowing?" I asked.

"Yes," Ruth said. "Aunt Kate raises chickens as well as flowers."

"On a floathouse?"

"Sure. Come and see."

I followed her to the rear of the house. A white leghorn rooster was strutting around his harem of seven or eight hens, monarch of all he surveyed. The hens were happily scratching in runs attached to the chicken house. The whole coop was screened in with chicken wire and floated serenely on its own raft. The chickens and their lord and master looked healthy and content in their marine residence.

"It's often hard to get fresh eggs, so Aunt Kate thought of this and it works fine. The kids take turns feeding and looking after them."

Flowers and chickens. This was indeed an amazing place. I couldn't wait to see the rest.

We explored the bunkhouse, which was out of bounds when the men were in camp. There was a workshop and machine shop for keeping the equipment in repair. Finally, we visited the school. It resembled any country school in that it had the usual complement of desks, a blackboard, a library table, maps and a wood-burning heater. There the similarity ended, for it was one of the few floating schools, if not the only one, on the B.C. coast.

Its existence came about through necessity, as well as the persistence of Kate Mann. Besides her two grown sons, George and Bob, there were her school-aged children, June, Bud and Eddie. When the education of these young ones became a problem, Kate organized a school. They had started out with the government correspondence courses, but the supervision of lessons took a large chunk out of Kate's chore-laden day, cooking, washing and ironing for the hardworking and hungry men of her family. With other children in the scattered community sharing the problem, building a school soon became a co-operative venture. Men gathered on weekends for a building bee. Kate and Harry's three children, plus four or five others from the area, gave them the necessary number to assure a teacher would be provided by the government.

There was one other problem. The other children lived too far away to commute daily, so the Manns' camp became a boarding school with the teacher, as well as the pupils, living in residence. Most of them went home on weekends, but Kate had them the other five days of the week. This added extra work to the meals and the washing, but in her eyes it was worth it to provide the children with schooling that otherwise would be denied them.

The children may have lacked some of the refinements and frills city children enjoy, but there were definitely other rewards. They had access to things a city child could never dream of. There was the ocean to swim in a few feet from the schoolhouse door, log booms to walk, rowboats for fishing and exploring, and there were marvellous rafts to build from material salvaged from the sea. And what city child's school has sailed merrily over the deep, blue waters of the sea—with the school in session—while a tug towed it, along with the other buildings of the camp, to a new location?

That afternoon the younger children returned from fishing in a rowboat, accompanied by their fox terrier, Palooka. They brought rosy cheeks and large appetites, but no fish. June was a pretty, blonde 14-year-old, and her brothers, Bud and Eddie, wore ear-to-ear grins. The dog, well-adjusted to marine living, walked logs as if he were a veteran boom man. But his favourite pastime was barking at the exhaust pipe of any departing boat.

In the early evening, the men returned in an outboard from their day's labour in the woods. I met these adult male members of the household that night when we sat down to supper. There was Harry Mann at the head of the table, a rugged but kindly, sandy-haired New Zealander, who wasn't even a mite surprised to find me at his already crowded table. There were Kate's oldest sons, handsome fellows reeking of the great outdoors. As well, there was Ray Gravlin, the teacher, bespectacled and intellectual.

The whole atmosphere was so different from the one I'd left—was it only two days before? After all the months on Village Island in the sole company of the G.A.s, I'd begun to feel very prim and proper.

Here, among these friendly people, my outgoing personality—which I'm sure the serious Miss Dibben always suspected lay under my professional veneer—took over.

Looking happy, Hughina (far right) poses with her two young friends—likely Ruth Mason (left) and Irene Dunseith.

I'd become accustomed to the narrow life on Village Island, had seen a bit of Alert Bay, which was much like any small town, and now I was being introduced to life in a remote logging camp by the genial Mann family. Until now, this land had seemed so harsh—beautiful but empty. But having been accepted so readily by people whom only days before I'd never heard of, I had to reassess my first impressions. The second look was much more to my liking.

Gas boats and tugboats took the place of cars, and although slower, were a much more relaxed mode of travel—weather permitting. And certainly there was no traffic problem. It seemed no one passed Manns' camp without stopping to say hello and have a cup of coffee. This dispelled the idea of isolation I'd grown used to. So often on Village Island I'd heard a boat in the distance, only to have the sound fade away, leaving me desolate.

Hughina (standing, at left) with the same two friends and an unidentified young man. Socializing with her new companions helped her overcome the prim-and-proper attitude that had started to rub off on her from the G.A.s.

The following afternoon, we heard the deep throb of an engine long before we saw the boat.

"That sounds like the *Sky Pilot*," said Kate. "I hope it is. We haven't seen Lea Gillard for ages."

As we watched from the float, a boat the size of a small tug turned toward the camp. I'd heard about this craft and her skipper-chaplain, Lea Gillard. The *Sky Pilot* was a mission ship sponsored by the United Church of Canada. She was stationed in Alert Bay, and although she didn't carry a doctor as the *Columbia* did, she gave yeoman service and help to all along the coast who needed it.

The *Sky Pilot* nosed into the log boom that lay off the float, and a young man hopped off and secured the boat.

"Why, that's Percy Wickett," I said, surprised. "He teaches at the Indian day school in Alert Bay."

Another man stood on the afterdeck, watching Percy with interest.

"Who's he?" asked Ruth.

"I don't recognize him," I said, shaking my head.

"He's probably a visitor from town," Kate speculated.

When the boat was secured, Lea Gillard emerged from the wheelhouse, waving to us as he did so. He jumped onto the boom, then turned and said something to the unknown man, who was obviously reluctant to leave the afterdeck. Percy and Mr. Gillard started across the boom, jumping easily from log to log, and soon joined us on the float. After the introductions were made, Percy turned to me.

"Imagine running into you here. How come?"

"I went to Kingcome with the *Columbia*, and they dropped me off here yesterday. I'm staying 'til the weekend. What about you?"

"I've been making the rounds with Mr. Gillard. It sure makes a nice change." He smiled when I nodded my understanding. "I bet you're glad to be away from Village Island for a while."

"I'll say. I'm just finding out what this country is all about."

Our chat was interrupted by Mr. Gillard.

"Lou!" he shouted to the man on the boat. "Come on. We're waiting for you." He turned to us and explained, "Lou is my wife's cousin, just arrived from Montreal. This is his first trip west."

Lou looked out over the log boom, still hesitating, then he seemed to take a deep breath before jumping heavily onto the first log. The logs rolled and bounced, and he clung to the side of the boat, looking as if he wanted nothing more than to climb right back on board and forget the whole thing. But he proved to be game. He let go of the boat and started to hop gingerly from log to slippery log. Foolishly, he hesitated on each one, which caused it to bob up and down, making his passage even more perilous.

"Don't stop now, Lou," Mr. Gillard yelled. "Just keep moving." But Lou hesitated, slipping and slithering with every uneasy step.

With arms held wide for better balance, he resembled a far-from-graceful ballet dancer. He progressed by inches, keeping us in breathless suspense. And it wasn't only his arabesque movements that held us spellbound, but also his sartorial splendour. He was wearing a pristine white shirt, open at the neck, khaki riding breeches, and shiny brown puttees up to the knee and folded neatly at the ankle over smartly polished shoes. Considering the task he was bent on, his attire was wildly incongruous. He looked as if he'd have been happier crawling on all fours.

But somehow he managed to stay upright, although at any moment we expected him to fall on the seat of his sharply pressed breeches. At last he tottered onto the float, decidedly shaken from his first brush with the wild and woolly west.

Mr. Gillard introduced us. His name was Lou Layhew.

"Now, come in and have some coffee," said Kate.

"I think I need it," Lou agreed, now quite relaxed and smiling. "But tell me, is it usual to have to walk logs before you get a cup of coffee?"

"No," laughed Kate. "Next time you come you'll be able to hop off the boat right here on the doorstep. The tug will be here any day now to tow the boom away."

"Thank God," he said fervently.

On closer inspection he proved to be a very presentable fellow. He had sleek blond hair, a trim moustache and a suave manner. Evidently he realized his apparel was a far cry from the jeans, heavy sweaters and sturdy boots that were the usual attire of the male in these parts. He felt called upon to explain.

"Before I left Montreal I thought I should have the proper clothes for this country, so I went to my tailor for a western outfit. This—" he gestured toward his pants and boots "—is the result. I guess he'd seen too many western movies."

Later, when the local boys got to know him better, they teased him unmercifully. He became known as "Horse Pants and Rattlesnake Boots."

"You must all stay for supper," Kate said. "And if you'd like to hold a service later, Lea, by all means do so."

"That's fine, Kate. I'd like to very much."

Lea Gillard was a friendly Newfoundlander, quick to smile, who looked more like the Atlantic fisherman he'd been in his youth than a missionary. His powerful frame, grizzled greying hair and clear, blue eyes seemed more suited to manning the wheel or walking the bridge. He was highly respected

Reverend Leander Gillard (right) and Lou Layhew surround Kate Mann, while a lanky Percy Wickett thwarts the photographer.

and fitted well into the logging community. Under his craggy exterior was a sincerity and firm belief in his calling. When he held a short service, many of the sometimes rough-around-the-edges loggers would attend, regardless of creed—or lack of it. Always obliging, his church was wherever he happened to be at the moment. Kate Mann's sitting room, someone else's kitchen or the deck of a floathouse, it was all the same to him. After the service, he would become one of the boys with no loss of dignity or respect.

After supper, as they were leaving for the *Sky Pilot*, Lea Gillard said to me, "We're going to Alert Bay on Sunday, Hughina, so we can easily drop you off at Village Island, if you like. I haven't seen Miss O'Brien and Miss Dibben for a long time. I'd like the chance to say hello to them."

I accepted happily, thinking of all my difficulties in finding transportation on the island, while here it all seemed so easy.

We walked them to the edge of the float.

"Be sure to come to the party Saturday night," Kate said as they started toward the boom.

"Don't worry, we'll be there," Lea Gillard assured her.

Lou looked dubiously at the log boom, then bravely launched himself off the edge of the float. This time, he jumped more quickly from log to log, so the bounce and roll was less unnerving. He made the side of the boat with ease and then turned and waved while his audience gave him a resounding cheer.

With the long winter over and the hazards of travel less severe, a community get-together in the school seemed in order. When the desks were moved to clear the floor, the school made a sizeable room.

Invitations had gone out by way of the gas-boat grapevine, so there was no way of knowing how many would come. I looked forward to this affair. The closest I'd been to a party in months was Miss O'Brien's social evening. We were all caught up in the frenzy of preparations. Everyone had a job, even eight-year-old Eddie.

"Are you expecting a lot of people?" I asked Kate the day of the party. "And will they have to travel far?"

"Many will have to start out at noon to get here by evening," she said. "The Scotts will come from Mackenzie Sound and the Wilsons from Minstrel Island. There'll likely be people here from Echo Bay and Bond Sound and, of course, Irene and Joyce from Simoom Post Office. You wait and see. You'll be surprised."

By early evening boats were coming from all directions. The log boom had been towed away earlier in the day, so the boats were moored alongside the floats. When all the space was taken, a second row was started, one boat being lashed to another. This necessitated a considerable amount of agile boat hopping.

There was all manner of boats, from small, trim gas boats to sturdy tugs with powerful diesel engines. One traveller's boat looked more like a sleek pleasure craft than a floating business enterprise. The *Sky Pilot* returned as promised, and Lou looked relieved to find the log boom was well on its way to the sawmill.

There was much loud talk and armchair logging among the men and happy greetings among women, who hadn't seen one another for weeks or months. No one came empty-handed, and soon there were mounds of food. I was sure we couldn't eat it all.

While the older folks visited, the younger ones gathered in the schoolhouse and danced to records on the windup gramophone. There was a singsong, with people bellowing at the top of their lungs—lots of enthusiasm but not much harmony.

Amazingly, the food disappeared along with great pots of coffee and considerable amounts of beer. No one thought of going to bed. As one guest said, after coming so far, there was no point in wasting precious hours of sociability in sleep.

I was awestruck that from this sparsely populated land so many people could gather in one place. For the first time I saw a cross-section of the hardy folk who faced danger and loneliness to wrest a living from this unyielding country. These were the Depression years, yet here there was no poverty, no starvation and no soup kitchens. Everyone had three meals a day and a roof over his head, providing he was willing to work. The women were as hardy as the men. Their work, often done in isolation with no female friends within miles, was equally difficult.

There were no social barriers, no status seekers, and each man was taken at face value with no questions asked. Gracious-mannered, well-educated people were on equal terms with the rough and ready transient who came to work a month or two before moving on. Here the preacher, the teacher, the logger and the travelling salesman were all linked by common bonds of independence and interdependence, each sure in the knowledge that every man must be sufficient unto himself, but if help were needed, it was there for the asking. It was the pioneer spirit of a lone frontier.

Morning came and, one by one, the boats left. Soon the float was empty except for the *June M*, the *Sky Pilot* and a few local boats. Morning's arrival also meant my holiday was at an end. Needless to say, I was a little the worse for wear from lack of sleep and unaccustomed exercise. What some of the men lacked in dancing finesse, they made up for in enthusiasm!

But there was nothing to be done. It was time to go. We all headed to the edge of the float.

Hughina (middle row, second from left) enjoys the company of her new friends. Kate Mann is in the front row, sitting third from left.

"Well, it's back to the grind, I guess," I moaned to Kate. "I'm sure going to miss you all—and the fun I've had here."

"We'll try to come for you on weekends when we can," she said. "And when school is finished in June, why not come here for a few days, then take the boat to town from Simoom Post Office?"

"Thanks. I'd love that!" I replied earnestly. "You know, I have a whole new outlook on this country. Thanks to you. It's so different from what I thought it was. And so much more friendly than it seemed when I first arrived on Village Island in the fall."

"It just takes getting to know the people," she said.

I couldn't agree more.

As the *Sky Pilot* pulled away from the float, Kate called, "We'll reserve the bathtub for you when you come next time."

They stood on the float waving goodbye: Kate and Harry, George and Bob, Ray, Ruth and the children. Kate's flowers formed a gay bower around my new-found friends, and I watched them fondly until the boat rounded a rocky point.

The *Sky Pilot* nosed its way through the water, weaving a course through the islands, and before long the familiar shape of Village Island loomed ahead. The old Indian wharf, the brown house and the sad little village looked just as I'd left them a week before.

Maybe they were the same, but I wasn't. I had a new hunger. I longed to see more of this country and its wonderful people.

I told the G.A.s about my holiday, and they were excited about my trip to Kingcome Inlet, but a bit amazed on hearing of all the people I'd met.

"I don't think your holiday was very beneficial," Miss Dibben remarked coolly. "You look tired and not at all well."

I didn't explain my weary appearance, certain the idea of staying up all night and dancing until the daylight hours would horrify their puritan souls. I simply went to bed immediately after supper and stayed there until eight o'clock the next morning.

*L*IFE WAS MORE LEISURELY EVERY day, as most of the children had gone on the traditional spring exodus to the fishing grounds with their families. Never again was I paid for doing so little. Although my salary covered only my teaching duties, somehow looking after the sick and afflicted took precedence over teaching, particularly when there were so few in school. But even the sick were few in number these days.

Of the people left in the village, there was only one who might need attention, and this possibility was remote. Emma Beans, Simon's wife, was seven months' pregnant. But as this was her fourth child, and the doctor had checked her last time around, I wasn't particularly concerned.

I liked Emma. She was a nice young woman who spoke English well. She'd attended the residential school in Alert Bay, where she'd been taught domestic sciences. She was a good cook and her house was always clean and tidy.

I walked into the kitchen of the brown house one day after school with nothing more important on my mind than trying to decide what to do between tea and suppertime. I found Simon waiting for me.

"You come quick!" he said, jumping to his feet the instant he saw me.

"What's the matter? Is one of the children sick?"

"No. Emma wants you. And she says come quick."

I grabbed the black bag and hurried along the path after Simon, all the while praying it was nothing serious. We were at the Beans' house in seconds.

"Emma in there," he said, pointing to the bedroom.

I went into the dark room, which seemed to overflow with a double bed. The only light came from a tiny window near the ceiling, and this had been nailed tightly shut. There was barely two feet of space at the foot of the bed and only just enough room for me to squeeze between the bed and the wall. In the gloom, I could see Emma's form under the grey blanket.

I was almost afraid to ask, but I said, "What's the matter, Emma?"

"I think the baby come," she said in a frightened voice. She sounded alarmed, but no more so than I felt. Seven months' pregnant. It was too soon. Too many things could go wrong. A situation such as this was always hanging over my head, but I'd pushed it away as being too improbable. Now, here it was. I could only hope I was up to it.

"Well, let's see what's going on," I said, sounding more assured than I felt.

I placed my hands on her abdomen and confirmed my worst fears. Emma was in labour, and the contractions were strong. I timed them and found they were coming at regular, five-minute intervals.

"Just lie quietly, Emma, and try to relax between the pains."

There was still a possibility this was a false alarm. I sincerely hoped so, but only time would tell. But it wasn't long before there was no doubt. Emma was going to bear a premature child.

The light from the window was useless. The room was far too dark, and I simply had to see what was going on.

"Simon," I called. "Bring me a light."

"Okay, Miss B. Right now."

I heard him scurrying around, and a moment later he appeared holding a coal-oil lamp. Its feeble, flickering light pierced the gloom to reveal Emma's face. Beads of perspiration stood out on her forehead, and she bit her lip, moaning with each pain. The light from the lamp was practically useless, for there was nowhere to set it down. Although Simon held it as best he could, it wavered and shifted in his unsteady hands.

"This light's no good. Have you got a strong flashlight?"

Simon raced from the room, and with him went the little light I had.

The contractions were almost continuous now, and I was sure, at any moment, the membranes would rupture. I was panicking. How could I manage to deliver a baby under such crude conditions—and in the dark?

"And bring lots of newspapers," I yelled.

Simon poked his head in. "No newspapers, Miss B."

"Find them somewhere," I yelled at him.

Again I was alone with Emma. The room was stifling, and the poor woman was fast approaching the last stages of labour.

"And hurry, Simon," I yelled again, but there was no answer.

I had nothing to work with—no rubber gloves, no rubber sheet, no sedatives and no time. If Emma had towels and extra sheets, I'd no idea where to find them, nor, I was sure, would Simon—if he ever came back.

Emma moaned, strained painfully with each contraction, and all I could do was murmur soothing words. But words weren't nearly enough.

I was hot and clammy and helpless, squeezed in the narrow space between the bed and the wall. The situation was impossible. There was only one option—let nature take its course.

Just then Simon dashed in. He'd been gone only minutes, but it seemed like hours. He rushed in carrying a large flashlight and a pile of newspapers. He beamed the flash into the gloom and it gave a fairly good light. At least it was an improvement over the coal-oil lamp.

"You stand at the foot of the bed and hold the light so I can see," I told him. "And keep it steady."

"Okay. Okay, Miss B.," croaked Simon.

"Raise your hips, Emma. I'm going to put newspaper under you."

While I spread newspaper over the mattress, I kept thinking, what terrible technique. All those months of learning about correct maternity care, and I end up making a birthing bed with yesterday's headlines.

I'd no sooner finished spreading the paper than Emma had a prolonged contraction. Her membranes ruptured with a vengeance.

"It won't be long now," I consoled her.

The baby was coming; I expected to see the head at any moment. Maybe everything would be all right, after all.

"Hold the flashlight closer, Simon. I can't see."

But it wasn't the head appearing. I looked more closely, trying desperately to figure out what part of the anatomy I was seeing. Then I realized, with sinking heart, Emma's baby was arriving in the breech position, buttocks first.

"Push, Emma. Take a deep breath and push," I said the words automatically, for I'd said them many times. But that had been in shining white delivery rooms, with me in a white uniform and a button to push to call for a doctor. There was no one to call in this dark and stuffy room to help Emma and her baby, except me and Simon. I didn't know if he'd been present at a delivery before, but he was in on this one whether he wanted to be or not.

"Come on, Emma. It won't be much longer."

After what seemed a lifetime, the baby's buttocks presented to the point where I could help it along. Together we eased Emma's baby into the world.

The child was stillborn.

Emma lifted her head and looked at me through glazed, hopeful eyes.

These house posts were owned by the Beans family and depicted wolves facing down the poles.

"I'm *so* sorry, Emma," I said softly.

She closed her eyes and lay back, quiet and still.

I turned toward Simon. "You'd better make a little grave for the baby. I'm sorry, Simon."

"Yeah. Too bad, Miss B.," Simon said sadly, shaking his head.

Emma lay limp and exhausted.

I waited for the afterbirth, praying it would be intact, then examined it as thoroughly as I could with the shaky flashlight; it seemed complete. Nevertheless, I had frantic thoughts of retained membrane, puerperal fever, septicemia, hemorrhage and every other complication in the book.

I'd forgotten the traditional custom in the storybooks of having gallons of water boiling on the stove. But there was enough so I could bathe Emma and make her comfortable. She told me where to find clean sheets, and when I removed the layers of newspaper, I saw the mattress had come out unscathed. Small comfort.

My drug supply didn't provide for such emergencies as this, so all I could give Emma were a couple of Aspirins.

"You must stay in bed until I say you can get up," I instructed. "You promise?"

"Yes, Miss B.," she said and smiled weakly.

Infection was my biggest worry, and I checked her temperature three times a day for a week. To my relief it never went over 99 degrees. Soon she was up and about, looking as well as ever.

One day when I called, she held out her hand and said shyly, "Here, Miss B., you take. It's for you."

On her palm lay a brooch, wrought in gold and engraved with a simple design of etched flowers. It was, and still is, a lovely thing. A sad but lovely token of a shared loss. Simon said thank you in his own way. For the rest of my time on the island, he transported me to Alert Bay for half the going fare, often taking no money at all.

This unfortunate emergency did serve to raise my stock with the G.A.s. Such a situation had never before arisen on Village Island, so from then on I was regarded as an authority in obstetrics.

Lucy the Cow

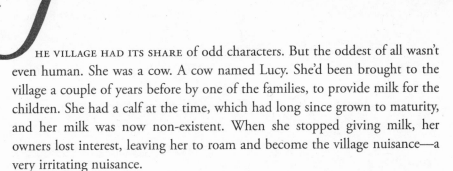

*T*HE VILLAGE HAD ITS SHARE of odd characters. But the oddest of all wasn't even human. She was a cow. A cow named Lucy. She'd been brought to the village a couple of years before by one of the families, to provide milk for the children. She had a calf at the time, which had long since grown to maturity, and her milk was now non-existent. When she stopped giving milk, her owners lost interest, leaving her to roam and become the village nuisance—a very irritating nuisance.

The village path was narrow and Lucy's girth generous, so when you met her there, it was always a battle of wills to see who would give way first. She would stand, feet planted firmly, and stare balefully at you as though daring you to pass. If she were anywhere in sight, I would arm myself with a stout stick, and if I met her face to face, I'd brandish my weapon and yell, "Move over, Lucy!" She usually gave way, but never graciously or gracefully, and only when she was sure she couldn't win.

As her owners had ceased providing her with adequate food, she foraged for herself. She would eat *anything* in range of her mouth. She had the appetite of a goat rather than a cow. She adored cardboard cartons and could demolish one in short order, chewing blissfully, a faraway look in her eye, as though she were a gourmet savouring the world's most exotic dish.

It was common to see Lucy careering through the village with a throng of teenaged boys in hot pursuit. Clamped firmly between her teeth, and waving like a sail in her wake, could be anything from a sheet to a shirt. She would first reconnoitre the village until she found washing on a clothesline, then she would pull and tug at whatever appealed to her taste at the moment. She'd happily devour it until someone spotted her, then the chase was on.

So Lucy became the scourge of the village, and at one particular point in my sojourn on Village Island, she had me wondering why I'd left Victoria.

One Friday afternoon the *Columbia* called and dropped off the parson. He'd come to spend the weekend and lead a Sunday service.

I had plans for Saturday that entailed a lot of hard work. The schoolroom floor was dirty, having had spring mud tracked over it day after day. It was past time to clean it up. The Sunday service was another impetus. So bright and early on Saturday, I lit the fire in the heater, then carried buckets of water from the well and put them on the fire to warm. Finally, armed with rags and a brush, I began the backbreaking task of scrubbing the floor. This took all morning, for the desks had to be moved, first to one side then back again. The floor was laid with rough planks, which made the scrubbing more difficult. But I finished by noon, and although my hands were wrinkled, my knees sore and my back aching, I looked at the floor with satisfaction, seeing a job well done.

Then I went to the house for lunch.

"Did you finish the floor, Miss B.?" Miss O'Brien inquired, impressed with my diligence.

"Yes. The scrubbing's done. After lunch, it should be dry enough to put a coat of oil on."

"I'll be glad to oil the floor for you," the parson said, taking me completely by surprise.

"Thank you. I'd appreciate that very much," I said, knowing if I refused, my poor knees would never forgive me.

Since the rest of my self-inflicted job was being done for me, I hiked through the woods and had a cup of tea with Mrs. Oiens. By the time I returned, the parson had finished, so between us we arranged the desks and made the room ready for church the next day.

Sunday dawned bright and warm with everyone bustling about getting ready for the morning service. Miss O'Brien rang the bell, and the people strolled leisurely along the path. With fishing season underway, there weren't too many of them, just the old people, some teenaged boys and a few children. After the service, we had our Sunday dinner. The G.A.s were in a festive mood, as they always were when the parson came to call.

After dinner the parson remembered something he'd left in the school, so he sauntered up the hill to retrieve it. Shortly after, the deep whistle of the

Columbia sounded on the clear air. This brought him scuttling back to the house for his bag. The kicker was skirting the rocks in the channel, and in a few minutes he was on his way once more. The brown house settled down for a quiet Sunday afternoon.

I went to my room and reread the previous day's batch of letters. Then I put a bit of thought into whether I'd read my new book, go for a walk along the beach or go out in the rowboat. I'd just decided the water looked too inviting to resist on this mellow afternoon when the sound of pounding feet brought me up with a start. A fist banged on the kitchen door and an excited voice yelled, "Miss B.! Come quick!"

I raced to the door to find Arthur and Alfred, two agitated teenaged boys.

"What on earth is the matter?"

"Miss B. You come quick. The cow. She's in the school."

"Lucy?" I said, as if there were a hundred cows' names to choose from.

"Yeah. Lucy, the cow. She make big mess, Miss B.," Alfred said, shaking his head.

"The parson," I seethed. "He must have left the door open."

I raced up the hill after the boys, with the G.A.s, who'd heard all the commotion, following along as fast as they could.

When I puffed through the schoolroom door, the boys stood back and said dramatically, "Look, Miss B."

I looked—at utter chaos! Desks were toppled, books strewn, pictures torn from the walls, and the floor, which had been fresh and clean, now resembled a cow barn, complete with smell.

Lucy stood amidst this havoc, chewing placidly on a piece of drawing paper. I could see one of the better drawings disappearing into her great maw.

The G.A.s and I stood in stunned silence and surveyed the devastation.

"Now, Miss B., let us discuss the pros and cons. We must decide on the best way to attack this problem," said Miss O'Brien, who was the first one to regain her speech.

About the only thing I wanted to attack was the cause of the problem, Lucy.

"The first thing to do is to remove Lucy," I said. "The big, lumbering beast. Just look at this room and my clean floor!"

"Shoo, Lucy. *Shoo*," cried Miss Dibben, waving her arms toward the beast. Lucy was unimpressed and continued her placid munching.

I picked my way carefully across the floor and got behind her, giving her a sound smack on the rump and a mighty push. All she did was lumber around a desk and devastate the floor in yet another spot.

The boys tried coaxing her. "Come on, Lucy. Come on," they cajoled. No response.

Alfred grabbed hold of her horns and pulled, but she tossed her head menacingly, so he let go.

"Boys, fetch some kindling sticks, please," I said.

Lucy (with the horns), seen here with her overgrown calf, Mollie, caused Hughina a lot of grief when she decided to attend school one day.

We whacked her across the rump, hard enough to sting but not do damage. This seemed to startle her somewhat, but didn't interrupt her chewing. We pushed and pulled while she held her place with a nonchalant switch of her tail. Our efforts were useless. She stood her sorry ground. By this time we were hot, cross and nauseated from Lucy's perfume in the warm room.

"Darn you, Lucy," I yelled, completely exasperated. "Get out of here!"

She gave me a sidelong look, then, surprisingly, started ambling toward the door. But desks impeded her progress, while the filth on the floor impeded ours, so two elderly missionaries, two excited teenage boys, one irate schoolmarm and one intractable cow put on a performance that outdid the wild dance of the hamatsa.

Once she made her first move, we pushed mightily on her rear end, while Alfred and Arthur brandished the kindling sticks, yelling furiously in Kwak'wala. Little by little, foot by stubborn foot, we manoeuvred her until we got her head through the door, then with our combined weight, we gave her a hefty push. For one horrible moment, I thought she might become wedged in the doorway, and I had the appalling vision of spending the rest of my life viewing Lucy's rear end. Then, with a toss of her horns, she popped through the door and lumbered down the steps. We trailed after, shooing her well along the path and away from the school. Unperturbed, she sauntered off, no doubt looking for more havoc to create.

It was a relief to be in the fresh air, and I breathed deeply to eradicate Lucy's stench from my nostrils. However, there was nothing to do but go inside again and attempt to restore order. I surveyed the ruin with sinking heart and could have wept from sheer anger and frustration.

Besides the toppled desks and the filthy floor, the library table was in a shambles, many of the books beyond repair. But by some magic of her own, Lucy had removed the brown paper covering the table, while leaving some of the books on it. She must have eaten the paper, for there wasn't a trace left. And where there had been a nice display of artwork around the room, there were only shreds of paper held in place by thumbtacks.

"My, my," said Miss O'Brien, who seemed frozen in place by the destruction. As was I. It was Miss Dibben who took charge.

"Well, Miss B.," she said, rolling up her sleeves, "We'd best get started."

She was right. Tears and bad temper wouldn't get the job done. "Boys, could you please get some shovels," I said. "I think that's the only way to tackle this mess."

We shovelled first, then with buckets of water and strong Lysol, we swooshed and swept, swooshed and swept, until our arms were about to fall off. By using elbow grease and hard labour for the rest of the afternoon, we got the room back to something close to normal.

The boys tethered Lucy at the far end of the village, so we could safely leave the door open to air the room. But it was days before it smelled like anything but a poorly ventilated cow barn.

"I think we all deserve a good cup of tea," Miss O'Brien said as she surveyed the room. "We've accomplished all we can here."

After tea I went for my favourite walk, along the old wharf then down to the rocky shore. When I got there I sat on a log and breathed deeply of the clean sea air. What I wanted and needed, more than anything else right then, was a good, hot bath. But Simoom and Alert Bay—and their bathtubs—were far, far away.

I could see no humour in the situation as I viewed the seascape that day. But later, when I told my story to friends, fully expecting their sympathy, it was met with uproarious laughter, and the story of Lucy, the educated cow, travelled far and wide.

The Search

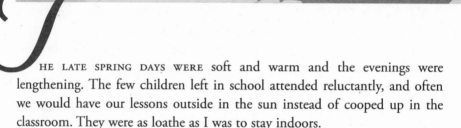

*T*HE LATE SPRING DAYS WERE soft and warm and the evenings were lengthening. The few children left in school attended reluctantly, and often we would have our lessons outside in the sun instead of cooped up in the classroom. They were as loathe as I was to stay indoors.

Eliza, Christine and Kathleen, the three TB patients in the preventorium, were as restless as the rest of us. They had made good progress over the winter months and had become quite active and healthy-looking. They were allowed a certain amount of exercise along with rest periods morning and afternoon. Occasionally they'd have a special treat. When the tide was high and the evening air warm, they were permitted to take the rowboat out in the village channel. Limits were set as to how far they could go and for how long, and they were good about obeying the rules. Mostly they puddled around, doing more floating than rowing, but it was a delight to hear their happy chatter wafting across the water.

One such perfect evening, the girls begged Miss Dibben to let them take the boat out.

"You may for a little while, but come in as soon as you hear the whistle," she cautioned.

"Yes, Miss Dibben," they chorused as they raced down the float.

"I'll give you half an hour," she called after them, "That will make it 7:30 and bedtime."

They scrambled into the boat, with Christine, who was the strongest, taking the oars. They pulled away from the float, making girl talk in a mixture of English and Kwak'wala.

Miss Dibben waved and went back to the Gables to prepare their evening cocoa. Miss O'Brien and I went into the sitting room, she to pore over her accounts, and I to read a new book from the mail-order library.

Sometime later I was vaguely aware of Miss Dibben's shrill whistle signalling the girls to return. Then all was silence again, so I returned to my book. Presently I heard a second whistle and then a long, harsh third. It slowly penetrated: something was wrong. I looked through the window to see Miss Dibben pacing the float and no sign of the children anywhere in the channel. Miss O'Brien was still absorbed in her accounts, and because of her limited hearing, she was unaware of the extra blasts on Dib's whistle.

I touched her arm and said, "Miss Dibben has signalled the girls three or four times, but they don't seem to be coming. Maybe we should see what's going on."

"Yes, indeed," she said, a frown instantly creasing her brow as she got to her feet. "I do hope nothing has gone amiss."

We joined Miss Dibben on the float just as she let forth another panicky blast.

"Is something the matter, Miss Dibben?"

"I can't understand it," she said, worry in her voice. "The girls don't answer. Can you see them anywhere?"

"No, I can't," I said. "I'll go along the wharf. See if they're beyond the islands."

I ran along the path and onto the old Indian wharf. From the far end I had a clear view down Village Pass. There was neither happy chatter nor splash of oars.

"There's no sign of them that way," I told the G.A.s when I got back to the float.

"I can't see them in this direction either," said Miss O'Brien, straining her eyes toward Turnour Island.

"Something has happened to them," Miss Dibben said, her tone tense. "I know they would have answered before now if they were close at hand. They always do."

The sun was setting in a blaze of pink and sapphire, and dusk was falling quickly. Soon it would be dark.

"I think we should organize a search," said Miss O'Brien.

"I'll go through the village and see how many boats are in tonight," I volunteered.

TB patient Christine Taylor sits in the *Hyuya-Tsi* with Reverend Alan Greene, before he took over John Antle's position as superintendent of the Columbia Coast Mission.

I hurried along the path, and the first person I met was Simon.

"How many boats are in tonight, Simon?"

"Three or four, Miss B."

I quickly explained the situation, then asked, "Could you round up the men and go look for the girls?"

"Sure. Okay. I go tell the fellas." And he was off on the alert.

I returned to a worried pair of G.A.s and, despite my own concern, tried to ease theirs. "The men are starting out right away. The girls couldn't have gone too far. I'm sure they'll be found safe and sound."

"But it's almost dark," said Miss Dibben. "If they are out among the islands they'll never find their way home."

"Try not to worry, Dib," consoled Miss O'Brien. "The good Lord will look after them."

The noise of engines starting rent the quiet of the evening, and we counted four gas boats leaving the floats along the village waterfront. For a time the flotilla skirted the rocks in the channel, then went out of sight and sound around the islands. Silence descended once more—this one more anxious than the last.

"It's cold out here. I think we'd best go inside and wait," said Miss O'Brien.

Knowing we couldn't accomplish anything other than stand and watch, Miss Dibben and I agreed.

I noticed the village women walking slowly along the path, coming from the opposite direction. We met them just as we reached the kitchen door. They were talking quietly in Kwak'wala.

"Ah eeh, ah eeh," they murmured, but this time, it was not a wail of mourning but a sound of concern and anxiety.

"Ladies, do come in," said Miss O'Brien, the gracious lady as usual. "I'll make a cup of tea."

"Oh, dear. Where can they be?" fretted Dib, now close to tears.

"Don't worry," Gertrude said with surprising calm. "The fellas will find them."

"I pray they will. But I keep thinking of those three little girls out there alone in the dark. And the cold! What will it do to them? A chill could set them all back, especially Eliza. It could kill her! Oh, why did I say they could go?" she moaned, awash in guilt.

"You're not to blame, Miss Dibben," I told her. "The girls have been out in the boats before and everything has been fine. How could you know tonight would be any different?"

"But what if the men don't find them?" she answered, putting into words the thought that was in all our minds. And asking a question none of us wanted to answer.

The waiting seemed endless. We sat around the sitting room, drinking innumerable cups of tea. The Indian women talked quietly in their own tongue, while poor Miss Dibben wept. Nothing anyone could say would console her.

I went outside and stood on the float in front of the house. I listened, but the only sounds I heard were soft night noises—the lapping of the water around the edges of the float, the cozy nighttime chatter of the birds. A fish jumped clear of the water, breaking the smooth surface with a splashy sound and causing wavelets to spread in ever-widening circles.

I looked across the water and thought about the girls, Christine, Kathleen and Eliza, alone in a rowboat, somewhere in that maze of islands. A few months ago these children had seemed so strange and foreign to me, speaking English badly, if they spoke it at all. At first I heard nothing but giggles and phrases in Kwak'wala, which frustrated me because I couldn't understand them. Then, slowly, as children have a way of doing, they won my heart. Each in her own way.

Christine was the sassy one, a leader who often needed a firm hand, but she was outgoing, and always full of chatter and questions.

Kathleen hadn't too many ideas of her own, or if she did, she preferred to keep them to herself; but she hero-worshipped Christine, following her lead in everything.

Eliza was a gentle girl, sweet and obedient, desiring nothing more than to

Eliza and her friend, Miss B.

please Miss Dibben and me. She so much wanted to be well. And because her condition was the most serious, she caused us the most concern. She and I were the best of friends, and she always had a smile for me no matter how miserable she might feel.

And now they were three lost girls, and I was sick with worry.

This rare photo of Christine, Eliza and Kathleen (left to right) was taken by Reverend Greene shortly before their "great adventure."

Then I tensed and listened. In the distance, I could hear the unmistakable throb of a motor. It drew nearer and my spirits rose. I watched a lone gas boat turn into the channel and come alongside the float, and those same spirits sagged. The boat had only one occupant.

"Any sign of them, Henry?" I asked, hopefully, thinking some other boat had found them and Henry was simply returning home.

He shook his head. "No. I come back to see if they come back."

"No, they're not here." *Oh, how I wished they were.*

"I go look again," he said, turning the boat back in the direction from which he had come.

Hours went by with no sign of boats or men. The women stayed on in the sitting room, speaking now and then in monosyllables, while the poor G.A.s sat together, praying quietly.

Midnight came, then one o'clock, and one by one the women rose and walked to the door, trailing out in a mournful procession.

About two o'clock I went outside again, this time walking to the end of the old Indian wharf. Fortunately for the searching men, it was a clear moonlit night. The islands on either side of Village Pass looked like black hummocks rising out of the still water. I listened, not too hopefully, while leaning on the rail. Then I straightened and listened more intently, for surely I heard a motor in the far distance. I strained to hear, and then I realized there was not just one motor, but probably four.

I raced back to the house.

"They're coming back! I can hear the boats!"

We gathered on the float, not daring to hope.

Simon, leading the flotilla, headed the *Helen B* toward the brown house, and in the stern we could see three forlorn little figures, wrapped in blankets.

Everyone talked at once.

"Where did you find them?"

"Are they all right?"

"Were they in danger?"

"They were halfway to 'Lert Bay! In the middle of Blackfish Sound," Simon told us.

We hustled the shivering children into the warm kitchen and gave them mugs of hot cocoa. Amazingly, except for being cold and frightened, they seemed none the worse for their adventure.

Little by little, with Gertrude's help, we sorted out their story. It seemed, on the instigation of a curious Christine, they decided to go exploring and ignore Miss Dibben's whistle. Their plan was to circumnavigate the island directly across the channel, but once out of sight of the village, they became confused in the labyrinth of rocks and tiny islands that dotted the sea. Christine, tired and frightened, didn't know which way to guide the boat. Then dusk crept up on them, and the tide turned, so they were caught in its ebb. They drifted then, and the tide carried them through the maze of islands and into Blackfish Sound.

The news spread rapidly through the village, and the people gathered to welcome them back. No one had the heart to chastize them for disobeying Miss Dibben's call. So they were greeted more as conquering heroes than the little culprits they were.

Needless to say, the girls were landlubbers for a long time to come.

Another Cup of Tea?

HAD PROMISED MURIEL BANFIELD by hook, crook, raft or rowboat I would get to Alert Bay for the May 24 holiday. I was determined not to spend it in the village. But for a while it looked as though I might have to build my own raft to keep my promise.

Good weather had arrived, the Natives were travelling constantly, and boat traffic flowed day and night. One day two or three local boats and a couple of visiting craft would be evident; the next day they would all be gone. I knew all these boats would end up in Alert Bay, where everyone would gather for the last festivities before the fishing season began in earnest. The village gradually emptied, with whole families disappearing at once. By the end of the week I had no children to teach, but had to stay until Friday to keep the records straight. I was beside myself with exasperation.

Scouting for transportation early in the week, I was willing, even eager, to accept a ride on anything that floated. I accosted anyone I met on the village path. My question was always the same.

"When will you be going to Alert Bay?" I'd ask.

"Maybe tomorrow. Or next day."

"Do you know of *anyone* going over Friday or Saturday?"

"Dunno."

"If you hear of anyone going then, please tell them I need a ride."

"Sure. Okay."

Usually the people were agreeable, but they weren't as impatient as I was—tomorrow, the next day or a week later—it was all the same to them. Probably whomever I'd spoken to would forget about me the minute I'd passed. I became more agitated as each day went by.

Friday came with nothing resembling a boat anywhere in sight. But there were still a couple of stragglers left in the village, so I told myself someone would surely happen by to pick them up.

I finished breakfast and went to my room. I was leaning dejectedly against the windowsill when I heard an engine. Anxiously, I wondered if the boat would keep on going or come to the village. When the sound grew louder, I ran out of the house and saw something resembling a boat floating up to a village dock.

It was broad in the beam, with a low-roofed cabin and a sizable well deck—and it overflowed with people. I'd heard of boats referred to as "old tubs," but this was the closest thing I'd seen so far to fitting the description. The *thing* was nearly as broad as it was long. There must have been at least 15 people on board; the gunwales were mere inches above the waterline.

But it was my only hope.

I looked at the sky, which was cloudless. I looked at the sea, which was without a ripple. I held my finger in the air, but could feel no breeze, so I decided to take the plunge, and I fervently hoped it would not be literally!

"Going to Alert Bay?" I yelled.

"Yeah."

"Is there room for me?"

"Yeah, yeah. Hokay."

That was all I needed to hear. I sprinted to the house for my bag, dashed back through the village, raced down the beach, scrambled onto the dock and jumped aboard. Breathless.

The people were strangers, except for a couple of village people and the odd familiar face from a nearby village. I didn't know who the others were or where they came from and, as usual, no one enlightened me. But I was glad the weather was calm; if not, we'd never have made it, considering the load on board.

I was becoming hardened to this type of travel, for if I hadn't, I might *still* be on Village Island. So I sat for three hours on the edge of the hard gunwales, squeezed between strange people who spoke not a word to me. I concentrated on the scenery and kept telling myself the fun I was going to have in Alert Bay was worth it.

We tied up to a dock in the Indian section of the town. I clambered ashore and hurried along the street to Muriel's boarding house. Along the way I noticed dozens of boats tied to every wharf and many more anchored offshore.

Alert Bay was bustling, and the street was crowded with Indian and White people from all the surrounding areas who had gathered for the celebrations.

"You made it," Muriel said as I walked in.

"Yes, but only just," I answered, flopping on the bed. "What I have to go through for a little fun. You should have seen my transportation this time. You'd never believe it."

"Oh, yes, I would," she replied, smiling.

I sat up. "Now that I'm here, what are we going to do?"

Muriel had the weekend planned perfectly, although any plan at all would have suited me. We were going to a play that evening, an epic entitled *The Red Hot Peppers*. The cast was all local talent, including Muriel, who had the starring role as Mrs. Pepper. We'd been invited to go for a picnic on Sunday with the Wastell family, and Monday was sports day.

I had to get back to Village Island for school on Tuesday morning, but with most of the families and all the children enjoying themselves in Alert Bay, I wasn't letting my return journey worry me too much. The weekend was shaping up wonderfully, well worth the morning's crowded ride.

That night the community hall was jammed with local inhabitants and visitors, both Indian and White, and the play was considered a smashing success.

Sunday, around noon, Muriel and I met the Wastells aboard their boat, the *Mary W*. She was a sturdy tugboat and compared with my transportation of the previous day, palatial. The Wastells, who operated a sawmill at Telegraph Cove on Vancouver Island, were long-time residents and respected citizens of the area. Mr. A.W. Wastell served for many years in the capacity of local magistrate.

Our destination was the mouth of the Nimpkish River, which empties into the sea almost directly across from Alert Bay on Vancouver Island's shore. The *Mary W* was to be anchored offshore, and we'd take the skiff to the river's mouth.

I was excited, for I knew that in 1792 Captain George Vancouver had visited the Nimpkish people here. And in 1936, pristine and untouched, it must have appeared much as it had to the first Nimpkish tribe who lived here so many years before.

It was better than anything I could have imagined.

A crystal river tumbled over shiny rocks, spreading in rivulets through the sand before disappearing into the sea. Meadows, lush and level, lay on either side of the river's mouth. And behind them—a cathedral of towering hemlock and cedar, silent and blessed, black cormorants and white-winged gulls its only parishioners.

The meadows had been cleared by the Nimpkish people when they chose this village site long ago. Now the only traces of their existence were mounds of clamshells. I imagined their great houses standing, the men in cedar-bark capes lazing in the sun, women drying fish and berries. I visualized their high-prowed canoes drawn up on the beach, ready for defence against an invading tribe, and children, brown and fit, playing naked in the sun.

The trees I now beheld could easily have been the same ones that had sheltered the village from the westerly winds so many years ago. What fate .had befallen these people to cause them to abandon this haven of security and plenty? Why had they gone, leaving only the meadows and clamshells to mark their existence in the distant past?

I hated to come back to reality, but when someone called, "Supper! Come and get it," I realized I was starving, as usual.

But many times during the fun and good times of the picnic my thoughts turned to the Nimpkish. They may have gone, but in this wondrous place, the spirit of their time remained.

Monday, the official holiday, was the gala day of the long weekend. It was the last chance for a gathering before fishing became a full-time occupation. Indian bands from all the surrounding villages had converged on Alert Bay. There were foot races, baseball games and football, as well as gas-boat and canoe races. Everyone entered into these activities wholeheartedly. The day sped by while we watched the sports and stuffed ourselves with hot dogs and ice cream.

The climax of the weekend was a dance in the community hall. Fortunately it was acceptable for girls to go to these affairs unescorted, so we dressed in our best "bibs and tuckers" and joined the crowd in the hall, stomping to the beat of a local band.

Someone touched my arm, and I turned to find Lou Layhew, minus his horse pants and rattlesnake boots, looking much more comfortable in an ordinary suit.

"Care to dance?" he said, then added, "It's much more fun than walking log booms."

We danced until the witching hour.

The next morning my conscience told me I should be back on Village Island to ring the school bell at nine o'clock. But with everyone from the village—except for the G.A.s and some of the older people—still in Alert Bay, there was nothing much I could do about it. But as soon as possible, I scouted

The significance of ceremonial totems could defy the untrained eye. In this one, the lower half of the Raven's beak opened into a ramp to admit guests to special events. The totem symbolically swallowed participants as they entered.

These striking poles stood in front of the Alert Bay chief's home and featured the Thunderbird, Grizzly and Nimpkish eagles.

for a boat ride home. Too tired to care what sort of a boat it was, my only requirement was that it point in the right direction.

It was a hot, cloudless day, and we travelled in the late morning hours. When I reached the brown house, not only was I late and exhausted from my strenuous weekend, I had a painful sunburn.

I was greeted by silence and looks of concern, convinced by this time the G.A.s had given me up as a bad job.

~

"Would you consider coming back for a second term?" Mr. Todd had asked when I saw him on that holiday weekend.

I was surprised to hear myself say "yes"—stunned, in fact.

Later, I wondered why I'd agreed, for had I been asked this question the first day, or even the first month after my arrival, I'd have returned an emphatic "No. Not on your life would I bury myself in this place for another year."

What had changed?

I realized that gradually, as the weeks became months, the country and its people had pulled me to them like a magnet. I loved the space, the freedom it afforded. I'd come to know people in the scattered settlements, and was enthralled by their kindness and good humour. Any tensions, on the surface at least, seemed negated by hard work and just-as-hard play. And there was such strength and power in them as they vied with the forces of nature to earn their living from the endless land and sea. Here, friendships were quickly made and each friend was of the utmost importance.

Because of this, I knew I had to stay on, for there were places yet to see and people I wanted to know better. Travelling on all sizes and conditions of boats, in every sort of weather, was an education in itself. Life was dull for long periods, that was true, but this made anything out of the ordinary a welcome change and laced it with excitement, for there was always the element of surprise.

When I told Mrs. Todd I was coming back, she said in typical blunt fashion, "I *am* surprised, Hughina. I had my doubts you'd last out the first year."

~

June arrived and I spent much of the time planning my departure for the summer. There were only three children, off and on, in school, and the village was essentially empty. However, no matter how little there was to do, I was required to stay until the last day of the school year. Then it was home for the summer. There was only one problem: money. I began writing frantic letters home.

It wasn't that my mother was trying to maroon me on Village Island. Rather it was the fault of my peculiar pay schedule. My salary was a respectable $90 a month, but I was to be paid quarterly—or so I had been led to believe. My employer must have had as much trouble as I in locating Village Island, for the cheque was often a month or more late. The fault lay with the powers that be in Ottawa, where my cheque originated from somewhere in the depths of the Department of Indian Affairs.

I would wait breathlessly as the due date drew near, and when the weekly mail arrived, I'd thumb through the pile seeking an Ottawa postmark. Passing weeks brought gloom, then desperation. Finally I would send a message to Mr. Todd, who in turn would jog one of the fuzzy memories resident in Ottawa. Eventually my cheque arrived looking—in all its $270 glory—like a colossal amount of money. But in cheque form it was useless.

I would endorse it and send it home to Mother. She would then return a money order made out to Miss O'Brien for three months' board and room, along with some cash for me. As the post office was forever being switched from Minstrel Island to Freshwater Bay to Alert Bay and back again, I never felt confident about receiving it. But somehow, that June, my mother caught up with the right post office and my money for passage home arrived just in time.

As I packed, I looked around my room. My cell with three doors and two windows. The sound of water lapping gently beneath the floor was soothing and pleasant, as was the smell of the sea wafting through the open windows. Now the rise and fall of the house in unison with the tide seemed ordinary.

The day after school closed, my Simoom friends came on the *June M* to gather me for a brief visit. As we nosed through the rocky channel, I waved to the G.A.s, the Oiens and the few old people still in the village. They had all gathered on the float in front of the brown house. I looked up at the school and barely resisted saluting the Union Jack fluttering in the soft breeze.

I DON'T KNOW WHAT MY FAMILY expected, but they seemed immensely relieved to find no great change in me since the Christmas holidays, other than my need to visit a hairdresser. My crowning glory was mute testimony to months spent in the bush. So my first phone call was to a beauty salon. The hairdresser looked at me with horror. However, she bravely plunged in with scissors, shampoo and permanent wave and soon all signs of my Village Island "coiffure" were gone.

The summer months flew by, as I was again busy with summer school and nursing. When October came I started preparing for my return to Village Island. This time I knew what to expect, but even the thought of icy feet and unreliable gas boats didn't deter me. I was looking forward to going back.

My plan was to spend a week with the Manns before settling in for the winter on Village Island. Because of this I travelled north on the small Union Steamship *Venture*, for it was only the smaller Union boats that called at Simoom Post Office. These friendly craft have long since disappeared from the coastal scene.

If you weren't in a hurry, these coastwise boats were fun to travel on. They called at all the out-of-the-way places bypassed by the larger Union and CPR steamers. Some of the ports of call might be no more than a wharf, a freight shed and a house. Then again, it might be a sizable community with houses, a general store, a large freight shed and a marine gas pump. Many were floating communities, built on large rafts at the foot of sheer, tree-covered hillsides rising steeply out of the sea.

People gathered on boat day, coming by gas boats from logging camps in the surrounding area, anxious for freight and mail from town. It seemed everyone knew everyone else, and I'd guess the crews of these ships had more friends scattered up and down the coast than they could count.

While the *Venture* was docked, the passengers would lean on the rail and watch the freight being unloaded, or, if there was time, go for a stroll—if there was anywhere to stroll. The ship traversed the length of many of the long inlets in the shadow of the towering Coast Range. Tops of drowned mountains thrust their heads out of the sea, forming hundreds of the islands that dot the coastline.

When the *Venture* reached Simoom Sound, all my friends were waiting: the Mann family, Irene and Joyce, and Ray, who, like me, was back for another year. At the end of my visit they took me back to Village Island on the *June M*.

I didn't expect to find any great change on Village Island, and I was right.

The G.A.s were waiting.

"Miss B., how well you look. What news from town?" Miss O'Brien greeted me with a wide smile.

"Did you have a pleasant summer?" inquired Miss Dibben politely.

After tea and imparting all the news I thought the G.A.s would find of interest, I retired to my room to unpack.

My cell was just as I'd left it, and the house still responded to the whims of the tide. The village was as sombre and dreary as ever, with not too many families yet in residence. Yet I had the odd sense of coming home.

I opened the school with an enrolment of seven. As the families gradually returned for the winter, the number of children increased to 15, which was an all-time high. Some of the wee beginners spoke very little English, which made my teaching duties more complicated. But the little dears were worth it. And, as before, the village ills cropped up daily so after tea, armed with the black bag, I'd be off on my rounds.

It didn't take long for the routine of each day to fall into place. One day, soon after my return, the usual dreary-looking gas boat chugged up the to float. A couple of young men were lounging in the well deck, and as I came down the hill from the school, they scrambled ashore and came toward me. Where to now, I wondered.

Wherever it was, I didn't want to go. I was tired and it was a bitterly cold November day.

"You come New Vancouver?" said one of the boys.

"Who wants me?" I asked.

The spokesman shrugged his shoulders.

"A fella," said the other boy.

"What's the matter with him?"

"He no wake up."

"Is he dead?" I exclaimed, startled by this terse revelation.

"Dunno," they shrugged in unison and stared at me, waiting.

This was all the information I was going to get, and I'd learned long ago it was useless to question too extensively.

"All right. I'll come. Wait for me on the boat."

I went into the house and collected the black bag, all the while wondering what situation I was getting into this time. It could be vital and urgent or nothing at all. I boarded the boat and sat shivering in the raw wind as we bounced over the choppy seas. The old village loomed into view, and soon the boys were tying up to a dock. They started along the path that led through the village, past the row of houses along the bank above the beach. No gentlemen these, for I was left to scramble ashore as best I could. I followed them along the path, and they led me to a shack at the far end of the village.

One of the boys pushed open the sagging door, and we entered an evil-smelling room. A fire burned in a rusty stove, and beside it there was a shabby table and chair. One tiny window let in the light, and beneath it was an old iron bedstead. A middle-aged man lay on a ragged mattress, fully clothed, and covered with a dirty blanket. He wasn't dead, but he was unconscious. His breathing was laboured, and he was burning with fever. The man was critically ill.

Other village people straggled in, and soon the room was crowded. No one said a word.

"How long has he been like this?" I asked.

"Dunno," a man said.

"Lo-o-ong time," someone else offered.

None of this helped, but I was sure the sick man must have been unconscious for a while. I looked at him, wondering what I should do, for I was far from help of any sort. He should be in hospital and by some means, I had to get him there.

"How many boats are in the village?" I asked.

"That one," said the boys, indicating the boat that had just brought me to the village.

It was an open boat with no shelter of any kind. The thought of transporting an unconscious man in it over miles of cold and choppy water was appalling, and yet to get a message to Alert Bay would take hours.

I went outside to get away from the fetid odour of the crowded shack and to breathe some clean, fresh air. I needed to think clearly. I stood on a high point of the bank above the beach, looking across the water. I was trying to form some plan of action when my gaze caught something moving into my line of vision. It materialized into a substantial tug towing a boom of logs. I watched as it made its leisurely way through the channel.

And then it hit me!

"All large tugs have a wireless!" I said aloud, although no one was in earshot. With my next breath I yelled, "Boys!"

They came sauntering out of the shack.

"Now listen carefully," I instructed. "You get in the gas boat, go out there, and stop that tug. Ask them to talk to Alert Bay on the wireless. Tell them to send a boat for the sick man. Wait a minute and I'll write it on a piece of paper!"

Luckily the black bag held a pad and pencil. So I wrote: "SOS. Critically ill man here. Needs medical attention immediately. Please contact Alert Bay or *Columbia* stat. Thank you. H. Bowden RN."

"Now hurry. You've got to catch the tug before it goes by!"

The boys raced off with great speed, for they loved this sort of excitement. As they ran along the path to the gas boat, my only hope was that this wild idea would work. I couldn't think of a plausible alternative.

The gas boat moved through the choppy water, closing the distance to the tug. Dusk was falling and the grey of the craft blended too well with the grey of the sea in the fading light. It looked so insubstantial bobbing on the waves. I watched and waited, and soon the people came out of the cabin to watch and wait with me.

The gas boat passed our lookout point and moved beyond the tip of the island, while the tug steamed steadily through the channel. As they drew nearer each other, I could dimly see one of the boys waving a makeshift flag.

The Natives and I stood motionless while this drama unfolded. I was still wondering what I'd do if the boys failed to intercept the tug. Just then it slackened speed and the gas boat gained on it. Only a few hundred yards separated the two boats, and now I breathed easier, for I was sure someone had seen the gas boat.

There was a murmur among the group around me as the boys reached the tug. Then the gas boat drew alongside, where it almost disappeared in the shadow of the larger craft. The two boats clung together for about 15 minutes. At last the boys turned back in the direction of the village, while the tug picked up speed and continued on its way. I followed the boat as it bucked its way through the chop, finally reaching the dock. The boys raced along the path toward us. One of them handed me a slip of paper. On it was written: Contact with Alert Bay has been made. Help is on the way. Good luck, whoever you are. Captain Wilson.

I waved my thanks to the captain, although I was sure he couldn't see me in the gathering dusk. There was nothing further I could do for this unknown man. The rescue boat would arrive in due course, and, if he lived or died, I could only hope it would be in hospital with proper care.

For once I heard the outcome—which was not always the case.

When the *Columbia* called sometime later, I asked the doctor, "Did you pick up a very ill man from New Vancouver a couple of weeks ago?"

"Yes," he said, "We were given your message by a tug in the area."

"Did he live?" I asked.

The doctor shook his head. "No. He was in the final stage of pneumonia and only lived a couple of days. He'd have had a chance if he'd got here sooner."

Such was life—and death—in this remote and far-flung community. A matter of chance and a passing boat.

Weather, Whether or Not!

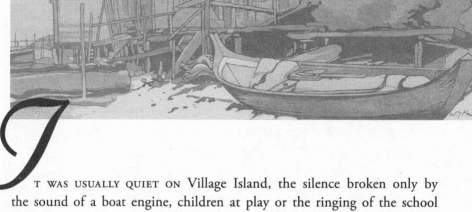

*I*T WAS USUALLY QUIET ON Village Island, the silence broken only by the sound of a boat engine, children at play or the ringing of the school bell—but it was never so hushed as during a fog. Outside the brown house, right on the water, the fog was at its thickest, enveloping everything in its grasp. At times the school, as well as the village, were completely blotted out. Then we lived in a cotton-wool world and the silence was deadly. It could last for days.

During these times, I was glad to be busy in school by day. After tea, I would grope my way through the damp white blanket to check on anyone sick and in need of attention. When I returned, the house always felt warmer by contrast and the coal-oil lamps brighter. After supper I was content to sit in my corner by the heater, preparing school work or reading.

One evening I was doing just this and thinking about the Christmas party I was arranging for the children. After the disastrous concert of the year before, I felt a party was all I could cope with. My thoughts rambled beyond the party, for I was eagerly awaiting Christmas vacation and a couple of weeks away from the island. This would be my first Christmas away from home, and I was looking forward to spending it with the Manns at Simoom. Thus I dreamed by the fire on this quiet, foggy night, while the G.A.s read and wrote letters in the lamplight. There was no sound to be heard except for the lapping of the water beneath the house.

Then a noise interrupted my thoughts, and I sat tense and listened. It grew louder until suddenly the peace was shattered by heavy pounding feet across the raft and a fist banging on the door. I raced to the door and found two teenaged boys beside themselves with fright.

"Come quick!"

"Come quick, Miss B.!" They were both terribly agitated.

I didn't bother to ask where or to what, just grabbed the black bag and followed them into the foggy night, beaming my flashlight on their hurrying legs. The gleam of the flashlight disappeared in the thick, white shroud that enveloped us. I groped my way after the boys, knowing that in places along the path a step or two to the right would land me on the rocky beach six feet below.

A glimmer of light pierced the fog, and I found we were on Dick Mountain's doorstep. I followed them into the kitchen–sitting room. It was jammed with people, both male and female, and a good number of children besides.

The room was filled with the sounds of mourning. The women were wailing and lamenting, rocking to and fro with shawl-covered heads, while the men stood around, talking in subdued tones.

"What on earth is the matter?" I asked, looking around. I expected the worst, at the very least someone with a heart attack or a stroke, maybe even someone lying dead on the floor. There was no sign of a body stretched out anywhere.

"Is someone sick?" I asked again.

"Her," said several frightened voices in chorus.

I looked around for the "her" and found the cause of all this commotion was a girl of about four, the youngest of the Dick Mountain brood. She sat quietly, looking frightened but otherwise healthy, except that her face, the hair on her forehead and the front of her dress were covered with blood, mostly congealed by this time.

"What happened?" I asked, but no one enlightened me. The men continued talking in worried tones and the women wailed on.

I looked more closely at the child, who stared back at me with round, frightened eyes. Except for the dried blood, she seemed fine.

"Will someone bring me a basin of warm water, please."

The kettle rattled on the edge of the enamel basin, and then it was handed to me. I washed her face and forehead and finally the top of her head. When the blood was removed, I found a minor scalp wound and a large bump. I snipped the hair away from the cut and applied some ointment and a dressing. Then I removed her dress and asked for a warm blanket to wrap her in.

At that moment she gave me a wide, beaming smile, and instantly the whole atmosphere of the room changed. The women stopped wailing and began talking normally again. The men continued their conversation, but now so casually, I sensed it could be about something as mundane as the price of fish or the weather. One by one the people straggled out while Mother went back to the dishes.

I was completely at sea. "Will someone please tell me what happened here?"

"She fell on the chair leg and all dat blood came," said her mother. "She cry and cry, and we scared when we saw all dat blood."

That was all the explanation I was to get.

I gathered up my bag and went out into the foggy night, alone this time, for my escorts had disappeared. I beamed my flashlight on the hard-beaten path, got my bearings and headed for home. It was eerie finding my way in the silence, and the walk I knew so well seemed suddenly unfamiliar. With relief, I found the steps to the raft. The lamp in the kitchen looked warm and welcoming.

I put my things away and went back to my chair by the heater.

"What was it this time, Miss B.?" asked Miss O'Brien.

"Dick Mountain's youngest fell and bumped her head. It bled freely so I guess it scared them. There was quite a commotion going on, but she's all right now."

I picked up my book, but somehow my thoughts kept returning to the scene of mourning in the Mountain house over a child with a minor scalp wound. It must have had great significance to the Native people, but never would I, so near yet a culture apart, understand it.

The fog had gone and in its place came the freezing cold. The ground was as solid as concrete, and the house cracked at every joint as it rose and fell with the tide. I dreamed of a few hours of constant warmth to thaw out my chilled bones. I hadn't been off the island for relaxation since I'd arrived in November.

During my daily rounds in the village, I had asked if a boat—any old boat—might be going to Alert Bay on Saturday. Then I visited the community house where Henry Bell's nephew, Jimmy Sewid, lived with his wife, Flora, and their four children. While putting warm oil in the aching ear of one of his little girls, I asked her father, "Do you know of anyone going to Alert Bay this coming Saturday, Jimmy?"

"Saturday?" he repeated, then nodded. "Yeah. Maybe I go to 'Lert Bay Saturday. Good idea! Yep. Go 'Lert Bay."

"Would you have room for me?"

"Sure," said the cheerful Jimmy. "You come to my house. Eight o'clock."

I spent Friday in happy anticipation. I would see my Alert Bay friends and, with any luck, I might be able to jump into a tub of hot, sudsy water. I was more than ready for any tub that presented itself.

At seven o'clock Saturday morning, I climbed out of my cot. It was bitterly cold—so cold I had to crack the ice in my water jug before I could brush my teeth, then thaw my washcloth in a pitcher of hot water before I could wash my face. I dressed speedily and had a good hot breakfast in preparation for the cold trip. I put my coat on over several layers of sweaters and scarves, and added woollen gloves to my bulky ensemble.

At eight sharp I walked along the path to Jimmy's house. My footsteps echoed in the frigid air as my boots crunched on the frost-swollen path. It was the only sound I could hear. There wasn't a sign of life anywhere.

I went to Jimmy's house and stood listening at the door, but all was silent. I knocked, and when no one answered, I knocked again. Knowing no village door was ever locked, I opened it a crack and peeked in. There was Jimmy, his wife and children and an assortment of relatives fast asleep on the floor around the wood-burning heater, all wrapped in blankets like so many cocoons. Jimmy stirred and looked up at me hazily as I let in a blast of cold air.

His look said, "What's that crazy teacher doing at my door in the middle of the night?"

This photo (c. 1910) shows Emma, Jimmy Sewid's mother; Henry Bell, his uncle, who later shared this community house with the Hanuse family; and James Sewid, Jimmy's father, who died tragically before his son's birth.

I quietly closed the door and trudged dismally back to the brown house. Oh, well. It was a good idea while it lasted.

After the fog and the freezing cold, the rains came. Such rain as I had never seen before. It poured without let-up for hours and days on end.

My room was a lean-to, added as an afterthought to the main house. In fact, the whole house seemed to be made up of bits and pieces. The roof was covered with tar paper in lieu of shingles, so when the rain came in such torrents, it sounded as if it might come right through the ceiling.

This pole belonged to Billie Beans, Simon's father, and was the last pole standing on Village Island a decade ago.

Then one night it did.

I was dreaming I was walking through the woods with rain falling from the branches all round me. It was no dream! I awakened to find water dripping uncomfortably close to my head and more falling on the foot of my bed. My feet, which had been warm with the aid of a hot water bottle and bedsocks, were damp and clammy.

I fumbled for my flashlight and turned it on the ceiling. I counted five places from which water steadily poured into my room. I got out onto the wet floor and shifted the foot of the cot, only to find I was under another torrent. I tried again, but the room was too small to allow many alternatives. Nothing worked. I gave up then and simply covered it with my raincoat. There was nothing I could do about it in the middle of the night, so I climbed back into bed, under my raincoat, and finally went to sleep. It rained steadily all night, and by morning I felt as if I'd slept on the beach. Getting dressed was a feat.

Called the White Man pole, this 25-foot totem was a landmark for years.

This community pole had no owner and was moved from time to time to a new site along the village waterfront.

The floor was one giant puddle, and no matter where I stood I couldn't avoid another waterfall. I arrived in the kitchen in a damp and dishevelled state.

The G.A.s looked at me in bewilderment.

"Whatever is the matter, Miss B.?"

"My ceiling is leaking like a sieve," I said. "I'll need some pots or buckets to catch the water."

"My, my, that will never do," said Miss O'Brien. "Shall we have a look, Dib?"

After they'd inspected the ceiling, Miss O'Brien came back into the kitchen and said, "I'll see Dick Charlie this morning. He must attend to this right away."

"Yes, indeed," replied Miss Dibben, firmly. "I'll find some pails. We'll watch they don't overflow during school hours."

After we'd placed an assortment of pots and pails in strategic places, I mopped the floor. During the morning, Miss O'Brien took a reluctant Dick Charlie away from his warm fireside to look at the roof.

The news wasn't good.

At lunchtime she said, "Dick said he can't fix the roof until it stops raining."

This was probably true, but I secretly wondered if he simply didn't care to work in the rain, although in this deluge I couldn't blame him. Now my only hope was the rain would stop. It didn't.

The days weren't so bad, as I had no great need to go into my room, except to empty the pails. The nights were a different story. I'd empty the pails last thing, then blow out the lamp and lie listening to the rain drumming on the roof, accompanied by Chinese water torture. The dripping water would sound a high ping in the empty pail, and gradually it would descend the scale to a deep plop. When the plopping hit the right note, I'd get up and heft the water out of the window.

The rain finally stopped, and Dick Charlie at last fixed the roof, but I found I'd become so used to the sound of dripping water, I had difficulty falling asleep without my liquid lullaby.

Edward Windsor and Friend

"MY DEAR, DID YOU READ this?" exclaimed Miss O'Brien. She was poring over a week-old newspaper.

"Read what, Miss O'Brien?" I asked, not bothering to look up, as I was intent on my own reading.

"Edward Windsor is enamoured with that woman. A blot on the royal family's good name. Disgraceful! How could such an indelicate situation arise? What of his duty to God and Empire?"

Edward Windsor was, of course, Edward VIII of England and "that woman" was Mrs. Wallis Warfield Simpson. This was December 1936 and, because of the brewing royal scandal, a momentous time on Village Island. The famous royal romance shook the very foundation of the brown house— down to the last log of the raft on which it rested. The G.A.s had spent many years in Canada, but to them this island was still a little bit of Olde England, so they took an event such as this right to heart.

We were always days behind on world news. Week-old papers arrived in bundles of six from Vancouver. Then there were the English papers and periodicals that were goodness-knows-how ancient when we got them, having come by boat across the Atlantic and by train across Canada. The G.A.s and I read all the papers and magazines and tried our best to keep abreast of world affairs, and the fact that our keeping abreast could be a month behind everyone else in the country didn't really matter in this remote spot.

Of course, all the English papers were filled with portraits of Mrs. Simpson, along with articles on her clothes, her previous husbands, her hairstyles and on and on ad nauseam. This information was discussed in the minutest detail with every meal. I'm afraid the G.A.s were rather hard on the poor woman, while I thought she was extremely smart-looking and very sophisticated.

Such shocking events as the death of King George V and the royal romance had the G.A.s beside themselves for up-to-the-minute news. It was about this time they finally accepted that radio was here to stay. There was one radio in the village, operated by batteries, of course, and it belonged to Chief Harry Mountain.

One evening, we were in the sitting room going over the newly arrived batch of papers. Miss O'Brien finished reading a particularly startling item, and then said—impatiently, for her—"This paper is a week old. It would be nice to have the latest news." She accompanied this statement with an exasperated sigh.

So I ventured, "Maybe Harry Mountain listens to the news. I know there's a broadcast at seven o'clock."

"I think I'll discuss it with him," she replied, as though reaching a long-considered decision. "I'm sure he wouldn't mind our taking up a few minutes of his time each day. Yes. I'll talk to him tomorrow. We must keep up with progress, you know."

And the goings-on of the royal family, I thought.

The next day Miss O'Brien approached Harry, and he immediately put the radio at our disposal anytime we wanted it, providing the batteries were charged.

"Harry thinks the best news broadcast is at seven o'clock, just as you said, Miss B.," she told me at lunchtime. "He has invited us to join him this evening." I could see she was excited.

After supper, Miss Dibben, Miss O'Brien and I trailed along to Harry's door. The chief's house was the best in the village, and one of the few painted ones. There was a veranda across the front, overlooking the sea, where Harry had a comfortable chair. He sat here on pleasant days, feet propped on the rail, watching the village world go by. He was a hard-working fisherman in season and owned a seine boat, which was moored in Alert Bay during the winter months. Louisa, his wife, was a frail, gentle little woman who worked hard to keep a clean and tidy house.

"Come in, ladies," said Harry, very proud and pleased to be able to accommodate us in this way, "and have a chair."

The sitting room, although small, was furnished with a couch and two armchairs. There was a wonderfully diverse collection of artifacts that would have made any collector green with envy. There were totems, masks, rattles and chests, as well as woven baskets and a food dish with an intricately carved ladle. Hanging on the walls was a priceless collection of photographs of Alert Bay in the early days, and of potlatches celebrated before the government had banned them. Sitting in the midst of these remarkable pieces of Indian heritage was the radio. It looked completely out of place next to Harry's ceremonial robes and talking stick.

Once we were all seated, Harry said, "Now, ladies, I'll get the news."

The impressive radio sat on a table in a corner, with the heavy batteries on the floor beneath. Harry made a great ceremony of connecting the batteries and adjusting the dials. A lot of static issued forth, with ear-splitting squeals, before the broadcaster's voice could be heard. In order for Miss O'Brien to hear at all, it had to be turned up full volume, and this made it hard on the rest of us. She sat close to the speaker, but even so, I don't think she heard too clearly.

So for half an hour several evenings a week, we would sit, with no one saying a word. Sometimes the static cut in, drowning out the announcer's voice, whereupon Harry would leap to his feet and adjust the dials. When the airwaves cleared, he'd again relax in his armchair. At the end of the broadcast we would rise, thank Louisa and Harry politely, and return to the brown house, where the rest of the evening was devoted to the pros and cons of world affairs in general and the royal romance in particular.

Soon it seemed Edward Windsor and "that woman" were a part of the family, although not the most desirable part. The G.A.s were aghast at the whole affair. As for me, with all this discussion, I felt an intimacy with them. I found the storybook romance most appealing, but I kept this opinion to myself.

The day of King Edward VIII's abdication speech, the brown house was close to a state of mourning. I almost expected Miss O'Brien to ask me to fly the flag at half-mast. The G.A.s went to Harry's to listen to Edward Windsor's emotional farewell and explanation to the British people as to why he must abdicate the throne to marry the woman he loved. I couldn't go to Harry's, as the broadcast on radio came during school hours. However, I heard all about it at the supper table that night.

"It really was very sad," concluded Miss O'Brien.

"Yes, indeed," agreed Miss Dibben. "Just think how one woman could shake the very foundation of the throne of England."

It took another week to dispose of Edward Windsor and Wallis Simpson. When they were laid to rest, we took on the new king and queen and their two princesses. They gave grist to the mill, and, just as avidly, we continued to read outdated papers and listen to Harry's radio. But this time all agreed the new royals were a laudable symbol of family and an asset to the Empire.

The Reef, the Privy and the Mountain Peak

"**M**ERRY CHRISTMAS, CHILDREN.**"

"Merry Christmas, Miss B.," they chorused happily.

I heaved a sigh of relief as the last of them went out the door, clutching a gift. There had been no concert this year, just a party with games and food and small gifts. I was worn out by the time it was over, and I'd have been happy to lock the schoolroom door then and there, but it wasn't to be. The room had to be tidied in readiness for church on Sunday. Also, there were reports to bring up to date and some requisitions for supplies to fill out. These I would dutifully send to Mr. Todd, who would forward them to Ottawa. In all probability my supplies would be as slow in coming as my cheque, so in desperation, I would often buy the necessities myself from my meagre personal funds.

Mrs. Oiens wasn't well, so when I completed my chores in the school, I walked through the woods to visit her. It was a cold day, and dusk had fallen before I returned home. The day ended at last, however, and none too soon for me.

I was relishing the thought of the next day, for then I would be on my way to Simoom Sound for the Christmas holidays. I'd had a letter from my friends saying they'd come for me on the weekend "for sure." My bag was packed and I went to bed in happy anticipation.

The sun was shining brilliantly when I awakened the next day. I hopped out of bed and looked through the window to find a smooth sea under a clear sky. This was going to be a wonderful trip; even the weather was obliging. It was a crisp, cold December day—just right for starting a vacation—and I was ready to go.

The morning hours dragged, but I filled in time by tidying my room and making last-minute rounds in the village. After lunch, I walked to the end of the old wharf, from where I could see the boat as soon as it came into view. I looked across the mouth of Knight Inlet. The panorama was one of clear and sparkling beauty, but empty. No boat of any kind crossed my line of vision. I watched and waited until I was so cold I was forced to return to the house.

Tea time came and there was still no sound of a chugging engine. I was trying to keep a stiff upper lip, but my spirits were getting lower with each sip of tea. By suppertime, darkness had fallen, and I knew there would be no *June M* arriving that day. I retired to my room feeling very sorry for myself and nearly in tears. And I went to bed with my heart in my boots, certain I'd been forgotten. The thought of spending my first Christmas away from home on the island, essentially alone, wasn't what I'd planned.

During the night there was a change in the weather, and Sunday dawned as grey as I felt. I sat around all morning, wondering what I was going to do for two dreary weeks. The weather worsened and the wind blew in strong gusts, capping an angry sea with white-crested waves. If, by some miracle, I hadn't been forgotten, the weather was so stormy I doubted the Manns would travel.

In the afternoon I was in my usual place with my feet on the heater and a book on my lap. Although I was trying to concentrate, my mind was filled with doleful thoughts and my ears attuned to the wind and waves pounding on the raft. I still harboured the faint hope that over and above the crash of the waves, I might hear an engine. Then I thought I did. But surely it was my imagination. I listened more intently.

A gust hit the house, drowning out all other sounds. Then it came again, a bit nearer, so I ran to the window. I didn't really expect to see the *June M*, but there she was: just rounding the end of the old wharf, skirting the rocks, plowing her dauntless way through the channel and heading for the float. A surge of joy and relief nearly drained me, but I grabbed my coat and raced through the house, leaving a couple of startled G.A.s in my wake. I ran to the float and grasped the line to tie the boat.

There was Bob, perched in the wheelhouse, grinning broadly, and Kate and June, and the Dunseith girls. Never had friendly faces looked so wonderful.

"Oh, Kate, I thought you'd forgotten me."

"Of course not," she said. "But we couldn't make it yesterday."

"It's so rough today I never thought you'd venture out."

"It's rough all right," said Bob. "So we'd better not hang around too long."

"I've been ready for days," I said and dashed to the house for my bag.

I wished the G.A.s a Merry Christmas, then hopped aboard the *June M*. Bob guided her back through the rocky channel, past the Indian wharf and into the open water of Knight Inlet. The cold and stormy day, the gusty winds and turbulent seas didn't worry me at all, snug and warm as I was in the cabin with my friends, talking and laughing, without a care in the world.

The light overhead swayed violently with the rocking of the boat as the waves pounded hard against her sides. We could hear the roar of the wind and, at times, water splashed into the well deck. After a while Kate got up and went to speak to Bob in the wheelhouse. I was vaguely aware she'd gone, but we girls were so busy catching up on all the happenings since we'd last met, it didn't register clearly. An hour went by while the boat was buffeted by wind and waves. Then gradually the violent rocking eased. We became aware of less noise and motion. Kate came down from the wheelhouse and sat beside us, looking pale and shaken.

"Kate, you look awful. Is something wrong? What's the matter?" I asked.

"There was plenty the matter for a while there. We nearly piled up on a reef!"

"We did? Was it that rough?"

"Couldn't you tell?" she exclaimed, staring at us in amazement.

I think we all looked sheepish at that point.

While we girls were having our cozy tête-à-tête in the cabin, Kate and Bob had been battling the elements. Our course lay across the wide mouth of Knight Inlet, with Village Island to the south and the larger Gilford Island off the northern shore. By the time we'd reached this open stretch of water, the wind had increased to gale force. This was the season of high winds off the Pacific Ocean, and they sometimes blow with sudden fury, battering the coast relentlessly. As we crossed the mouth of Knight Inlet we were caught in one of these violent windstorms.

Kate realized, when the heavy seas began washing into the well deck, that Bob might be in difficulty and had quietly left the cabin to join him. The wind was blowing in heavy gusts and the seas were wild. Wind-whipped spray washed over the prow of the *June M* and over the windows of the wheelhouse, cutting visibility, at times, to zero. Islands, rocky bluffs and headlands are a guide to all mariners and, on a night such as this, it was easy to lose sight of a familiar landmark.

Kate gave us a graphic account of the events in the wheelhouse.

"Sure as hell we're off course," Bob said to her as he struggled with the wheel. "The wind must be 50 miles an hour. Maybe more. Can you see anything through this damned spray?"

"No. Nothing," Kate had said.

"I don't like it," growled Bob, squinting to see through the wheelhouse window. And then he yelled, "Look there. God! I bet it's that blasted reef off Seabreeze Island." With that, he swore long and hard. "You've gotta help hold the wheel, Ma."

The tumultuous seas, spume blown high by the wind, were breaking over the reef, a reef looming ever closer.

"Hold her, Ma. That's it. We gotta swing her hard over. Brace yourself and hold on!"

The nose of the boat finally turned, struggling hard against a wind and current bent on her destruction. With their combined might, Bob and Kate held the wheel hard over, arcing us away from the jagged rocks.

"Once we were past the reef we got our bearings again," concluded Kate. "So everything's all right now."

"Why didn't you call us?" we wanted to know.

"We were too busy trying to figure out where we were. And when we realized the reef was just ahead, all we could think of was getting around it."

Sometime later, her subdued audience poked its collective head out of the cabin door and looked around. We were in the lee of the islands now, and although the wind was still blowing hard, its force was less violent under their protection.

"Hi," Bob said from his perch in the wheelhouse. "Tough trip, eh?"

We smiled and nodded; none of us had the heart to tell him we hadn't noticed. When the welcoming lights of the camp flickered in the distance, we retired to the cabin again, feeling a little let down. All of this excitement had gone on with none of us being aware anything was amiss.

—◈—

The windy weather continued for the next day or so. Even in this sheltered cove, where the buildings were secured in deep water, the floats rocked almost as badly as did the brown house on a stormy night.

One night the wind reached a peak close to hurricane velocity. It screamed constantly, lashing the sea into great undulating waves, dashing spray up the steep, rocky shoreline, while the floats and anchoring cables creaked and grated.

By morning the wind had died down, but not before leaving havoc in its wake. Before breakfast the men checked the floats for damage.

"One of the skiffs has disappeared. It must have blown right off the float. We've lost a few shingles and your planters are a mess," Harry told his wife as he sat down to the table. "I wonder what's happened in the woods. That gale must have taken out a few trees."

Just then George came in and announced in crushed tones, "The privy's gone."

"Oh, no," said the household with one voice.

"Yep. She's disappeared," he said sadly. "Blown down the sound, most likely. She could be miles away by now."

"Gee, George, that's tough."

"Yep. It's a shame all right."

The household was sympathetic and George was very upset.

Beauty, someone once said, is in the eye of the beholder, and to George the privy was a thing of beauty. He was justly proud of it, for it represented days of single-handed labour. He'd searched the woods for a straight-grained cedar tree, determined there be nothing but the best in this project. When he found the perfect tree, he cut it down and spent hours sawing it into just the right lengths. Then he split roof shakes to the correct thickness. He packed all the boards carefully out of the woods and let them age and dry.

George had a good reason for building this important edifice. With only one bathroom for a large household, he grew tired of lining up for his turn. A bunkhouse had been added recently, but it was sleeping quarters only. This motivated him to build the privy for his own use—with seats to spare.

When they saw him hard at work on it, everyone who passed by would smile and ask, "How's the privy coming along, George?"

"Fine," he'd reply. "She'll soon be finished."

"Glad to hear it. Are you going to have open house to celebrate?"

George's privy inspired a lot of ribald humour and teasing, but he took it in good part, for he was determined to have his "six-holer."

When at last it was tied beside the bunkhouse, it was strictly for men only. But it proved to be a boon for everyone, and George basked in the glory and praise for the excellence of his labour.

Another member of the camp was as upset as George at the loss of the privy: Norman Jewett. New to the camp, Norman was a cheerful, good-natured fellow, but he was also very modest. So modest, in fact, he didn't like to be seen going into the privy, so he devised his own devious route. The door of the bunkhouse could be seen from the main house, and Norman discovered that by climbing out a side window, he wouldn't be in the line of vision of female eyes in case bed-making or dishwashing coincided with his necessary trip around the corner. So George had a kindred spirit in Norman to console him now the privy was gone.

During the morning the wind abated, the restless sea calmed, and the floats ceased their undulating. The men disappeared after breakfast to carry on their various tasks, leaving Kate, June and me to do the dishes and tidy the house.

Presently we heard the engine of the *June M* starting.

"Who's taking the boat out?" asked Kate.

I went to the window. "It's Bob," I told her.

"I wonder where he's going ."

"Maybe Dad asked him to go to Dunseith's store for something," said June.

Just then Harry came in for a cup of coffee.

"Where's Bob off to?" he asked.

"I don't know. I thought maybe you did," answered Kate, turning back to her chores.

We forgot about Bob as the morning hours passed. Kate was baking one of her enormous batches of bread, and I was waiting for the cinnamon buns to cool, idly watching the ever-changing sea from the kitchen window. Then I became aware of a boat on the far horizon, travelling slowly in our direction.

"There's a boat heading this way," I told Kate.

"Can you tell who it is?"

"No, I can't make it out."

June went outside for a clearer look. "It's Bob and the *June M* and he's towing something."

We watched as the boat drew nearer, then Kate exclaimed, "My goodness. It's the privy. I wonder where he found it. Imagine him going off to look for it without a word to anyone."

"Wait till George hears this. Come on, June. Let's go tell him."

We raced along the float calling, "George! George!"

He came out of the workshop, still looking gloomy.

"What's going on?"

"Bob's found the privy. He's coming in now, and he's got it in tow."

We waited on the edge of the float. When Bob guided the boat alongside, we grabbed a line and made her fast. Sure enough, at the end of the tow line was the privy, slightly battered and waterlogged and half-submerged on one side.

"Gee, kid, where'd you find her?" asked George, grinning from ear to ear.

"I just went scoutin' around," said the nonchalant Bob. "She was hooked up on some rocks a couple of miles down the sound."

"It must have been tough gettin' a line on her by yourself," said George, admiration in his voice.

"It was pretty tricky all right," Bob replied modestly. "But here she is, so let's get her back up. And we better anchor her tighter this time."

Everyone gathered to pay tribute to Bob for his single-handed rescue of the privy. There was deep discussion as to how to go about erecting "her" and making sure "she" wouldn't take off down the sound again. The most willing helper of all was Norman, who was as happy as George to see the lady back where she belonged.

⁓

The donkey engine deep in the woods had a breakdown, so it was decided to suspend logging operations until after Christmas. This meant the men were around camp all day.

"The cookhouse needs a good cleaning. Any volunteers?" Kate asked, recognizing a good opportunity when she saw one.

"Sure. We'll clean it for you," said the ever-enthusiastic Norman. "Come on, gang, let's go."

He rounded up June, the younger boys and me, then, armed with buckets, mops and scrubbing brushes, we tackled the clean-up job. The cookhouse was a new acquisition that had arrived only days before and had been tied alongside the other floating buildings. The kitchen in the house had become too small for preparing the large meals essential to these hardworking people.

The cookhouse was one big room with many windows, furnished with a long table and benches on either side in lieu of chairs. As well, there was an oversized cookstove, a deep sink and lots of cupboard and counter space.

"Okay, kids. Let's get this place in shape. Have to have it nice and clean for Christmas," Norman said, grabbing a broom and attacking the floor. His cheerful attitude was contagious, so we happily scrubbed and scoured until everything shone.

"That looks just fine," he said, after he'd made a tour of inspection. "Now, I think we should decorate for Christmas. Let's go cut some evergreens."

Norman, Bud and Eddie went off in the rowboat, and while they were gone, Kate brought out silver tinsel and red bells. The boys returned with a boat load of evergreen boughs and with these we transformed the plain, utilitarian cookhouse into a room filled with Christmas cheer. The air was permeated with the scent of fresh-cut cedar and pine to blend with the tantalizing odours of Christmas baking.

Everyone was filled with Christmas spirit, but none more than Norman. He fairly oozed goodwill and glad tidings.

"Which day should we go to the Scotts'?" Kate asked Harry on Boxing Day morning. "I told Mrs. Scott in my letter we'd make it during the holiday, providing the weather didn't close in."

"It should be safe enough to go tomorrow," Harry replied. "The barometer's holding steady, so I don't think we'll get another big blow for a while."

Our destination was Scotts' camp, about 40 miles north of Simoom Sound at the head of Mackenzie Sound. Irene and Joyce, as well as Ray and Norman, went along, so the boat was loaded. Some relaxed in the well deck or lounged on the cabin roof, while others stayed in the cabin out of the cold. We whiled away the afternoon as the *June M* plied her competent way with Harry at the helm. We watched the islands and mountains slipping by, and as daylight faded, we saw groups of lights dotted along the darkened shoreline.

We turned into Mackenzie Sound and darkness followed quickly, but it wasn't an inky darkness, for the sky was clear, cloudless and studded with stars. As we rounded the next point, our chatter faded into silence at the sight ahead.

Before us was a sight of uncommon beauty.

The snow-covered peak of magnificent Mount Stephens sat in silhouette against the blue-black sky, its white crown glittering and incandescent under a luminous moon—and all of it reflected in detailed perfection across the water, with not a ripple to disturb it. The stars themselves seemed to have fallen from the sky to lie shimmering in the sea, a carpet of diamonds at the mountain's base. Nature had given us the perfect Christmas greeting, and it was a sight to take one's breath away.

The spell was broken as the boat turned out of the moon's path and made its way toward the lights of a camp in the sheltered bay.

The Scotts' camp was a substantial and well-established floating community. At this time five families were in residence, as well as extra crew. The houses were well cared for and comfortable, with proper plumbing and electric lights. I never got over my amazement at the touches of civilization that cropped up in these out-of-the-way places. As well as the houses for married couples, there was a large cookhouse, bunkhouses for extra crew and, lastly, a floating badminton court enclosed by a high wire fence. We had enormous meals in the cookhouse, and when we finally went to bed, we were made comfortable in the bunkhouses.

In the morning, we had a brisk game of badminton, and I came to appreciate the wire fence. Given the kind of badminton we played, it would have been a full-time and *very* chilly job fishing our errant shuttlecocks out of the ocean.

When the hour for leave-taking came, we did so reluctantly. But it was time to go home. We piled aboard the *June M* and headed into Mackenzie Sound, leaving the hospitable Scotts, badminton and the unforgettable Mount Stephens in all its white and shining glory behind us.

Mrs. Oiens Entertains

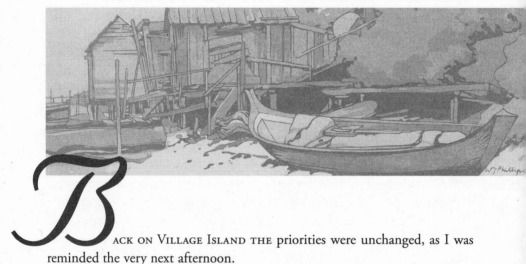

BACK ON VILLAGE ISLAND THE priorities were unchanged, as I was reminded the very next afternoon.

"Miss B., you forgot to raise the flag this morning—again."

"I'm sorry, Miss O'Brien. I'll remember tomorrow."

I never forgot to light the fire; if I had, the children and I would have been icicles. And as a matter of course, I saw to the brushing of teeth and the blowing of noses. But the blessed flag? It was always a blind spot, and it worried the G.A.s to no end when the Union Jack wasn't flying high on the little hill.

It was easy to remember on a pleasant morning, but on a stormy day I cursed the thing. With icy fingers, I'd untie the knot and untangle the cords, which had become snarled in the wind. Then, in all probability, the pulley at the top would seize and I'd yank and tug, all the while muttering nasty things about king and country. When the pulley gave way, it could be with a sudden jerk, and the flag would sail to the top of the pole. If it happened to be raining, it would hang there like a soggy rag. On mornings such as these, I was ready to chuck the whole blooming lot into the middle of Blackfish Sound and head south.

I did have Christmas parcels and mail waiting on my return, and this brightened my life considerably. In the evening, toasting myself by the heater, I would read and reread the mail from home. Then I would retire to my room and light the smelly coal heater. When the chill was off I'd undress with the speed of light and don my night attire—which added up to almost equal the number of garments I'd just removed. The frosty air was oozing through all the cracks and crannies of the house at low tide and when the wind blew, it was like living in a cold locker.

Things were definitely back to normal.

That night at tea time, Miss Dibben said, "Mrs. Oiens has invited us to a belated New Year's dinner on Saturday."

"That's nice of her," I said, pleased at the idea. "She's feeling better, then?"

"Yes, much better," Miss O'Brien replied. "She waited for your return before having the dinner. And she'd like you to spend the night if you'd like to."

"How nice," I said, already looking forward to Mrs. Oiens' cooking and a change of scenery. "How are we getting there?"

"By boat. Mr. Oiens will come for us late morning."

Mr. Oiens called for us about 11 o'clock. It was snowing hard, and a bitterly cold wind was blowing, slanting the snow in icy needles. We wrapped up warmly, but still the wind cut like a knife—and the snow was more blinding than fog. Mr. Oiens guided his gas boat through the rocky channel and around the shoreline as if by instinct, and found his wharf where there appeared to be nothing but a white wall.

As he secured the boat, he said to Miss O'Brien and me, "Ladies, you go into the house where it is warm," then added, "Just a minute, Miss Dibben, and I will guide you."

He placed his great paw under her arm and almost carried her along the path. I'm sure she couldn't see a thing in this white world, for I found it hard to see even with full vision. Mrs. Oiens was waiting for us at the door.

"Come in, come in. Out of the awful cold. Aye, it's a bad one today." She hustled us inside, then turning to me, she said, "Glad I am to see ye, lass. And how was your holiday now?"

"Just fine, thank you. And I'm glad to hear you're feeling better."

"Ah, yes. I'm some improved since you last saw me. The good doctor came and gave me some new pills. What a nice young man! Now, ladies, here I go prattlin' on again. Lay your coats on the bed and warm yoursel's by the fire. Dinner will be ready in a wee minute."

The kitchen was cozy and welcome after our cold trip. Pots were bubbling on the stove, and the tantalizing smell of roasting chicken filled the house. We clustered around the sitting-room heater while Mrs. Oiens busied herself in the kitchen with last-minute preparations, all the while keeping up a running commentary.

Mr. Oiens ties up at the G.A.s' wharf. He would bring them vegetables and, in season, blessed them with fresh strawberries.

The sitting room was also the company dining room. A round table, which ordinarily sat under a window, had been pulled out to the centre of the room. It had been extended with leaves and covered with a white cloth. This was the only time I ever saw it used as a dining table.

Mrs. Oiens was a truly excellent cook, and as she had so little opportunity to entertain, she was making the most of this occasion. There was plump, tender chicken, savoury stuffing, a variety of vegetables, pickles, relishes, light and airy buns with fresh butter, and delicious gravy. If ever a board groaned, hers did! Finally, we were groaning too.

"Have some more plum pudding, ladies. Eat up. Eat up," she urged. "For there's mince pie and tarts as well."

"No, thank you," said Miss Dibben. "Not another morsel."

"It was a wonderful dinner, but I couldn't possibly eat one more bite," Miss O'Brien added.

Both women looked about to burst. I'd never seen either of them eat so much.

"Come now, lass. How about you? Just a touch more."

"Really, I couldn't, Mrs. Oiens," I said, rubbing my stomach for effect. "But it was a marvellous dinner."

She positively glowed as praise was heaped upon her. And our immobility she took as a rare compliment.

When, sometime later, we could at last rise from our chairs, Miss O'Brien said, "I think we should get back to the village before dark, if Mr. Oiens will kindly take us." She nodded in his direction.

"Yah," he agreed. "The snow, she's almost stopped. If you like, we'll go now."

After the G.A.s left, I helped Mrs. Oiens with the dishes.

"Now, tell me all about your holiday, lass."

So I started from the beginning and told her all about the trips and parties and about the people I'd seen, a lot of whom she'd known at other times in other places along the coast. She was an intense listener, avid about every detail. I sensed she took vicarious pleasure in my activities, as she so rarely left the island.

It was a pleasant evening, not only the conversation, but because I was warm all over for the first time since leaving Simoom. At bedtime, I was ushered into the guest room, where I crawled between cold sheets, but with the aid of a hot water bottle, I soon warmed up and slept soundly in a bed that stayed level all night long.

The next morning was brilliant with snow—a Christmas-card sort of day. Mr. Oiens took me home through a dazzling miracle of winter. The rocky islands wore glistening white crowns, the evergreens were festooned with feathers of soft snow, and the sea, under a flawless sky, shone as though polished.

When the village came into view, I scarcely recognized it. No longer grey and dreary, it was gilded in silver white. The totem poles, wearing new white wigs, appeared jaunty and rakish, and the children romped along the path, yelling happily while fighting a boisterous snowball war. All combined to lend the place an air of unusual and welcome liveliness.

Mustard Plasters and All That

SCHOOL WAS IN FULL SWING with an attendance of 12—unless someone slept in or the family decided to go visiting. Education was still low on the list of village priorities, except with Gertrude Hanuse, who made sure Wilfred and Stella attended regularly. Fluent in English, they were bright children who worked hard at their studies.

But the others were mastering a few skills. Quiet Emily could recognize words on flash cards and could count quite well. Margaret Rose knew her ABC's and was learning her numbers better each day. Twelve-year-old Matthew, who only attended sporadically, still struggled with the grade three reader, but he was a fine artist and rendered beautiful drawings of boats and Native symbols.

Teaching the group consisted of hammering home the three Rs. With patience and luck, I hoped something might stick. With so many disruptions to the school year, and no proper resource material from Ottawa, it was difficult to get and keep their attention. When I inquired about improved material, I found that Ottawa, a few thousand miles away, wasn't much interested in the Mamalilikulla Indian Day School. There was little I could do, other than to work with what I had.

Then, just when I thought things were going fairly well, the village was hit by a serious flu epidemic.

It had raged along the coast for most of January before striking our village about the end of the month. From then and all through February, I did more nursing than teaching. It was a virulent flu, often complicated by pneumonia, and a number of deaths resulted, one being the Anglican vicar in Alert Bay. At first the village had only isolated cases, but finally whole families were laid low. Many of the children were very ill, running high fevers with the added misery of severe earache. The *Columbia* hadn't called in weeks, being kept busy visiting places where there was no medical help at all.

The number of remedies was limited. There was the sweet-tasting cough mixture, which the people loved, Aspirin, rubbing alcohol, camphorated oil, laxatives and cod-liver oil. In 1937 treating flu involved labour and ingenuity, as antibiotics were yet to be discovered.

Each day I gave tepid sponge baths as an aid to reducing fever. I took temperatures, gave alcohol rubs and dripped warm oil into aching ears. I made so many mustard plasters, the thought of them curdled my stomach.

Very often I was in the village before school in the morning, again at noon and always after school. The children fell ill one by one, so the numbers in class fluctuated daily. I made calls to Turnour Island, Harbledown Island and Midsummer Island, and travelled on every imaginable kind of boat—except sleek, fast ones. In these other villages, I carried out the same routine, as much as time would allow.

Miss Dibben stayed isolated with the tubercular children, taking all her meals in the Gables. Miss O'Brien worked along with me, and during school hours made frequent trips through the village. At noon, she'd give me a progress report, and if there was time, I'd check on whomever needed attention.

I'd already met many of the people who lived on the surrounding islands and could now recognize most of their boats. So now, when a gas boat chugged up to the float, I usually knew where I'd be going. One day, however, a boat arrived with people aboard whom I'd never seen before. There were six or eight in the group, and they were a poor-looking lot. One of the men came ashore and I met him on the float. His clothes were ragged and dirty. The stale odour of fish and eulachon grease assaulted my nose, even though I stood several feet away.

In guttural tones he said, "You come—?"

He mentioned a name I didn't recognize.

"What did he say, Miss O'Brien?" I asked, for she had come to stand beside me on the float.

She poised, listening intently through her ear trumpet, as he repeated the Indian name a couple of times.

"I can't be sure where they're from," she said at last, looking confused.

"Sick people?" I asked the man.

"Yeah. Ve-e-ry sick."

This was the first time I'd felt real uneasiness. I'd had dozens of trips with the Native people and had never been afraid except, sometimes, of the condition of the boats or the weather. But this time the place and people were unknown, even to Miss O'Brien.

"Well, I guess I should go," I said reluctantly.

"You do as you think best," she answered, but I felt even she, who had been in this country so long, was a bit dubious.

I collected the black bag and such medical supplies as I thought might be necessary. It was difficult to tell what or how much I'd need. Then I boarded the open—very dirty—boat and settled myself on the edge of the gunwales. The people stared at me stonily.

I knew we were crossing Knight Inlet and heading in the general direction of Gilford Island. We followed the coastline and meandered through the islands that were so familiar and yet, at this moment, unfamiliar. At last we rounded a point that protected a sheltered cove and I saw a desolate and forlorn cluster of ramshackle houses.

They might have been deserted except for smoke curling from a tin chimney here and there. Most of the shacks were built on pilings on the beach, but a few stood above and behind on a grassy knoll. Some were in ruins, with

These children and most of the other villagers were hit hard by the flu epidemic that spread along the coast, including Village Island.

missing doors and windows and steps, giving them the appearance of blind and toothless old men. Between the houses were totems, some leaning wearily, others collapsed, as though from exhaustion. The place had an aura of decay. It was hoary with age and there was a dank, dull look about it, as if no sunlight ever reached it. Great evergreens climbed the hill behind, casting gloomy and sombre shadows that were reflected in the sea.

This was obviously a deserted village. The people must have been a wandering band who took up residence whenever the spirit moved them and they found an uninhabited spot such as this.

The boat was made fast to what was left of a wharf. The people climbed slowly out of the boat, and I followed them along broken planks onto the pebbly beach. One of the men indicated I should follow him. He led me along the beach to a shack that sat on spindly stilts. We walked up a couple of splintered steps and into a bare room. There was no furniture save a wooden bench, a table and a rusted stove. A fire was burning, but it would have been impossible to heat the room. The windows were broken and through the cracks and knotholes in the floor, I could see the beach below.

Through the gloom I saw why I'd been brought to this place. On the floor, rolled in blankets, lay a young girl. I knelt beside her and felt her pulse. It was very rapid, and the skin on her face was dry and shiny pale. Her breath came in short, sharp gasps. She was extremely ill.

I wondered desperately if I could make these people understand how sick the girl truly was, and that in one short visit, I could do nothing for her.

There were other people in the room and from the floor, I looked up at them. They gazed back at me like expectant children, as if they thought I could cast a spell and make this young girl better on the spot.

"She's ve-e-ry sick," I said slowly, knowing full well I wasn't telling them anything they didn't already know. "She *must* go to the hospital in Alert Bay. She must see the *doctor*."

Unconsciously I raised my voice as if speaking to the hard of hearing. I was sure their dialect was different to that spoken on Village Island. Not that my yelling would change that.

"Go Alert Bay. You understand?" I directed my question to the man who seemed to be the leader.

"Yeah, yeah. Go 'Lert Bay," he nodded.

"Is there another boat?" I asked. "Gas boat?"

"Boat. Yeah. Hokay," he agreed.

"Where is it?" I asked.

He went to the door and pointed to a craft tied to a broken-down wharf farther along the beach.

"All right, then. You take the girl to Alert Bay."

"Hokay," he agreed.

I turned back to the young girl, who stared up at me through fever-dimmed eyes. I wondered who she was and where she came from and wished with all my heart there was something I could do to ease her suffering.

The spokesman said something to another man, and I watched as he left the room. He walked along the beach toward another gas boat, so I presumed my instructions were going to be carried out. The head man indicated I should follow him, so I stumbled along the beach behind him. He took me to other houses, where there were sick people, maybe a dozen in all, but none as ill as the young girl. I doled out Aspirin and cough mixture, and they smiled, seeming pleased to receive this bit of attention. Most of them would have recovered just fine, I thought, without any of my pills or elixirs.

Every house I entered was in the same sad state as the first shack, where the young girl lay on the bare floor. How these people lived, and on what, was difficult to tell. But the acrid odour of dried fish and eulachon grease was everywhere, so I could only presume they weren't starving.

When I'd seen all the people who needed attention, I said to the man, "The girl. She will go on the boat now?"

"Yeah. Go 'Lert Bay."

I could see activity in the shack and watched as she was carried through the door and along the beach to the waiting boat.

This was all I could hope for. Wearily, I climbed aboard the gas boat that had brought me to this unknown village.

Whether the girl reached the hospital I never knew, and if she lived or died I never heard.

ABOUT SIX O'CLOCK ONE MORNING there was a tap on my bedroom door.

"Miss B. Could you come?" It was Miss Dibben's worried voice.

I immediately clambered out of my warm bed to open the door.

"What's happened, Miss Dibben?"

"It's Eliza," she told me. "She's suddenly much worse."

"I'll be there as soon as I dress."

Eliza was the most seriously ill TB patient in the *Hyuya-Tsi*. Over the months, while under Miss Dibben's care, she'd improved somewhat, and the doctor had been fairly optimistic on his last visit, but over the past few days, there had been a distinct change, and both Miss Dibben and I were very concerned about her.

I dressed quickly and dashed up the hill to the preventorium to find Eliza comatose, her breathing bubbly and laboured.

"When did this happen?" I asked a distraught Miss Dibben.

"She called me about five o'clock and said she didn't feel well, then she seemed to doze off to sleep. I checked her again just before I called you and found her like this," she said, then turned her worried eyes to mine. "She's dying, isn't she, Miss B.?"

I checked Eliza's pulse and found it weak and thready; she was unconscious.

"I'm afraid she is, Miss Dibben."

Miss Dibben closed her eyes as if to shut out this terrible news. News she'd heard far too often in her time on the island. She worked hard, caring for the children, and with her limited vision, it was doubly difficult. On the surface she seemed stern and strict, but she was fond of these unfortunate children. Each loss was a terrible blow.

I was fond of Eliza too. A nice child of about 12, she never complained about her life of inactivity and always co-operated with any effort that might help to make her well.

"Why don't you have breakfast and I'll stay with her," I said.

We took turns having breakfast, and then we both stayed with Eliza, although there was nothing we could do for her now. We did screen her from the other two girls, Christine and Kathleen, by hanging an old bedspread between the beds.

Eliza's mother was dead, and her father and grandmother lived in Alert Bay, but there were two aunts in the village. We sent them word of Eliza's serious condition, and soon two figures with shawl-covered heads appeared from the village. They stood on the path below the *Hyuya-Tsi* and looked up at the windows. When I looked down at them, they shook their heads sadly, saying, "Too bad, too bad."

Eliza passed away about eight o'clock the following morning, and we were left stunned and shaken by her sudden demise. When we told her aunts they started wailing and lamenting. Other people from the village soon gathered on the path, adding their cries until the morning air was filled with the sound of grieving.

Miss Dibben went out and spoke to Eliza's relatives, and when she returned, she said, "Miss B., the family would like you to prepare the body for burial."

"All right, Miss Dibben." I said, nodding, while dreading the task ahead. "It's probably just as well considering the infection involved."

When I indicated my agreement, the women nodded solemnly.

"I'll arrange for a short memorial service," said Miss Dibben. "And I've

Eliza's death broke everyone's heart. Here she is seen with Miss O'Brien.

asked Miss O'Brien to prepare the school. The men must see about a coffin and a boat too," she added, almost to herself. I got the impression she wanted to busy herself to keep from thinking about Eliza. It was too difficult. Too much of a loss.

I knew her heart ached at losing this child and admired her all the more for her self-control. The details, the planning, all would be properly seen to.

After I bathed and dressed Eliza in her double wardrobe, we placed her in a makeshift coffin, which the men had put together hurriedly. They carried it to the school and set it on the floor in front of my desk. Miss O'Brien rang the bell and its mournful clang echoed through the frosty air.

The schoolhouse was filled with the village people, who sat quietly while Miss Dibben read passages from the burial service in both English and Kwak'wala. After the service, the men carried the coffin to a waiting gas boat. I walked to the end of the old Indian wharf and, for the second time, watched the start of the final journey of a child too young to go, another tragic victim of TB.

I waited until the boat was out of sight, then turned to head back along the wharf. I was tired and depressed by the events of the morning, yet now I must ring the bell and transform the church-cum-morgue into a school again.

Frustration

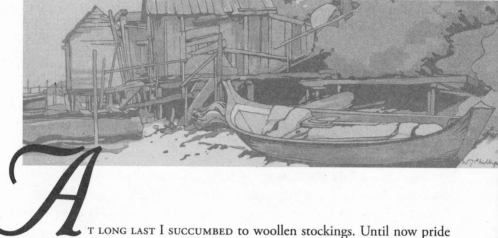

*A*T LONG LAST I SUCCUMBED to woollen stockings. Until now pride had prevented me from wearing them. Thick ugly things! But when ink froze in the inkwells, I gave in.

But, oh, how I hated them! Not only were they bulky, making my legs look like the underpinnings of a piano, they itched most dreadfully. I had to admit, they were warm, and as we'd had no visitors in weeks, it didn't much matter what I looked like. Orphan Annie came to mind. Then, just as I'd started to forget my dowdy appearance, we had unexpected arrivals.

I'd dismissed the class at noon and went outside to find the *Sky Pilot* tied to the float. Sitting at the kitchen table were Reverend Dance from the Anglican Diocese, United Church parson Leander Gillard and the sartorially correct Lou Layhew. And there I was in woollen stockings thick as tree bark. I quickly sat down at the table, and shoved my legs out of sight.

"We've missed seeing you at the Bay," Mr. Gillard said.

"I'll be there when the weather improves," I told him, pulling my skirt firmly over my knees under the table.

"I hear you spent Christmas at Simoom," Lou said with a smile.

"News does travel in this country," I replied. "I guess the gas-boat grapevine has been busy again. But tell me what's new in Alert Bay? It seems like ages since I've been there."

So while Mr. Gillard and Reverend Dance were in deep discussion with the G.A.s, Lou brought me up to date on Alert Bay, telling me all the trivial things that take on such vast importance in the backwoods. Then he invited me to a dance coming up later in the spring. Although there was no assurance I'd get there, I was delighted to be asked—especially since I was wearing woollen stockings.

After lunch I said my goodbyes and headed back to the schoolhouse.

"We'll see you later," Lea Gillard said. "I have a call to make on Gilford Island and Miss O'Brien is coming along. We'll be back when school is out, as she'd like the parson to hold a service."

When I returned to the house after school, Miss Dibben announced, "Cheeky Joe sent a message. He said to tell you he's sick and wants you to come and see him."

"Who brought the message?" I asked, for there was no gas boat tied to the float.

"Some boys from New Vancouver. They're visiting in the village at present. They tied the boat to one of the other floats."

When Mr. Gillard heard of Cheeky Joe's plight, he said, "We'll take you over. Maybe Lou and I could help."

This was the first time I'd made the trip to New Vancouver on a substantial boat and it was a marvellous change, seeming to take no time at all. We found Cheeky Joe lying in his rumpled bed, looking quite ill.

"Hello, Joe. What seems to be the trouble?" I asked.

"Me sick. Me ve-e-ry sick," he moaned.

"*Where* are you sick?"

"Sick all over," he groaned.

"Tell me where it hurts—as best you can," I persisted.

"Hurt all over," he moaned. "Me ve-e-ry, ve-e-ry sick."

Cheeky Joe did look miserable. He was flushed and had a high temperature.

"What do you make of him?" asked Mr. Gillard.

"He probably has the flu," I guessed, then frowned. "He really shouldn't stay here alone. The doctor should check him."

"We could take him to the Bay," offered Mr. Gillard immediately. "Lou and I could easily get him aboard the *Sky Pilot*."

"Joe," I said, leaning close so he could hear me. "Mr. Gillard will take you to the hospital in Alert Bay. Then the doctor can help you."

"No! Me no go hospital!" he roared, as much as he could roar in his weakened state.

"But we can't do anything for you here."

"No. No go hospital." He was adamant.

We talked and cajoled to no avail. He refused to be moved.

"Joe medicine man. Use own medicine," he said stubbornly.

Evidently he was practising some of his own medicine already, for the head and foot of his bed and the corners of the room were festooned with cedar boughs and eagle down.

"Joe," I said, curious and a bit exasperated. "Why did you send for me when you won't pay attention to what I tell you?"

Ignoring the question, he rolled over and turned his back to us.

"What should we do, Mr. Gillard? We can't take him by force. I can give him Aspirin, but he really should be properly examined."

"I'd say leave him where he is. Some of the older people have a real fear of hospitals," Mr. Gillard told me. "I'll report him to the doctor when I get back to the Bay. Get him to come here."

Mr. Gillard was right. There was nothing to do but leave Joe to his eagle down and cedar boughs. Coming here was useless, but at least I had comfortable transportation and congenial company on the way home.

I was really worried about Cheeky Joe, as he was obviously a very sick man. It was sometime later when I met someone I could ask about him. I was surprised to learn he was as hale and hearty as ever.

"Then the doctor came?" I said.

"No. No doctor. Joe's medicine man. He cure himself with eulachon grease," my informant told me proudly.

So much for White man's medicine, I thought.

One afternoon, about a week after I'd seen Cheeky Joe, I found a man waiting to speak to me after school. The usual open gas boat was tied to the float.

When I got closer I realized the man was from Turnour Island. "Hello, Arthur. Anything wrong?"

"You come. Mary's baby, he sick. Julia say you come."

As usual at this time of year, it was a cold and blustery day—a woollen-stockings kind of day. I wrapped up warmly, but still I shivered when we headed into a biting wind. Sometime later, I climbed onto a wharf behind Arthur.

"You come," he beckoned.

I followed him through the village, which looked like the other villages in the area except for being larger. It had the same grey totem poles and a community house, along with some fairly good houses and a number of tumbledown shacks, all of them facing the sea.

When I entered Mary's house, the heat in the room hit me like a fist. I could scarcely breathe. The one room was filled to overflowing with a double bed, a couple of chairs, a table and a stove that was roaring hot.

Julia, the baby's aunt, whom I knew from her frequent visits to Village Island, was there along with Mary, the mother.

"What seems to be the trouble, Julia?"

Her tone was flat, her words without inflection. "The baby, he sick. Maybe he die."

The infant was wedged in a narrow wooden cradle close beside the kitchen stove. He was bound tightly in his blankets. Even if he'd had the strength, it would have been impossible for him to move. All I could see was his face; it was sickly bluish-white.

"How long has he been like this?"

"Few days now," she said with a shrug.

"First off, he needs some breathing room and fresh air," I told her as I loosened the covers. The baby didn't stir and his body burned with fever.

"This little fellow should be in hospital. Why didn't you take him before now?"

"Dunno," was her reply.

"Tell Mary he must go to Alert Bay right away."

Mary had been sitting quietly in the background, letting Julia do all the talking. She understood very little English, so Julia translated into Kwak'wala. Mary nodded and replied in monosyllables.

"Mary say, hokay. She get Johnny to take her to de Bay!"

"Good," I said. "Tell her to go today. Don't wait until tomorrow. He'll get better in the hospital, but you must get him there right away. You understand, Julia?"

She nodded, this time vigorously.

"The most I can do now is bathe him and make him more comfortable, but it won't make him better," I told her as I prepared to sponge his hot little body. "Now, you make sure Mary understands. It is *very* important. Is Johnny in the village?"

"Oh, yeah. Johnny will take." They both nodded in solemn agreement.

As the two women were willing to co-operate, and after I'd done what I could, I thought it safe to leave.

When I stepped outside, the chill air was a welcome relief after the hot and stuffy room. Arthur was waiting on the boat, and I climbed aboard, confident the infant would soon be on his way to hospital. The return journey, in the late afternoon, was just as cold as the earlier one. Before we were halfway home, I was practically blue, but for once my travelling companion realized my plight.

"Here. You take," said Arthur, handing me a heavy green blanket.

"Thank you," I said through chattering teeth.

I wrapped it around me.

Arthur grinned and said, "You all same Indian woman now."

And that was all right by me. The blanket was wonderfully cozy and warm.

The following day not too many children came to school. There had been an undercover potlatch the night before, which most of them had attended. Consequently they didn't get up in the morning. No doubt the whole village was suffering from potlatch hangover. After supper I retired to my corner with a book, the cares and ills of the village and surrounding area far from my thoughts.

I heard a knock on the door, but as Miss O'Brien was in the kitchen, I paid no attention. In a few minutes, she came into the sitting room.

"Miss B.," she said. "Julia and Mary are here. They're asking for a burial layette for the baby."

"What?" I exclaimed. "Wasn't he taken to the hospital?"

"No, I don't think so," Miss O'Brien said, shaking her head.

I strode into the kitchen to face the two girls—Mary looking sheepish and Julia, belligerent.

"What's the meaning of this? Didn't you take the baby to the hospital?"

"No," Julia said, immediately on the defensive. "Him going to die. We come for burial clothes."

"You promised to take him to Alert Bay yesterday." I was close to yelling and I know my face was grim. "Why didn't you keep your promise, Julia? Why don't you give him a chance?"

For a brief moment, the women looked at me, their expressions unreadable. Then without another word, they stalked out of the kitchen.

I turned to Miss O'Brien, angry and frustrated. "Why? Why are they so exasperating sometimes?"

"They have their own ways," she answered quietly, "which to us appear ... childish or irresponsible. But they are all God's children, so we must be patient and try harder to make them understand."

Right then, I wasn't at all sure I had the patience required.

There was little I could do about making the people in the outlying villages follow my suggestions. I certainly had no authority over them. All I could do was explain and hope for the best. I was hired and paid only as a teacher. Therefore, the powers that be would have taken a jaundiced view if I had personally conducted every patient to the hospital. If such had been the case, I'd have spent a great deal of time travelling to Alert Bay.

Young Village Islanders peer intently at the camera, except for one little girl who seems highly amused at the baby's efforts to get a look at the action as well.

Much later, I met Julia in the village.

"What happened to Mary's baby?" I wanted to know.

"Johnny took Mary and the baby to Alert Bay. The doctor fix so he got better."

I couldn't believe my ears. Maybe the occasional display of bad temper had its merit. "I'm very glad to hear that, Julia."

I sighed in relief. A happy ending. I could use all of those I could get.

Our Darling

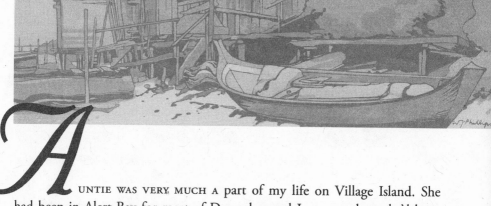

AUNTIE WAS VERY MUCH A part of my life on Village Island. She had been in Alert Bay for most of December and January, where she'd been a patient in St. George's Hospital. Now she was home in her tiny grey house with her brother Sam. Although she told me she was a "little bit good," I still checked on her frequently.

"Ah, Kwunuk," she'd say when I opened the door.

"Hello, Ubumpus. How are you today?" I'd reply, for we were still playing the game of mother and daughter.

Auntie would then carry on at great length in her Native tongue. I would listen and laugh with her, never really clear as to the trend of the conversation. Not that it mattered. We enjoyed each other's company and her health remained stable.

Not so for poor old Sam. He seemed to be getting older and more rheumatic every day.

It was difficult to tell the age of many of the older people, and when I'd ask, the answer would simply be, "Oh, him born lo-o-ong time ago," and judging from Sam's appearance, he no doubt was. With his wrinkled face, wispy hair, lack of teeth, and stiff joints, he might have been anywhere from 70 to 90.

He seldom left home, except for the one time when he caused such a sensation in the missionaries' kitchen. Nor did he have much to say, even to his own people. Having lived with the talkative Auntie for so long, perhaps he'd lost the art of making conversation—or given up trying. She rarely let anyone get a word in edgewise.

During the cold weather, Sam kept more and more to the house. When I'd call, I'd find him sitting up in his tumbled, none-too-clean bed, looking like an ancient statue. Most of the time he never uttered a word, but once in a while he'd mutter to himself. On such occasions, Auntie would cease to be chuckly and would become very serious. She would carry on at great length, her eyes never wavering from mine, trying desperately to make me understand. I tried, but it was hopeless. She spoke too rapidly and I assimilated far too slowly.

One day, after one of these singular conversations, I met Gertrude on the village path. "Will you come to Auntie's with me, Gertrude?" I asked. "She keeps trying to tell me something, and I've no idea what she's talking about."

"Sure, I'll come."

We walked back to the house, and I stood by while they carried on a long conversation. Finally Gertrude turned to me and said, "Auntie says Sam talks to himself. Sometimes he even talks to people who aren't there and who've been dead for a lo-o-ong time. Auntie says she's scared."

"Tell her not to be scared, Gertrude. It's just because he's old and sick. This happens to lots of old people. Tell her not to worry."

Gertrude spoke in rapid Kwak'wala to Auntie, who listened intently and nodded. Then she replied at length in her own tongue, her tone low and serious.

"What's she saying now?" I asked.

"She say, if Sam keeps on, pretty soon she'll see people who aren't there, too."

I had to smile before telling Gertrude to assure Auntie that Sam's visions weren't contagious. I never was certain she believed me.

I called almost every day, although there was little I could do for Sam now. One day I knocked, opened the door as usual—then stopped cold. Sam had been out of bed and was just now in the act of climbing back in, giving me a full view of his posterior—a posterior clad in pink silk long johns. The legs of this dashing garment were tucked into thick, woollen socks, and he had topped his luscious pink undies with a suit coat, much the worse for wear. Completing the ensemble, perched on his head at a rakish angle, was a bright red toque trimmed with a gay pom-pom.

After the visit, I returned to the brown house and said to Miss O'Brien, "Have you given Sam any clothes lately?"

She thought for a moment. "Why, yes. A week or so ago, I gave him an Alert Bay mission box."

I speculated for a long time on who in Alert Bay wore long johns made of pink silk.

During the next couple of months, Sam grew weaker. Sadly, he died during the latter part of March. Auntie took it very hard.

Sam's earthly possessions were taken to the island across the channel, where they were burned in a bonfire on the beach. He was prepared for burial by his relatives and laid in a coffin that had been brought from Alert Bay. He was returned to the Bay for committal in the Indian graveyard.

It was a most elaborate coffin, covered in grey and decorated with ornate handles. There was a silver plaque on the lid and inscribed on it, in flourishing script, were the words: OUR DARLING.

The villagers had their own brand of humour. This figure, wearing a chief's hat, was known as a *Daduquala*, who looked out for the coming of a wife's parents.

I had made my entrance into Sam's life as it drew to a close, he an old man of set ways and unknowable visions. And while the epitaph didn't describe the man I knew, it was gratifying to discover, in the dim and distant past, old Sam had been someone's much-loved darling.

Skookum Chuck

"**W**OULD YOU COME AND SEE Kathleen, Miss B.? She's feeling miserable and has a sharp pain in her chest."

"I'll be right there, Miss Dibben."

I went to the preventorium to find the little girl crying and feverish.

"Take a deep breath, Kathleen."

"Can't, Miss B. Too sore," she sobbed.

"Do you think she should be in hospital?" Miss Dibben asked in worried tones.

I nodded. "I think that's best. She probably has a touch of pleurisy, so the doctor should check her."

This was Thursday evening. We discussed the pros and cons with Miss O'Brien, and it was decided she would arrange a village boat to make the trip the next afternoon. That done, Miss O'Brien turned to me.

"I'm sure it would be permissible for you to close the school at noon so as to accompany Kathleen," she said. "After all, this is something of an emergency."

I was sorry for Kathleen, and worried, because she was one of the TB suspects, but I was also looking forward to the trip. I hadn't been off the island since Christmas, and this would be my first visit to Alert Bay since returning in the fall. I could only wish it were to be under happier circumstances.

Kathleen was bundled up warmly, and we were underway early Friday afternoon. Blackfish Sound was choppy, but otherwise the trip was uneventful.

We went straight to the hospital, where Kathleen was examined by Dr. Ryall, then admitted as a patient. My duty done, I had some time to visit for a while, so I arranged with the two boys to pick me up Sunday afternoon.

"Two o'clock at the hospital wharf," I told them.

I stayed with the Todds, shopped on Saturday and then had dinner at the Nimpkish Hotel with Lou Layhew and Kay Weymouth, one of the Alert Bay teachers. It was a novelty eating in a public place and ordering from a menu.

Boy, am I bushed, I thought.

Sunday after lunch, I checked on Kathleen. She still looked too pale, but at least she was where she should be and getting proper care. Which was more than I could say for a lot of the sick people I was taken all over the countryside to see. I left her, feeling very positive.

At the hospital wharf, I found Lou and Kay waiting to see me off. I almost wished the boys would be late so I could visit longer, but this time they were right on time.

"Hope you make it," Lou said dubiously, when he saw the shabby old craft chugging up to the dock. But I was unfazed by it. I was becoming so accustomed to this mode of travel, I seldom gave it much thought. As far as I could see, there were no obvious holes in the hull, and the engine was running, so it was about what I expected.

"Don't worry," I said, stepping confidently onto the boat. "I've been on worse than this."

They both waved as the boat pulled away from the wharf. I waved back until they were out of sight.

I sat on the ledge in the stern and watched the hospital and the totem poles disappear. It was a fairly pleasant day, not too cold, with a bright afternoon sun. With any luck, I had no more than three and a half hours to sit on my hard seat.

I watched vaguely as the familiar shapes and colours of the islands slipped by and I knew Blackfish Sound was close at hand. Then daydreams took me away from the present and my surroundings. I lost track of time and place, for how long I didn't know.

Suddenly I was yanked from my reverie by the roar of water. This shouldn't be, I thought, not on such a calm day. I looked around. Blackfish Sound had vanished and nothing looked familiar. The boys, whose existence I'd temporarily forgotten, were nosing the boat into a narrow channel between strange rocky islands.

Ahead was a confined passage in which the sea churned and boiled, forming a great witch's cauldron of surging green water.

Riptide!

It reached out, clawed at our flimsy craft, then wrenched it into the maelstrom. Whirlpools, deceptively smooth around the circumference, swirled in great circles, then cascaded into a sucking vortex. I could see holes in the dead centre of each whirling pool—funnels descending into the bowels of the earth for all I knew.

The hair on the back of my neck stood straight up as the sickening, gurgling sound filled my ears. The boat shuddered and spun like an old man hit by a prizefighter. Was the engine still running? I couldn't tell. Nothing could be heard save the ceaseless roar of the ocean.

I thought the boys had taken leave of their senses to have come this way and they must be as terrified as I was. I wrested my gaze from the threatening tide and glanced at them. Instead of their eyes bugging out, as I'm sure mine were, they were manoeuvring the boat around the eddies in a very masterful way. They skilfully negotiated the final run, then we were away from the islands, in open water.

I sat limp and exhausted while the young mariners started talking cheerfully. Once we reached the comparatively calm water, when I could get the wheels and cogs of my brain functioning again, I looked behind. The whitewater was plainly visible in the narrow channel between the islands, but which islands they were, I never knew. In some way, known only to these fellows, we were passing Freshwater Bay and heading into Village Pass. Only then did I start to breathe normally again.

We reached the brown house, and I wobbled onto the float, my knees still knocking. When I offered the boys the money to pay for my transportation, they said in unison, "No. You keep."

With that, they turned the boat around and chugged away.

I stood on the edge of the float, watching their departure and completely in the dark as to why they'd refused my fare. Usually they were eager for the money we paid for our trips to and from Alert Bay.

And why had they taken this roundabout, hair-raising side trip? Was it to give me a thrill or was it to test their navigating ability? As not one word of explanation came my way, I never found out.

Life and the Party

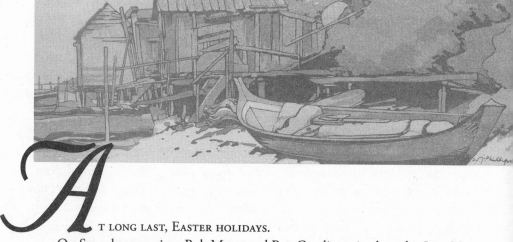

T LONG LAST, EASTER HOLIDAYS.

On Saturday morning, Bob Mann and Ray Gravlin arrived on the *June M* to take me to Manns' camp. Although the camp was only a few hours journey from Village Island, it took two days to get there. We stopped at Simoom Sound around noon and spent the rest of the day visiting with Joyce and Irene Dunseith. In the evening, we all went to a party at Echo Bay. Its name was derived from the way sounds bounced off the sheer rock cliffs that guarded one side of the bay's entrance. First settled in 1912, at one time it had been the site of a mill. It was a port of call for the Union Steamships, and in 1936 boasted a store and hotel.

As was the custom in these parts, the party went on all night. Dawn came and people either retired to their boats or started for home. But a few hardy souls in our group decided to go on a picnic.

Our destination was Broughton Park, on an island of the same name.

Among my friends were the Wilson family, whom I'd met during my visits with the Manns. Jack, Tommy and Rita lived with their parents, "Mom" and "Pop" Wilson, on Minstrel Island. They were of Irish stock, hardworking, big-hearted and jolly. They were pioneers in B.C.'s logging and fishing industry.

It was the Wilsons' boat, a sturdy tug, that led the flotilla to the picnic. The smaller gas boats were towed behind, travelling the easy way. Jack eased the tug into a bay and nosed its prow onto the beach, which shelved off sharply into deep water. We scrambled onto the shore, then climbed a steep bank. At the top we found a level, grassy area surrounded on three sides by tall trees.

In the long ago, this had been an Indian encampment. The cleared area had been the site of a longhouse; its rectangular shape was still clearly defined by mounds of white clamshells. Trees surrounding the site provided protection from the winds in winter and cool shade in summer. The island-dotted sea was visible in three directions and would be an ideal place for a lookout. A sentry, standing on the steep bank above the beach or better still, high in the branches of a tall tree, could warn his people well ahead of the approach of an enemy.

Mounds of clamshell indicated that an ancient people inhabited this place for a long time. Every other sign of their existence had vanished, but they had left this lovely green and shady spot for us to enjoy our picnic and we made the most of it.

By the time we arrived at the Manns' on Sunday evening, I was exhausted. All this socializing was such a switch from my cloistered life on Village Island. I lacked the stamina for it.

Not so the hardy Manns. "We're having a party here next Saturday," Kate told me minutes after our arrival.

"So I heard. Surely, I'll be rested by then," I said as I departed for the bedroom.

Kate's spring garden was in full bloom, and it seemed impossible a year had gone by since I'd first set eyes on this place. I was still amazed by the floating flower garden.

The next couple of days passed quietly, with the men working full-time in the woods. I helped Kate in the cookhouse, mainly as a dishwasher. Then I joined June, her younger brothers and Ray in the rowboat to fish and explore. Once we went ashore and into the woods to watch the logging operations.

There was always something to see or do at the Manns' camp.

It was Wednesday evening. We'd just finished listening to the ten o'clock news on the battery radio. Harry switched it off, and the men straggled out onto the float in the direction of the bunkhouse. The rest of us were preparing for bed in the house when we heard George come back.

"There's a boat coming into the float, Harry," he said. "But I can't make out who it is."

We gathered outside and watched as it came closer.

"Hello, there!" Harry called. No one answered but the craft drew closer.

Harry walked along the float and caught the line the man on board threw him. He made the boat fast, then stepped into the well deck. The two men talked quietly for a few minutes, and then Harry called, "Kate, come here!" He sounded urgent, tense.

We watched curiously as Kate stepped aboard and a woman and two little boys emerged from the shadows of the cabin. Kate helped them off the boat. The woman seemed to wilt when she stepped onto the float, and the two boys started to whimper.

As Kate brought them into the house, she said, "Someone put the kettle on, please. She needs a hot drink."

Soon the pale, quiet woman was sipping hot tea beside the kitchen range, while the two boys gulped mugs of cocoa. They were blond, blue-eyed cherubs who clung tenaciously to their mother's knee. Bobby was three years old and his brother, Davie, was 14 months.

Kate went into the pantry and I followed her.

"What's happened?" I whispered.

"I'm sorry I couldn't explain, but I didn't want to talk in front of her," she replied in low tones. "It's terribly sad ... Their oldest boy wandered off this afternoon." She paused briefly and took a breath. "He fell into a slough. When they found him, he had drowned. He was just five years old. They have his body on the boat."

"Oh, Kate! How awful!"

"Yes. It doesn't get any worse than losing a child."

"No," I agreed, and for a moment we were both silent. "Have they come far?" I asked. I couldn't help but think of the agony of a long trip with your dead child only inches away.

"A long way. From way up Wakeman Sound," she said, slowly shaking her head. "It must have been a nightmare trip for them."

"What's going to happen now?"

"I don't know. Harry and the men are talking about it. They'll come up with a plan."

"Maybe I could help with her little boys," I suggested, wanting to do something.

"All right." She nodded. "And I'll go and see what's been decided."

We went back into the kitchen, and I coaxed Bobby and Davie into the living room. They were sleepy and tired, so I tucked them up on the chesterfield and stayed with them while the others gathered in the kitchen.

Presently Ray and Norman joined me.

"What's happening?" I asked.

"The parents are taking the boy's body to Alert Bay and Kate and Bob are going with them," Norman said. "They're in no condition to go alone."

"Harry and George are going to Wakeman Sound," Ray continued. "It seems this fellow had a contract to salvage some old logging equipment, and a tug is on the way to pick it up. He hasn't finished the job, and there's no way to intercept the tug. George and Harry are going to try and get there in time to finish up and load it for him."

"And the little ones?" I asked, stroking a sleeping blond head.

"I'm not sure if they plan on taking them or not," Ray said.

"Why couldn't we look after them?" I suggested. "I think it would be easier on all concerned."

"Good idea," Norman said. "Between you, me and Ray here, I'm sure we can handle it."

It was after midnight before everything was arranged. Kate and Bob left with the parents, heading south to Alert Bay, while Harry and George, aboard the *June M*, headed for Wakeman Sound.

After they'd gone, Norman and Ray helped me carry the children into the room where I slept, for I felt they wouldn't be so lonely if they were with me. I undressed them, put them into bed, then gingerly crawled in between them. None of us were used to such close quarters. They fussed and squirmed for most of the night, and I was thoroughly kicked in the ribs and stomach. I did manage a *few* hours sleep. When I wakened, I lay on the pillow looking at the chubby faces of Bobby and Davie. I smiled lazily at them while they stared, wide-eyed, at me. Then, suddenly, I sat up, all vestiges of sleep gone.

"Horrors!" I exclaimed to Bobby and Davie.

"Glaggle," replied Davie.

Here I was, chief cook and bottle-washer for a logging camp, as well as nursemaid for two strange children. Granted, the logging operations had been temporarily suspended and the crew depleted, but it was still a formidable job for a girl who couldn't boil water, let alone flip pancakes. Despite my mother's best efforts in this regard, my knowledge of cooking ran an extremely short gamut, from coconut macaroons to opening a can of soup. I didn't feel this covered the meat-and-potato situation in which I now found myself.

But for the present, the most important items on the agenda were Bobby and Davie. They didn't seem *too* unhappy in their new surroundings, although Davie was whimpering. I decided a trip to the bathroom and breakfast would likely cheer him up. I stoked up the fire in the kitchen range and ran water in the tub. I was about to put them in when Norman appeared at the kitchen door.

"How are the little guys?" he asked.

"They're fine," I said. "I was just going to put them in the bathtub."

"Let me do that," he offered.

Soon I heard great splashing and gales of laughter.

"Where are their clothes?" he called from behind the bathroom door.

I took him the clean clothes, and presently he appeared with the boys dressed and shining.

"You're quite the paternal type," I said.

"I like kids," he answered.

And so, between us, Norman and I looked after the boys. Maybe because they had the undivided attention of one, the other or both of us, they were as good as gold. I was terrified they might fall off the edge of the float, so we never let them out of our sight.

Somehow we managed to eat three square meals. Everyone rallied to the cause, and with helping hands and no end of good advice, the day went smoothly. Then, toward evening, June reminded us of something we'd all forgotten.

"What about the party Saturday night?" she asked.

"My gosh, the party," we answered in chorus.

Kate had sent out invitations by way of the gas-boat grapevine a couple of weeks ago. There was no way to rescind them. The party would be on, so we might as well face it. It was impossible to tell how many might come. There could be anywhere from 20 to 80, and at this time of year, it was more apt to be the latter. It all depended on the weather and how far the grapevine extended. The question was, could we manage the necessary preparations?

Help arrived that evening in the petite form of Joyce Dunseith. Irene and Joyce, along with a couple of girls from Echo Bay, had gone on an overnight fishing trip to Kingcome Inlet, travelling in Irene's boat.

When the girls called by on their way home, we told them of the events of the last couple of days.

"And now we have to get ready for the party Saturday night. How will we ever get all that baking done when none of us can cook?" I was worried and it showed.

"I'll stay and help," Joyce volunteered with a smile.

"That's wonderful, Joyce. You're a lifesaver."

Next day, with Joyce at the helm in the cookhouse, we started on a mountainous task—or so it appeared to us. Although no woman came to these affairs empty-handed, we knew Kate always had plenty of food on hand. And we intended to do her proud.

Ray decided he was going to bake a cake.

"After all, I can read, and anyone who can read should be able to follow a recipe," he said seriously in his best teacher-voice.

Although it took a long time to measure and stir, beat and pour—as he checked each step in meticulous detail—the cake turned out, if not a masterpiece, at least well enough to satisfy Ray. When it came out of the oven, he beamed with pride, while we waited in suspense until we were sure it wasn't going to collapse with a soggy hollow in the middle.

"I'll make the icing," Norman announced.

"Have you ever made icing before?" I asked.

Norman shrugged. "No, but I've watched my mother and there's nothing to it."

The icing wasn't too lumpy, but somehow he overdid the quantity, so we used what was left on cookies and cupcakes, then ate the rest. Most of our cookies were edible, although some were hard as bullets. Even the seagulls wouldn't eat them. We peeled pots of potatoes for salad and boiled dozens of eggs, some for the salad, some for sandwich filling. I made coconut macaroons, which was my one claim to fame in the culinary line. They turned out beautifully, all softly golden and light as air.

After we'd prepared the mounds of food, we started cleaning the house, the school and the cookhouse. Everything was swished into a semblance of order, on the surface at least.

Harry and George arrived home Friday evening. Since Wednesday night, they'd travelled to Wakeman Sound, finished the salvaging job and loaded the tug. In all that time, they hadn't had a wink of sleep. Such was the spirit of the coast dwellers. Upon their arrival, they had something to eat, then fell, bone-weary, into bed.

Kate, Bob and the children's father returned Saturday morning, leaving the mother with Mrs. Dunseith at Simoom. Norman and I looked on sadly as the father gathered up his small sons for leave-taking, for, in a very short time, we'd grown attached to these blond cherubs.

Both Bob and Kate were physically and emotionally exhausted from the trip.

"What about the party tonight?" asked Kate, the weariness evident in her voice. "We'll never be ready."

"Don't you worry about a thing," we told her. "Go to bed and get some rest. We have everything under control—we hope." I added the last to tease, but it was half a jest at best.

Kate was too tired to argue but did manage a wan smile before heading for her bed.

The party was mere hours away, but by the time the first boat was heard in the distance, we were ready. It turned out to be one of the larger gatherings of the year. By ten o'clock the floats were jumping and the party was in full swing. It was a great success.

The following morning my restful holiday was at an end, and I was so tired I could barely see. I'd had fun, but lurking in a corner of my mind was the memory of raw tragedy—the loss of a child. The danger of accident, and even death, was something many of the coastal people faced every day of their lives, and always with the knowledge there might be no help or means of communication within miles.

Yes. Life, like the party, had to go on, but at times the cost was high—tragically high.

The Radio and the Maple Tree

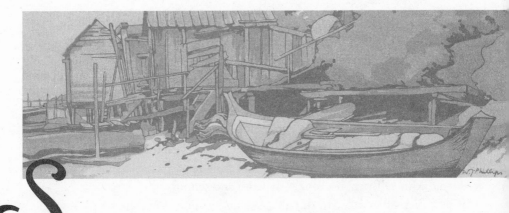

SINCE THE ABDICATION OF EDWARD VIII of England, the new royal family had become our intimate friends. The papers and periodicals from Great Britain were filled with pictures and articles about the king and queen and the two young princesses, Elizabeth and Margaret. Coronation plans were going on apace, and I'm sure the powers that be in England would have been surprised by the furor it was causing in this remote spot on the B.C. coast.

We discussed the royal family and all their kin ad nauseam, from the dowager Queen right down the line to the last possible link with the British throne. Not only this, but we had the exciting prospect of a radio in the offing. And as if that were not enough, there were to be coronation-day celebrations in Alert Bay in which the whole countryside would participate. This was more excitement, all at one time, than we'd had during the better part of the two years I'd been a resident on Village Island.

Before the royal romance and the abdication, week-old or even month-old news was accepted. However, since December, having listened faithfully to Harry Mountain's radio, week-old news was now too stale. There was constant talk about getting a radio of our own. And when it was learned King George VI would broadcast his coronation speech, the plans were quickly put on the front burner.

Miss O'Brien made a trip to Alert Bay to consult with Mr. Earl Anfield, the principal of St. Michael's Residential School, and he had ordered the radio for her from Vancouver. Now it was only a matter of time until we had our own source of news. I admit I was as enthusiastic about this purchase as the G.A.s.

"I've heard from Mr. Anfield," Miss O'Brien announced one day. "He and Mr. Todd are coming to install the radio as soon as it arrives, so we must decide on the best possible position for it in the sitting room."

At last the great day arrived.

The Indian department boat *Gikumi* eased to the float, and Mr. Todd, Mr. Anfield and the radio—with all its component parts—came ashore. The chosen corner had been cleared, so the men immediately set about setting up the apparatus. It was placed on a table by the window, with its heavy batteries set on the floor beneath. The aerial was hooked up, then strung out the window to a pole on the roof. The G.A.s stood back while this was going on, quite awed, for it looked so technical and complicated.

"When the radio is not in use, be sure to detach the batteries. If you don't they'll run down, and then you'll have to have them recharged," Mr. Anfield told Miss O'Brien, his tone instructive and serious.

"Yes, of course, Mr. Anfield," she nodded, but I felt she wasn't at all clear as to what was going on. She stared at the radio as if at any moment it would go up in smoke.

"I think we're ready," announced Mr. Todd, nodding at the scientific wonder in our midst. We stood by expectantly.

He switched it on and adjusted the volume. Squealing static filled the air at first, then finally music. After giving us a demonstration on the care and control of the radio, the gentlemen departed. Now the G.A.s were on their own with this symbol of progress. It might be a taste of modern living and a one-way contact with the outside world, but I sensed they were both a bit afraid of the monster.

It was never used except for the evening news, and the procedure quickly became a ritual. When the announcer's voice came through the static that accompanied every broadcast, the volume was immediately turned up. It had to be so loud for Miss O'Brien's sake that I found it hard to bear. After a few times, I retired to my room where I could hear the whole broadcast comfortably through the walls.

Now that the radio was installed, we turned our attentions to the coronation-day celebrations. Alert Bay would be the focal point, and all the scattered communities would be taking part. The opening event would be a parade, and it was expected to be the largest ever seen in the area. Each school in the district would be represented, including the Mamalilikulla Indian Day School.

This was all very thrilling, although the children weren't too clear at first as to what was going on. After all, the coronation of a king in England was beyond the comprehension of Native children living on an island reserve in B.C. However, once they understood what a parade was and learned of all the festivities that were to accompany it, they talked of nothing else.

There were, more or less, a dozen children on the roll, unless they were searching for seaweed or clam digging—then I was lucky if four or five turned up. But now, with so much excitement in store, the attendance was more regular. And perhaps it helped when I said firmly, "You must all come to school every day if you want to be in the parade, for we have a lot of practising to do."

With this admonition, seaweed and clams were finally shoved into the background. Temporarily.

"How are you going to have the school represented?" asked Miss O'Brien.

"I don't know yet. I'd welcome any ideas."

So we discussed the pros and cons. Pros and cons were served up with every meal, mulled over and discarded. Mainly the problem was lack of materials. The teachers in Alert Bay had a source of supply readily available, whereas I had to use whatever was on the island, essentially nothing at all. Time was slipping by, and I was becoming a bit frantic. What could I possibly do that would be simple and pertinent to the Indian people?

Then an idea came to me. At first it seemed so simple it bordered on silly. At supper one night, I said, "I think I might have an idea for the parade."

"Do tell, Miss B.," Miss O'Brien said eyeing me over her teacup.

"Yes. What is it?" queried Miss Dibben.

"If the parents will permit, I was thinking of having the children wear their family blankets. Each family would be represented. The blankets are wonderfully colourful; they should make a nice showing."

After some consideration, Miss O'Brien agreed. "Yes, I think that's the best idea to date. Of course, we'll have to consult the parents."

Next day I conducted a door-to-door canvass and found all the parents in agreement, so everyone was happy with this simple plan.

I'd seen most of the blankets at the potlatch, where they had shown up so beautifully in the glow of the firelight, with the buttons sparkling and flashing in all the rainbow hues. The first blankets had been introduced many years before by the Hudson's Bay Company, and the Indian people had quickly adapted them to their own use as ceremonial robes. There was one rarity in the collection, an item of artistry and unusual beauty. This was a Chilkat blanket, a most prized possession.

The Chilkat tribe is a branch of the Tlingit Nation, which occupied the area of the coast we know as the Alaska Panhandle and of which Skagway, Alaska, is now a centre. The Mamalilikullas of Village Island were members of the Kwakwaka'wakw Nation, centred around B.C.'s central mainland coast and the adjacent parts of Vancouver Island. So it was always a mystery as to how this blanket reached this destination. Perhaps it belonged

The Chilkat blanket in this photo is the same one worn by Henry Bell in the earlier 1910 community house photo. It was made at Fort Rupert by a Walas Kwakiutl woman, who learned the weave from a Tlingit slave over a century ago.

to an unfortunate prisoner captured in some long-ago war.

The Chilkat blanket was one of the few textiles woven by the Indian people. A pale yellow and blue combined with a lot of black on a background of greyish-white, it was made from mountain goat hair wrapped around a core of cedar bark. The stylized design, a most intricate one, was surrounded by a plain five-sided border and finished with a deep fringe, measuring at least 12 inches. The weaving was close, making the blanket heavy and, I'm sure, waterproof.

Each child brought his or her blanket to school so we could organize ourselves and start practising. I lined them up according to height, and, with Gertrude's help and advice, draped the blankets in approved Indian style. Some of the little ones were slightly swamped, but with a few extra folds at the top, the lower edge didn't drag on the ground. Finally, we marched along the village path to the far end and back again, much to the amusement and delight of the people who came out to watch and applaud.

"Somehow we must be identified," I said that evening, "I'd like to make a banner of some kind."

"I might have some material you could use," Miss O'Brien told me. "I'll see what odds and ends I have tucked away."

She delved into her cache of extras and brought out a few yards of unbleached cotton and some strips of red fabric.

"This will work just fine," I said, now enthusiastic about what a splash the school would make. "We could sew red borders on the white cotton and print the name of the school in blue."

Little by little the banner evolved. We stitched the red cotton in folds on either end of the white material to make loops through which to slip poles.

One of the village boys, a talented carver, made two Thunderbird totems about five inches high. These were painted and mounted on top of the poles. Then I blocked out in large letters:

MAMALILIKULLA INDIAN DAY SCHOOL
VILLAGE ISLAND, B.C.

We coloured them blue. In the upper corners, the boys drew Indian motifs, and we painted them in traditional colours. When it was finished, the overall effect was striking. The name and designs were bold and colourful and left no doubt as to where we had come from. We could march proud.

Once the banner was complete, we had a full dress rehearsal, with Wilfred and Matthew, the tallest boys, leading off. We marched smartly through the

Some of Hughina's students are shown wearing their family button blankets, all ready for their dress rehearsal.

The symbolic designs on the backs of the children's blankets are impressive.

village, with the banner flying high, while the G.A.s and the people again came out to watch. We were a resounding success.

I went to Alert Bay on a Saturday to receive instructions regarding the parade and to get a list of the songs we were to sing. It was planned that the children from all the schools in the area would congregate on the grounds of St. Michael's Residential School after the parade to form a massed choir. They would sing "O Canada," "The Maple Leaf Forever," "Land of Hope and Glory" and "God Save the King."

After I'd dealt with official business, I visited with Kay and Percy and some of the other teachers. It was then I learned of all the elaborate preparations they were making for their classes. There were to be kings and queens and princesses in crowns and robes. Britannia would be there in all her glory, along with all sorts of symbolic costumes. The teachers were going to no end of work and trouble.

"What are you doing with your kids?" Kay asked.

When I told her they were wearing their family blankets, it sounded so uninspired I was embarrassed.

"But we have a beautiful banner," I added quickly, trying desperately to make our entry seem a bit more exciting.

I had the feeling she was not impressed.

I returned to the village, feeling deflated, but it was much too late to change—even if I could think of something more grand. All we could do was carry on with the marching and practising the songs. The G.A.s were so enthusiastic, I hadn't the heart to tell them of my misgivings.

"I think we should have a ceremony to commemorate this great occasion," Miss O'Brien said to me one day. "Something which will make a lasting impression on the children, remind them of the significance of the coronation and instill patriotism."

"What did you have in mind?" I asked, unable to imagine what would accomplish this lofty ambition.

"I think we should plant a tree," she said. "A maple tree would be appropriate, and it would be a living monument to our new king."

As this was obviously important to Miss O'Brien, I nodded my agreement and for a time put aside my worries about the Alert Bay parade.

Miss O'Brien scoured the woods and found a sturdy sapling which the bigger boys helped her dig up. Then she had them prepare a hole near the flagpole, and at the appointed hour for planting, she came to the school. The children, dressed for the occasion in their family blankets, stood in a semicircle around the spot where the tree was to be planted. They looked very solemn, as befitted such a patriotic moment, but I secretly wondered if the significance of this event had any real meaning for them. I'm sure they couldn't imagine the need for planting another tree on an island filled with them.

Miss O'Brien made a speech on the theme of duty to king and love of country. Then, with the help of the boys, she planted the tree. We raised the flag and sang "God Save the King."

The ceremony was complete. If Lucy the cow didn't decide it was salad, King George would have his tree.

Parades–Ugh!

As the Alert Bay coronation celebrations drew near, Mr. Todd gave me an extra day off to arrange transportation. He was all too aware of my difficulties in this regard.

Coronation day was Wednesday, and the parade was to start at nine o'clock sharp. As I had to be there to conduct my little brood, I'd planned to go on Tuesday. But as was often the case on Village Island, my travel plans were changed.

I learned the village people had decided to go en masse on Monday, so I knew, by Tuesday, the island would be deserted, no people, no children and certainly no boats. So, all of a sudden, I found myself packing my bag, rolling up the precious banner and scrambling for a boat. I chose one from a neighbouring village. It was large and clean, and looked reasonably safe. I counted 14 passengers on board. This time I decided to sit inside, out of the weather, for I had to protect the banner. It was a raw, cold day and the Blackfish Sound crossing was very rough—rough enough to make five of the Natives seasick. But not me!—which just goes to show what a hardened old mariner I had become.

I'd been invited to stay with the Todds, but when I walked in, Mrs. Todd exclaimed bluntly, "What on earth are you doing here today? I already have a houseful."

"I'm sorry," I said, embarrassed and somewhat disconcerted. "But it was either come today or swim tomorrow. There isn't a single boat left in the village. All the people and the kids are here."

"Well, if you don't mind sharing a bed, it's all right," she said in her usual forthright manner. "But I'll have to put you in with Miss Thomas. She's here from Cape Mudge and the Hallidays are here from Kingcome Inlet, so all my extra beds are full."

"Whatever you have is fine with me. And I really am sorry," I said, wishing I had an alternative.

Now the sleeping arrangements were settled, Mrs. Todd seemed to soften. "Yes, well, have a cup of tea now. You look cold."

I took it gratefully. "The weather doesn't look too promising, does it?" I said, sipping my tea and peering through the window at the leaden sky.

"No, it doesn't," she answered. "And if anything happens to ruin the parade, I don't know what Mr. T. will do. He's been planning it for weeks, and it's been such a lot of work."

It was grey and gloomy for the rest of Monday, but Tuesday was a fairly pleasant day, so everyone's spirits rose.

The community was bursting at the seams. The hotels were full and anyone who had an extra bed found it occupied. There were dozens of boats tied to every available wharf, and more anchored offshore. Many of the boats had sleeping quarters, so the lucky owners had no worries as to where they would spend the night. The whole town was more active than I'd ever seen it.

One of the projects of the festivities was a house-decorating contest. As I had time to spare on Tuesday, I said to Mrs. Todd, "Would you like me to decorate the house?"

"I certainly have no time for such things, but go ahead if you want to. I don't know what you'll use, though," she said, with questionable enthusiasm.

Just then Mr. Todd came from the office for a cup of coffee.

"I'd like to decorate the house, Mr. Todd. Have you anything I could use?"

"Well now, I think there's some leftover bunting and flags," he said. "I'll get them for you."

I'd thought of doing this just to fill in time, but soon Mr. Todd was up the ladder hammering tacks and draping red, white and blue bunting between veranda posts. We added strings of small flags and a single large flag in the centre. Then we stood back and admired our handiwork. Impressive, or so I thought.

"Come and see what we've done," I called to Mrs. Todd.

"All right, but I think it's a waste of time," she said as she came out onto the porch. Nevertheless, when she viewed it from the roadway, she admitted it looked "presentable enough." I think she was secretly pleased with our labour, as most all of the buildings in Alert Bay had some sort of decoration. The whole community looked very gay and festive.

The atmosphere was anything but festive when we awakened the following morning. The changeable weather of the past week had—as we had all secretly dreaded—turned to torrential rain.

Mr. Todd was most upset at this turn of events. I felt terrible for him. He'd spent weeks organizing for today—an onerous undertaking, considering the widely scattered communities and difficult communications.

"Maybe it'll ease up by nine o'clock," he said, trying to sound optimistic. "Anyway, we'll have to carry on. Can't change plans at this stage."

He was right. Rain or no rain, the parade must go on as scheduled. Too many people had worked long and hard to disappoint them now.

The marshalling point was the playground of the Indian day school. From there we would march the length of Alert Bay's one and only street, a walk of about two miles, to the grounds of St. Michael's Residential School. I left the Todds about 8:30 and squelched along the road with the banner over my shoulder, rolled up tightly against the weather. When I reached the school, I rounded up my group, who were all on time for a change. They clustered around me, wrapped snugly in their blankets. At that moment I'd have gladly worn one too, for the rain was heavy and relentless. Although I was wearing a raincoat, a beret and rubber boots, I might as well have been in a bathing suit. In no time my beret was sodden. I could feel the moisture creeping under the collar of my coat, the dampness soon spreading over my shoulders and chest. My feet were drenched before we reached the starting point.

The parade entrants were gathering, and soon the schoolyard was filled with groups of unhappy people, standing with shoulders hunched, shivering in the downpour. Many of them, representing Indian bands from the outlying villages, were dressed in full tribal regalia. I guessed many of the costumes hadn't seen the light of day for years and many more had *never* been seen by White people. It was a splendid array. Had the day been bright and sunny, to better show off the colours, it would have made a truly exciting spectacle.

People milled about until order was eventually created by Mr. Todd, who blew signals on his whistle while sorting out the various groups. The flag-bearers took their places at the head of the procession, followed by the band. At nine o'clock sharp, the musicians struck up a marching tune, and the parade was underway along the muddy street.

The children and I waited our turn, delaying to the last possible moment the unfurling of our beautiful red, white and blue banner. When our signal came, the boys took the poles proudly and held the banner high, where it

The people standing close to the fence are the Village Islanders (the *Mamalilikulla* banner can be seen at the side). Hughina recalled that the ones standing in front, with the ceremonial cradle adorned with a whale, were from Fort Rupert.

flapped in the wind and driving rain. The children, to my delight, all started on the same foot, and we were off, marching smartly.

As soon as the first big drops hit the banner, the paint began to run. Before we had gone a quarter of a mile, it was wet and soggy, looking more like a dirty old sheet than anything else. The banner and I might be soaked and bedraggled, but not the children. Wrapped in their blankets, they were snug and warm; the weather seemed to have no effect on them whatsoever. I pulled my inadequate coat closer and sloshed along beside them, cold and utterly miserable, wondering if the end would ever come. I was dimly conscious of people lining the street and applause, the sound of which mingled with the rain drumming on my head. The music of the band floated back through the downpour, and I concentrated on putting one foot in front of the other in time to the rhythm. After what seemed an eternity, the residential school came into view; the end of this ghastly hour was in sight. Finally, we tramped through the totem pole gateposts and onto the school grounds.

I looked down at the dozen black-eyed children now clustered around me, and they grinned happily, their faces damp and shining.

I couldn't help but smile. "You did very, *very* well," I said, through chattering teeth. "And you marched beautifully."

"You're wet, Miss B.," said Wilfred Hanuse in innocent understatement. I was waterlogged.

"Yes, and freezing to death," I answered, touching his dark head. "How about you? Are you cold?" I said to the children.

"No," they chorused. "Blankets nice and warm."

How I envied them. The blankets, an idea I'd thought uninspired, had probably saved the youngsters from pneumonia. I glanced up.

"Our poor banner didn't do so well. It's a mess," I said.

"Yeah," agreed the children. "Too bad."

It was still flying high between the Thunderbirds, but now its blue paint ran in rivulets over the white fabric. The designs in the upper corners were indiscernible blobs of mixed colour, and the carved and painted Thunderbirds were a pale washed-out grey.

The last of the parade straggled into the grounds. A more dejected congregation of people and children one could not imagine. There were poor little would-be queens and princesses in golden crowns with gold paint running down their faces. Royal robes were sopping wet and filmy dresses were streaked with mud. I learned many entries had dropped out before they reached the end of the route; some hadn't started at all.

"May I have your attention, please," Mr. Anfield called through the loudspeaker. "We'll try and get this over with as quickly as possible, so everyone can go home and dry out. But first we'll announce the names of the prizewinners. However, everything else has been cancelled for today."

There were prizes for the most original entry, the best comic entry and the best Native display. Each announcement was followed by applause and cheers. I clapped vigorously, not only to cheer them on, but to warm my hands.

Then I heard Mr. Anfield saying " … and a case of canned milk goes to Mr. Todd as first prize for house decoration."

Mr. Todd was standing beside Mr. Anfield, and he looked in my direction, giving me a broad wink. I smiled to myself, wondering what Mrs. Todd would

After the parade, the Mamalilikulla banner remains intact (except that the colour ran in the torrential rain) as the elders await announcement of the prizes.

Traditional button blankets look striking on these parade participants.

say. She would be the one to reap the benefits of our labour after all.

The list droned on and the rain poured down. I was only half-listening as my thoughts were fixated on the warm towels and hot tea to be found back at the Todds'.

"And now we come to the school entries from Alert Bay and surrounding areas," boomed Mr. Anfield. "The first prize of $10 goes to the Mamalilikulla Indian Day School, Village Island."

I looked up with a start, scarcely believing my ears. Then I looked at my blanketed children, who were jumping up and down—and yelling.

"That's us!"

"We won first prize!"

"Hooray for us!"

Hooray for the blankets, I thought, as I again praised the children for their wonderful marching.

Just then I saw Kay walking toward me, looking just as wet and miserable as me.

"Congratulations," she said graciously.

"Thanks, Kay. But I'm sure we only won because the blankets didn't fall apart in this miserable torrent. I think we won by default."

She laughed. "I wouldn't say so," she replied. "It was an appropriate entry, and your banner was beautiful before it got wet."

"Maybe so, but I'll always feel we won because of the weather."

I dismissed the children and trudged back to the Todds' through the deluge. As I squelched along the road with the soggy banner over my shoulder, my step was lighter. Two first prizes in one day were pleasant to think about, no matter how we got them.

I went into the kitchen and started peeling off my wet coat when Mrs. Todd came in. She'd watched the parade from the shelter of her front porch.

"How did it go?" she asked.

"We won first prize for schools," I told her. "And did you know you won a case of canned milk?"

"I did?"

"Yes," I said. "Your house took first prize for decoration."

"Well, of all things … " She looked pleasantly surprised. Her thanks were genuine, and I felt less guilty for being the unexpectedly early guest.

She was still smiling when she said, "As for you, young lady, you'd best get out of those wet clothes while I make you a hot drink."

My raincoat was damp and clammy and my beret so wet I had to put it over a dinner plate to stretch it back into shape. When I removed my blazer and the scarf I'd worn around my neck, Mrs. Todd looked at me in alarm.

"What happened to you?" she asked, staring hard at my sweater.

I looked down at my bosom, where it appeared I'd been stabbed in the chest! A great red patch spread over the front of my white sweater—a sweater I'd knitted slavishly so I'd have something new to wear in the parade.

"It's the red scarf," I cried. "It's soaking wet and the dye has run."

"Never mind it now. Take it off and get dry," advised Mrs. Todd in her terse way. "As for the sweater, we'll see what we can do later."

What we could do was nothing at all, so for the rest of the time I wore my sweater backward, as luckily, it was the same coming and going. Under my blazer the red stain didn't show at all.

By Thursday the rain had let up enough to allow some of the delayed sporting events to be run off in the residential school grounds. There were all manner of foot races covering all age groups. After the races, Kay, Sadie and I, along with the rest of the spectators, walked down to the beach to watch the boat races.

The first race was for gas boats, and the course was the circumnavigation of Cormorant Island. A dozen or more boats lined up in the bay, and at the crack of the starter's gun, the engines growled into action with roars, bangs and popping backfires. Then they were off in a cloud of spray, and I was surprised to see how fast some of them could travel. They *never* travelled that fast when *I* was aboard. Once the boats were out of sight around the end of the island, the excitement was over for the time being. It would be a while before they'd appear again in the opposite direction.

Next, the war canoes lined up in the bay. These old canoes, with their graceful lines, high prows and brightly painted figureheads, were large enough to hold a dozen men. The Indians were skilled boatmen, and it was thrilling

Hughina noted on the back of this photo: "The end of the canoe race: I think Kingcome won. The boys from here, New Vancouver and Turnour Island (all in one canoe) were second. They looked so nice as they all wore yellow shirts. They were the only ones who had a uniform."

to watch the canoes gliding over the water, paddles flashing rhythmically in perfect unison.

The war canoes were followed by the dugouts. These small craft, which had been hollowed out of a straight-grained log, were not as spectacular as the war canoes, but when paddled by a couple of sturdy boys, had great speed. They fairly flew over the water, light as leaves. The spectators, strung out along the beach, shouted and cheered as their favourite crossed the finish line.

Just as the canoe races ended, we again heard the sound of the gas boats as they neared the last point. They roared into sight then, making a mad dash for the finish line, while the great war canoes and the dugouts stood by giving

Jimmy Sewid sits at left at the front of this canoe, practising for the coronation ceremonies. Simon Beans, the Hanuse brothers, Robby Bell and other Village Islanders man the oars. Hughina had written on the back of this photo: "Jimmy Sewid ... is one of the very finest boys around here. Everyone likes him. Believe it or not, he's been married since he was about 15 or 16 and is the father of a family of four."

them a clear path for home. As the gas boats raced past them, the contrast between the ancient and the modern mode of travel was indeed startling.

The next day was Friday, which meant I'd been away from Village Island for almost a week. Probably in few parts of the British Empire had there been such an extended celebration for the coronation of King George VI. And still none of the Village Island people made any move to return home. Without transportation, I was obliged to stay another day and I intended to enjoy it. The weather was clear enough to hold the previously rained-out football and baseball games, so we watched them all.

The grand finale was a dance in the community hall. By Saturday, when I finally boarded a boat for the village, I was worn out from the week's events.

In addition, I had a full-blown head cold.

My sorry condition wasn't lost on the G.A.s on my return to the island.

"Miss B., you always look as though you need a day in bed after one of your outings," Miss O'Brien said, wagging a finger at me. She wasn't smiling, and I wasn't sure if she was serious or not.

"I know, Miss O'Brien, but you've no idea what I went through during the parade," I said, quickly adding with a bright smile, "But the school took first prize. We won $10. The children were perfect, just perfect."

"That's wonderful. Congratulations, dear," she replied, mollified by this exciting news. "We'll have to decide on something very special to buy the school."

As I closed the door of my bedroom behind me, I could almost hear the pros and cons buzzing in her head.

Then I carefully unrolled the ruined banner and removed the rain-washed Thunderbirds from its folds. I would keep them as souvenirs. In years to come they would remind me of my marching children and their rain-soaked moment of glory.

*T*HE FIRST WEEK AFTER THE big doings in Alert Bay was grim. My head cold lingered and bloomed, and, as if that weren't enough, I was faced with teaching some Saturdays to make up for the extra days I'd had off during the celebrations.

The first Saturday after my week off, I got up as usual, raised the flag and rang the bell, all the while being tempted to go back to bed and forget the whole bally thing. Many of the families were still absent, no doubt carrying on the festivities, so my roll call was down to four. I spent a miserable day, for I was full of sniffles and feeling grouchy and hard done by. I'm sure the poor children in class felt much the same.

I left school in the afternoon to find the usual old gas boat at the float with a couple of teenaged boys aboard.

Here we go again, I thought crossly, as the boys hopped off the boat and came toward me.

"What is it?" I asked, giving my nose a blow and trying to contain my bad temper.

"Cheeky Joe say you come quick," said one of the boys.

"Cheeky Joe! I was under the impression he was keeping everyone healthy with eulachon grease," I said, but my sarcasm was lost on the boys. It didn't make me feel any better either.

I gulped a cup of tea, collected the black bag and boarded the boat. The boys nosed it out into the channel, laughing hilariously at jokes exchanged in Kwak'wala, and ignoring me as usual. But I really didn't mind, for the sun was warm and the air mellow and soothing.

When we arrived at New Vancouver, I went directly to Cheeky Joe's house and knocked on the door. I was about to open it when Cheeky Joe himself appeared, looking hale and hearty.

"What's the trouble here, Joe?"

"Her," he said, indicating a low cot on which lay Mrs. Cheeky Joe. It was my first encounter with his wife. In fact, I was a little surprised to find he had one. As soon as she saw me she started to groan and writhe in agony.

I began with the routine questions.

"Where does it hurt?"

"She got bellyache," Cheeky Joe answered.

"Let's have a look," I said.

First I took her temperature, which was normal, as was her pulse. I poked her tummy all over and found no rebound pain, distension or tenderness.

"What you do to make her better?" demanded Joe.

"I think I'll give her an enema," I said.

"Hokay, hokay. Dat good idea. Yeah," he said, nodding his approval with the gravity of a consulting specialist.

I don't know if he realized what I was going to do, but he grinned enthusiastically and made no move to leave the room.

While I was preparing for the procedure, I looked around the house. Cheeky Joe had festooned every corner, as well as the door and window, with cedar boughs and eagle feathers. I suppose, since none of this medicine had worked on Mrs. Joe, he'd been forced to take a chance on me.

Giving an enema to a groaning, uncooperative woman who couldn't understand English and was lying on a cot not more than a foot off the floor was a back-breaking, nerve-wracking task. When it was over, I made her as comfortable as possible and gave her an Aspirin.

"If she isn't feeling better tomorrow, take her to the doctor in Alert Bay," I told Cheeky Joe, who had watched the whole procedure with keen interest.

"Sure, sure," he agreed, giving me his snaggle-toothed grin.

"I'll leave some pills, but don't give them to her all at once," I instructed. "Just one at a time."

I doled out six Aspirin and some soda mints. Then I gathered up my things and said goodbye to Cheeky Joe and his missus, who was much quieter now.

I trudged along the path through the village, which seemed eerily quiet and deserted, and made my way toward the dock. Once there, I stopped and strained my eyes in disbelief—it was empty!

From where I stood, on a slight rise, I could see every wharf along the village waterfront, and there wasn't a boat of any description to be seen. I panicked for a moment. How was I to get home? Then I spotted two young men farther along the beach.

"Yoo-hoo!" I yelled.

They turned, then sauntered my way. I met them by the dock where the vanished gas boat had been tied.

"Where's the boat that brought me here?" I asked.

"Gone 'Lert Bay," they informed me cheerfully.

"Gone ... " I repeated stupidly. I was too surprised to be angry.

"Yep."

"Are there any other gas boats around?"

"Nope. All boats gone 'Lert Bay." They grinned. Either they were being friendly or laughing at my predicament. I couldn't tell which.

I'd never been in a situation like this before. Whoever came to fetch me always waited to take me back to Village Island. Now, here I was, marooned with Cheeky Joe.

"Look, I have to get back to Village Island. There's got to be a boat around somewhere." I looked around, hoping to see one magically appear, but there was nothing but a few logs bumping the shoreline, and I didn't feel my prowess as a log paddler was up to the job.

I waited while the boys had a long discussion in Kwak'wala. Then they turned and beckoned me; I followed them along the beach for a way. They stopped beside a narrow dugout that had been pulled up in the weeds above high-water mark.

I looked at it in horror.

It was ancient, no more than eight feet long, its centre barely wide enough for one person to kneel and paddle. At one time it might have been a moderately sized tree, but after being adzed, whittled and burned out in the belly, it was a far cry from what I considered even mildly adequate transportation. I was aghast, couldn't take my eyes off it.

"We take you back," one of the boys said cheerfully, nodding at the contraption in the weeds.

"In that?" I couldn't conceive of it floating, let alone carrying three passengers.

"Sure. Be hokay."

They each picked up a paddle and, grasping the canoe, one on either side, pushed it along the sand into the water. I looked at the dugout and then across the water in the direction of Village Island. It wasn't *that* far, I told myself—the truth being there was no choice other than to take a chance on this awful, old antique.

Hughina's lone option to return home across the open channel was in a dugout canoe similar to this one.

The boys were already in the canoe, paddles at the ready, one kneeling in the prow, the other in the centre. The only place left was the stern. I gingerly stepped in, but before I could sit down, the thing tipped sickeningly from side to side. The boys balanced it with the paddles until I squeezed myself in. There was nothing to sit on, so I had to assume a squatting position. It was then I realized there was water in the bottom of the boat.

"It's leaking," I cried in alarm, now certain all of us would wind up on the ocean's rocky bottom.

If the boys heard me, they gave no sign. They were already busy, paddling across the ocean and ignoring me. I watched the water level with horrified eyes, and when it didn't change, I concluded—hopefully—it must be rainwater, collected during our recent downpours.

No matter where it came from, it was mighty uncomfortable to sit in. It didn't help that I was wearing a heavy tweed skirt that soaked up the moisture like a sponge. I couldn't move, wedged tightly in the stern as I was, and I scarcely breathed for fear the aged craft would tip. I sat rigidly, not moving a muscle, while my rear end got colder and wetter by the minute.

The boys laughed and talked while they paddled in the general direction of Village Island which, frankly, I never expected to see again. We skimmed at a fair rate of speed over blessedly calm water, but I hung on to the sides of the boat as if we were in a hurricane. On most trips I'd had with the Native people, I could always appreciate the beauty around me no matter how cold or uncomfortable I was. But not this time. I was too busy saying my prayers, my eyes tightly shut.

I'd no idea how long I sat, cramped, wet and immobile, but as we rounded the end of one of the islands, there was the village—just ahead. Only then did I allow myself the luxury of a deep breath. As we drew closer to land, my vise-like grip began to lessen. With a few more paddle strokes came a grinding sound, and the canoe hit the pebbly beach.

I tried to hoist myself out of the canoe, but I was wedged in so tightly I couldn't move. And whatever signals my brain was sending to my legs were being ignored. I couldn't get any leverage.

The boys hopped out onto the beach and turned to look at me.

"Can you give me a hand, please," I croaked, surprised at the sound of my own voice. It was like nothing I'd ever heard before.

They each took an arm and hefted me to a very wobbly standing position. My knees were cramped, my skirt was soaking wet, and my legs felt boneless and unreliable. I managed a feeble "thank you" before tottering along the beach to the house.

When I entered the kitchen Miss O'Brien took one look and me and exclaimed, "Miss B., whatever happened to you?"

"You'll never believe what kind of a trip I had this time," I said, giving my nose a good blow.

"Sit down. I'll make you a nice cup of tea, and you can tell us all about it," she said, certain a good cup of tea could set everything to rights.

"Thank you," I said, "but I think I'll change first, if you don't mind." I sloshed to my room, my soggy skirt slapping wetly against my now-restored land legs.

After I'd changed and was drinking my tea, I told the G.A.s of my misadventure. It was then I learned the strip of water I'd just crossed in the ancient dugout was known as "Beware Passage."

A startling discovery for a girl who couldn't swim a stroke.

The Parson and the Anvil Chorus

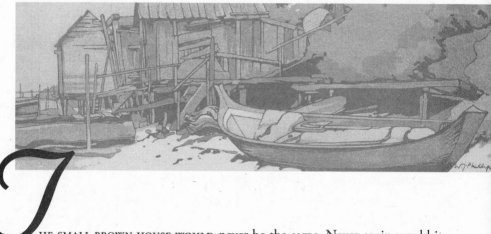

*T*HE SMALL BROWN HOUSE WOULD never be the same. Never again would it rise and fall with the tide or rock us to sleep on a stormy night. Somehow it didn't seem normal to walk through the sitting room, when the tide was low, without listing to starboard. I rather missed its tipsy appearance, although it had never been in keeping with the sobriety of its occupants.

The reason for the sober change of personality was that Miss O'Brien, at long last, had decided to put the house on pilings. Now and forever more, it would be level. As well, there was a spanking new walkway and float to which visiting boats could be tied. The reconstruction was needed to render the house plumb, so Bill Foster could install an oil-burning unit in the kitchen range.

"I wonder what time Mr. Foster will arrive," Miss O'Brien remarked at breakfast the morning the change was to take place. "He said he'd be here for certain today. I expect he'll be able to finish the job by noon."

"I hope so," replied Miss Dibben. "The oil burner will certainly lighten your load. It should be so much easier than carrying and stoking wood."

"I'm sure it will be, Dib," she agreed.

There was no doubt both women were looking forward to a level house and a warmer one.

As I was raising the flag to the top of the pole—after the better part of two years it had almost become a habit—I saw Bill Foster's boat heading for the float.

I forgot about Bill as I went into the schoolroom and waited for the few children to arrive. About an hour had gone by when we were interrupted by a knock on the door.

"Come in," I called, a bit surprised, for this kind of interruption was rare. The door opened and two men walked in, one of whom was the Reverend Alan Greene, director of the Columbia Coast Mission. The other I didn't know.

"Good morning, Miss Bowden," Reverend Greene said, smiling affably. I hope you don't mind our dropping in so unexpectedly. We're making our rounds of the coastal outposts and this is our day for Village Island." He nodded toward the other man. "May I present Dr. Thomas Connold. Dr. Connold is presently serving the Pender Harbour area but is taking this tour to see the rest of the territory."

Important visitors. The G.A.s would be in a dither, I suspected.

We spent a few minutes discussing the school, the village and the area in general. Then Mr. Greene said, "Mr. Todd tells me you won't be back next year."

"No," I replied. "I feel two years is long enough." And much more than I planned, I thought.

"Have you enjoyed your work here?"

"Quite honestly, there have been times when I've wondered what I'm doing here, but these will be years I'll never forget. I wouldn't have missed the experience for anything. And I don't think I'd have said this two years ago, but I've grown to love this country."

"Wonderful people in these parts," said Dr. Connold.

"There certainly are," I agreed, then smiled. "If you know where to find them."

Both men smiled back. They had spent long years on the coastal mission and well knew the empty miles between neighbours.

Just then Miss O'Brien bustled in the door.

"Forgive me, Miss B., but Reverend Greene and Dr. Connold must leave right after lunch, and it would be nice to have a service while they are here.

"Of course, Miss O'Brien. I'll dismiss the children for the rest of the morning."

"Tell the people the bell will ring for service," I told them as the three of them walked sedately to the door and then, once outside, went rushing down the hill with Miss O'Brien in the lead.

I immediately set about converting the school into a church. Within minutes Miss O'Brien was back to distribute the hymn and prayer books.

I rang the bell, and presently the village people, few in number now, came strolling along the path. Miss Dibben took her place at the organ and the service was underway. Both gentlemen took part, for Dr. Connold was an ordained minister as well as a medical doctor. By the time the service was over it was lunchtime, so we went down the hill to the brown house.

And then the fun began.

Since he'd arrived at nine o'clock, Bill had been working on the installation of the oil burner, but things hadn't gone well. As we walked onto the float with our distinguished guests, we heard a stream of unmistakable cuss words, interspersed with hammering and banging, issue from the open kitchen door. Miss O'Brien couldn't hear all this racket, of course, but Miss Dibben certainly did. The look on her pious face was one of true horror. Even the parsons looked startled.

We walked into a kitchen that looked as if it were undergoing a demolition rather than an oil installation. Miss O'Brien looked stunned. "Oh, dear. How am I going to prepare lunch," she murmured.

The stove was dismantled and Bill was unhinged. There were bits and pieces all over the place—tools and tool kit, stove lids, pipes and oil-burner parts—and all of it under a layer of soot. Combined with the black soot was the blue air created by Bill. It was obvious, as we picked our way over and around the pile of junk that had once been a stove, that he'd been having a bad time.

"Please, go right into the sitting room and I'll attend to lunch," Miss O'Brien said evenly, but I could see the bewildered look on her face. The poor woman didn't know where to start.

"I'll start the fire in the heater," said Miss Dibben. "We'll boil the kettle in the sitting room."

"Yes, Dib. Good idea," murmured Miss O'Brien. "And I'll make some sandwiches—somehow."

Eventually the kettle boiled for tea. We sat primly in the sitting room, eating sandwiches and soot-flavoured cake to the accompaniment of crashes, bangs and cussing from Bill in the kitchen.

We talked politely, pretending to enjoy our lunch and valiantly ignoring

Reverend Alan Greene's tea with the G.A.s happened at an awkward moment.

the cacophony from the other room. The gentlemen were hearty about it all, while the poor G.A.s were extremely embarrassed by the whole incident. The meal finally ended and the guests departed to the tune of the "Anvil Chorus" as rendered by Bill Foster.

Unrepentant, he struggled and swore for the rest of the afternoon, and by evening the stove was working—more or less.

It never was an efficient oil burner, for the stove was old and the drafts all wrong. Or maybe it couldn't stand the shock of being level after so many years of yielding to the whims of the tide.

As far as I could see, all it did *efficiently* was make an unpleasant smell.

The Final Cup of Tea

*J*UNE ARRIVED FULL OF WARMTH and summer sun. I hated being cooped up in the school on these lovely days. With the windows looking out on nothing but forest, the room seemed dark and gloomy. It was impossible to concentrate on the three Rs with the birds singing in the trees and the sea lapping gently on the shore.

There were only four or five children attending school and these were the wee beginners. This was the time of year when a particular type of edible seaweed was to be found, a great delicacy among the Indian people. As it was women's work to find it, the women and the older children would go off to search in the rowboats. Education always took second place to a project such as this.

Once in a while, for a change in diet, Miss O'Brien served this Native dish. It must have been an acquired taste because when I first tried it, I thought she'd made a horrible error and cooked a rubber boot by mistake. It had an odd, salty flavour and required a considerable amount of chewing so that as well as providing iodine, it gave the teeth and jaw a good bit of exercise. However, when served with boiled rice and clam juice, it became quite a palatable dish.

The staple diet of the Native people was dried fish and eulachon grease. I'd often find them having a meal when I made my rounds, and sometimes they'd invite me to join them, although I seldom did. There would be a large bowl of grease on the table and dried salmon in front of each person. The accepted manner of eating was to break off a piece of fish and dip it into the grease. Slabs of bread, strong tea and canned milk—and maybe some jam—rounded out the meal. Probably the Natives were the original "dunkers."

Fresh eulachon has a rich and delicious flavour but becomes rancid when kept any length of time. In this state it has an acrid odour I found nauseating. The odour clung to hair and clothing and, in an enclosed atmosphere, was overwhelming. I learned to tolerate the smell, but I never did develop a taste for eating it.

After school on these tranquil days, I'd walk along the bank to my favourite sunning rock. I loved to watch the sea's ever-changing moods, the patterns of light dappling its surface. Sometimes I'd use the rowboat, the sun warming my back as I pulled lazily on the oars. There were days when the water was so smooth it was impossible to tell where the rock disappeared into the sea and where the reflection began. The oars cut through the water effortlessly and I would row as if in a trance, enchanted and dreaming.

Although I was alone on these short journeys, I was no longer lonely. I knew now this country was full of people with kind hearts and welcoming smiles. I would miss them. But my time on Village Island was rapidly coming to an end. With my departure date in sight, I wondered how I was going to breathe in the city after all the months in the wide-open spaces of this magnificent and untrammelled land.

Through the week, I scouted around for transportation to Alert Bay on the weekend, for I wanted to say goodbye to my friends. It was hard to tell, at this time of year, how many boats might be around on Friday afternoon. Surprisingly, when the time came, I had a choice of four, all from neighbouring villages. I boarded the one that looked the best but, as usual, I made a mistake. It turned out to be the slowest and most odoriferous. By the time I reached the Todds', I'm sure they couldn't tell the difference between me and an eulachon. The first thing I did was have a bath.

"Do you realize this is probably the last bath I'll have in your tub?" I said to Mrs. Todd. "When I think of all the weeks and months I've gone without, I don't know how I stood it."

"These two years have been good for you," she replied. "I had grave doubts you'd adapt. You've surprised me."

I was wondering if this was a compliment when Mr. Todd asked, "You're sure you won't change your mind about coming back next year?"

"Thank's for asking, Mr. Todd, but no. I don't think teaching is my calling." I smiled. "And I've had enough of island living. But there's so much about this country I'm going to miss. And one of them—oddly enough—is the wide-open feeling of the sea and travelling so close to it on small boats." I laughed then, at myself and how far I'd come from that first ride with Mr. Cameron on the *Black Raven*. "Granted, I'd have liked a better selection of craft to choose from, but it's been a great experience and, at times, a lot of fun."

"Muriel is leaving, so there's going to be an opening for a village nurse," Mr. Todd persisted.

I shook my head. "Thanks, but I want to get back to bedside nursing again—real nursing. And maybe this time do more than hand out Aspirin and advice that isn't always heeded."

My sentimental journey continued as I said goodbye to the teachers and hospital staff, then Muriel, Kay, Sadie and Lou. On Sunday I boarded the same slow boat to return to Village Island. It would be my last trip in an Indian gas boat.

I had one more goodbye to say—to Mr. and Mrs. Oiens. Fortunately, Mrs. Oiens invited the G.A.s and me to tea on my last Friday afternoon on the island. It gave me the perfect opportunity.

It was strawberry season. Mr. Oiens had a large field where he grew enormous and delicious berries that he sold in Alert Bay and on Minstrel Island and to the people in the outlying communities. The field had a southern exposure, and the fruit thrived mightily. He didn't allow anyone near his strawberries as a rule, but as this was my last visit, he let me roam at will to gorge on his sweet, sun-ripened berries. They were ambrosia, the nectar of the gods! After I'd eaten my fill, we went to the house for tea and more berries, this time smothered with thick, rich cream.

There was another reason I was allowed the freedom of the berry patch, for by a peculiar coincidence, I'd become a heroine in Mr. Oiens' eyes.

One day, earlier in the spring, I had walked through the woods for my weekly visit with Mrs. Oiens. We were sitting in the kitchen drinking tea, chatting as usual, and Mr. Oiens was in the woodshed, just outside the kitchen door, chopping a supply of kindling. Suddenly we heard a yell, and the next moment he appeared in the kitchen, white and trembling. Blood was flowing from the index finger of his left hand and running down his arm. The finger was severed almost through the second joint; only a tag of skin held it in place.

We helped him to a chair into which he collapsed.

"Och! Aye! What to do, lass?" asked a rattled Mrs. Oiens.

"Have you any absorbent and bandages? Get them quickly!"

Mr. Oiens sat white-faced and groaning. When Mrs. Oiens brought the dressings, I swabbed off the blood, fitted the finger into place, bandaged it firmly, and applied a splint to keep it immobile.

"Tea! He needs, good strong tea," exclaimed Mrs. Oiens.

I thought he needed more than that, but didn't discourage her. "Have you any pills for pain?" I asked her.

"Aye. The good doctor left me some last time he called."

"Then give him two with his tea," I told her. "You'd better lie down for a while, Mr. Oiens."

"No. She'll be all right now. Yah. She'll be all right," he said, shakily drinking his tea.

"You'll have to keep the hand still for a few days," I told him.

"Yah. Yah. I will."

I was just as disturbed by this experience as the Oiens. I know he should have medical attention, but in his condition he couldn't have navigated the boat, let alone started the engine.

After school, for the next three days, I hiked through the woods to check on him. He wasn't having too much pain and, thank heaven, there was no sign of infection. On the fourth day, I felt it was safe to

This welcome pole stood outside Henry Bell's house for decades before vandals rolled it into the sea.

have a look, so I gently removed the dressings. To my great relief, the finger was healing beautifully. By the end of the week, there was no doubt the union was perfect. Eventually there was a small scar and the only other evidence to remind him of the accident was a stiff joint.

So Mr. Oiens insisted I eat my fill of strawberries on this Friday afternoon. It was the last time I ever saw the Oiens. It saddened me to say goodbye to

Mrs. Oiens. Hers was a lonely life, and she was so eager for affection and companionship. She had been my staunch friend while I, for a little while, had taken the place of the daughter she had never had.

My trunk was packed and the small room emptied of my possessions. It looked just as it had two years before when I'd arrived. Back then I was wondering why I'd come. I was nervous, afraid I'd made a terrible mistake coming to this remote place.

I thought differently now. I had come to know a type of life found only in the outposts of our society. I had met some of the first citizens of Canada and learned something of their culture, art and music. Had I not stayed, I would have missed seeing the hidden inlets of the limitless B.C. coast. And I would have missed knowing the dear, old G.A.s who, I'm sure, never entirely approved of me, but were just a little sorry to see me go.

It was the people I'd miss the most. In these vast isolated areas a single individual can seem small indeed, but when the chips are down and help is needed, that individual serves a unique and valuable purpose.

To quote Mrs. Todd, who said in her usual forthright manner, "This country has made a woman of you."

I believe she was right.

Final Episode

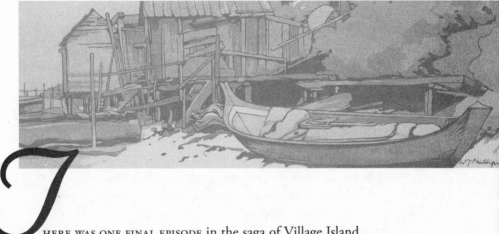

HERE WAS ONE FINAL EPISODE in the saga of Village Island.

When I left, I took with me the prize money we'd won on coronation day. As I was spending a few days in Vancouver, it was decided I should buy something very special for the school. The G.A.s and I had many sessions of pros and cons at tea time, mulling over ideas. Finally, we decided on a wall clock, for it would be a permanent reminder of our moment of glory.

I visited several shops while in Vancouver and told my story. Through one of the larger stores, I was able to purchase a handsome clock at a wholesale price. It was wound with a key and had a swinging pendulum. The store arranged for shipment, and I later heard from Miss O'Brien it had arrived safely and had been hung with due care.

Some months later, I was talking to someone from Alert Bay who had recently been to Village Island.

"By any chance, did you see the clock in the school?" I asked.

Then I heard the tale of the handsome timepiece.

It had been hung appropriately, wound with the key, and the gleaming pendulum swung rhythmically back and forth, ticking away the minutes.

It fascinated the children who watched it—almost mesmerized them. In fact, it became so irresistible to one of them he or she swiped both the pendulum and the key—thus silencing the clock forever.

Afterword

Miss Kathleen O'Brien, M.B.E.

Prior to establishing her *Hyuya-tsi* on Village Island, Miss O'Brien was a public health nurse in Alert Bay for three years. In an interview with Harry Wolcott before her death she said, "Our job was to live a Christian life of kindliness … The government had no provision for TB cases … Alert Bay could not keep them. I wish I could have been more helpful."

Hughina remembered her well. "At the time of the coronation of King George VI of England, shortly before I left Village Island for the last time," she says, "Miss O'Brien was named to the King's Honours list and awarded membership in the Order of the British Empire in recognition of her service to the cause of the Native people on Canada's west coast.

"She had left her comfortable life in England to come to a small, primitive village amid the wilderness of the British Columbia coast. Through her efforts the Mamalilikulla school was built, and out of her own funds the preventorium was established to comfort children suffering the scourge of tuberculosis. She gave order and purpose to life in the village, as well as a touch of Christianity. And she bettered the health and welfare of the people.

"When Miss O'Brien at last retired in 1945 at the age of 70 and returned to live in England, life in the Mamalilikulla village was never the same. No one came to take her place.

"I found her different and full of oddities, but kind and gentle too. Brash youth looks at life through thoughtless eyes, but later from the pinnacle of middle years, I can see her for what she truly was—a good and selfless woman.

"Such devotion to a cause I'll never see again."

Miss Kate Maria Dibben

"Miss Dibben," Hughina recalled, "was as devoted to her charges on Village Island as Miss O'Brien. She worked under a far greater handicap, for she suffered from glaucoma, which caused her agonizing pain at times. She bravely carried on her chosen work with Christian zeal. Sadly, she eventually became totally blind. She lived the last years of her life in Alert Bay."

On now-abandoned Village Island, pristine water laps against an empty shoreline where the little brown house once tilted with the tides.

The People of Village Island

On a cold Saturday morning in December 1936, Hughina Harold entered Jimmy Sewid's home to find her hopes for a ride to Alert Bay dashed. Her sleepy, volunteer captain was not up to the task, and she retreated home very disappointed. This event belied the future of the 22-year-old fisherman, who later became an energetic and effective spokesman for his people. James Sewid's life was documented in *Guests Never Leave Hungry*, published in 1969. After many young Mamalilikulla families (including James's) moved to Alert Bay, James Sewid became the first elected chief of his people in 1950 and an activist in the restoration of First Nations traditions, such as the potlatch. (Based on revelations in his autobiography, it was most likely Jimmy Sewid who was behind the hamatsa mask on the night Hughina witnessed a potlatch.) James Sewid died in 1988 in Campbell River.

Simon and Emma Beans were James Sewid's lifelong friends. In 1963, Simon, James and their friend Henry Speck decided they would build a new community house in Alert Bay. "He was part of everything I had been doing over the years," Sewid wrote. Before this new project was finished, Simon died from a heart attack while hunting alone up Knight's Inlet.

Like many Mamalilikulla men of their era, Wilfred Hanuse and his brothers raised their families in Alert Bay. Wilfred and his sister Stella had been the shining stars in Hughina Bowden's 1936 classroom, and 14 years later it was Wilfred who nominated James Sewid for the position of chief. Only six weeks later, Wilfred and his brothers, Fred and Alex, were at the centre of a great tragedy. During a December storm in 1950, the three sons of Harry and Gertrude Hanuse were lost at sea only miles from their homes.

Indian agent Murray Todd, with wife Myrtle at his side, served in Alert Bay until 1952. While later criticized for his efforts to suppress the potlatch and other Native traditions, Todd earned wide respect and friendship among the Natives of Village Island. For James Sewid, Todd was "just like a father to me."

In 1940, Murray Todd and Earl Anfield, the principal of St. Michael's, were instrumental in helping Sewid become the first Native fishboat captain to buy his boat from B.C. Packers in Alert Bay.

In 1950, after the demise of village day schools, Todd orchestrated both the Alert Bay amalgamation of the Nimpkish band and James Sewid's followers on the Industrial Reserve, and the resurrection of the day-school program in the outer villages.

Clergy and Doctors

Dr. David Ryall served for nine years at St. George's Hospital in Alert Bay and made the *Columbia* his main link with the coastal villages. In 1941 Dr. Ryall joined the Royal Canadian Air Force. St. George's remained a key element of the Columbia Coast Mission (CCM) until 1965, when it was turned over to a private corporation.

The 100-year-old Anglican Church in Alert Bay, as it appeared when Hughina went to visit the area in 1985.

Reverend B.H.L. Dance was never in full agreement with the social and medical aid priorities of the CCM. Hughina Bowden's impressions of Dance were well-founded, based on his 1936 report to his superiors. The broad demands placed on the *Columbia* meant he "was unable to carry out adequately his religious duties." In the mission's annual report he recorded his fear that CCM's flagship was being reduced to an itinerant hospital ship.

Leander Gillard, a Newfoundlander who loved both the sea and the church, commanded the *Sky Pilot* between 1935 and 1941. The United Church's Alert Bay mission was closed the year after he departed to become a navy chaplain. He retired from that role in 1958 and died in Victoria in 1966. Along the coast, he left a legacy of good humour and goodwill.

The Schools

Mamalilikulla Indian Day School was started by Kathleen O'Brien and the first teacher, Miss M.E. Nixon, who left in 1931 and was succeeded by a procession of women, including Hughina Bowden, over the next decade. During this time the winter population of the village rose moderately from approximately 95 to 108 residents. After 1940, no teacher was provided and an aging Miss O'Brien confined her own activity to conducting religious services and caring for sick children in her preventorium.

The lack of a school pushed James Sewid and many of the family men of the village to relocate to Alert Bay. A new school was opened in the 1950s, and, under the pseudonym "Blackfish Indian Day School," this site became the focus of Harry Wolcott's 1967 dissertation, "A Kwakiutl Village and School" referenced in the foreword. Harry was one of the last teachers at Mamalilikulla before the school closed permanently in 1964.

St. Michael's Residential School at Alert Bay proved a mixed blessing. Both government and Anglican church policy encouraged Natives to send their brightest children to Alert Bay. Earl Anfield, principal of the residential school, was widely respected by both his peers and his students.

St. Michael's Residential School in Alert Bay was guarded by a Thunderbird and Grizzly pole.

The crumbling school as it appeared in 1985.

Index